Starboard at Midnight

Starboard *at* Midnight

Helen Behr Sanford

The Darwin Press, Inc.
Princeton, New Jersey

Publisher's Cataloging-In-Publication Data
(Prepared by The Donohue Group, Inc.)

Sanford, Helen Behr.
    Starboard at midnight / Helen Behr Sanford.

    p. : ill. ; cm.

    ISBN: 978-0-87850-200-4 (hardbound)
    ISBN: 978-0-87850-201-7 (paperback)

    1. Behr, Karl Howell, 1885-1949. 2. Tennis players--United States--20th century--Biography. 3. Bankers--United States--20th century--Biography. 4. Survival after airplane accidents, shipwrecks, etc. 5. Titanic (Steamship) 6. Shipwrecks--North Atlantic Ocean. I. Title.

GV697.B45 S72 2011
796/.342/092   2011928793

∞ The paper used in this publication meets the minimum requirements of the American National Standards Institute for Information Sciences—Permanence of Paper for Printed Library Materials, ANSI Z39.48-1992.

Upper cover photo provided by Martin Schwartz:
martyphoto1@gmail.com

All photos in this publication were provided by the author.
Printed in the United States of America

Published by: The Darwin Press, Inc., Princeton, NJ 08543-2202
www.darwinpress.com

To Ed Breisacher—
my deepest gratitude

Contents

Sonnet xv

When I consider everything that grows
Holds in perfection but a little moment,
That this huge stage presenteth nought but shows
Whereon the stars in secret influence comment;
When I perceive that men as plants increase,
Cheered and checked even by the selfsame sky,
Vaunt in their youthful sap, at height decrease,
And wear their brave state out of memory:
Then the conceit of this inconstant stay
Sets you most rich in youth before my sight,
Where wasteful Time debateth with Decay
To change your day of youth to sullied night;
   And, all in war with Time for love of you,
   As he takes from you, I ingraft you new.

—William Shakespeare

Author's Note

*I*WAS ALONE WHERE I LIVED at Pretty Brook Farm the night my intrigue began. Firelight animated books lining the room's floor-to-ceiling shelves. Music subdued the fire's crackling where I sat in the midst of a vast library—Shakespeare, Pearl Buck, Zane Grey, Rumer Godden, Melville, C. S. Lewis, Churchill—under the portrait of a man whose eyes followed my every move. On a whim, I shifted a chair near the hearth in order to gain access to the cabinet behind it. When I raised the black iron lift-latch, it burst upward. The door flew open as though pressure from something enclosed there needed immediate release.

Before me, bulging with pictures, letters, and newspaper articles, were my grandfather's scrapbooks that I had never seen before. As I turned the pages, I was captivated by pen-and-ink illustrations of Karl Behr kissing Helen Newsom with a ship sinking in the background. Columns of text supported headlines above them: *Love in a Lifeboat; Love Blooms from Disaster*. The memorabilia, which had been sequestered in darkness for decades, was suddenly monumental to me. After I discovered it, somehow, my life changed.

The fire in embers, I replaced the albums and climbed the stairs to my bedroom where I studied another black-and-white photograph of my grandfather that was on my desk. It was just his face, the face of a man I had never known since he died six months before I was born. The handsome features that composed his earnest demeanor—a pleasing nose, a distinguished mouth, a youthful, combed-back hairline—were overlaid by traces of duality. An aura of experience intermingled with innocence; apparent introspection overshadowed triumphant resolve. Ambiguities insinuated that I had as much to learn from him as about him.

In my early twenties at the time, I peered at the photograph, wondering where he'd been when it was taken and whether or not, once the session ended, he'd engaged the photographer in conversation, or simply hustled out the door. Without a spoken word from him, a raised brow, a propitious lick of lips, even a blink, I was aware, of course, that I would never know him really, and that I could only inform my intuition into his sympathies, into the mystery—what I wanted to believe might be a continuance of souls.

Considering these quandaries as I was getting ready for bed, I walked across a small hallway and was moving through my sister's room when I experienced (as Helen recounts to Karl in Chapter 7) a phenomenon that struck me as a revenant, or some kind of ghost.

Whether imagined or not, although decades have passed since that night, I remember the sound and sensation of the occurrence as if it happened a minute ago. Ever afterward, I harbored intuition that there was something my grandfather had never been able to clarify. And I hoped that by being his messenger I might bring his name— transfixed in memory—to light.

Along with his photo albums, my grandfather (known as "Pappy") wrote a 185-page unpublished memoir from which this recounting is derived and further conflated by my research. I was able to learn more about Karl through people who knew him: his two sisters, my father (Karl Jr.), and my father's three siblings. For the purpose of helping me present my grandfather's character, I have introduced three fictitious characters: Charlie, Jack, and Sarah, based upon real people Karl might have known. With the exception of these and the few mentioned in "Research and Commentary," all dignitaries, acquaintances, colleagues, and events in regard to Karl come from his true life story.

On the other hand, although I knew and adored Helen and grew up only a short walk from her door, I had no memoir or memorabilia from which to garner details about her. Therefore, although her background, friends, family, and educational history herein are authentic, my depiction of her emotional landscape, as well as that of *her* grandfather, is based upon an assumption that personal histories might be woven from common threads—albeit some more mine than hers.

In this book, present-tense chapters titled in italics with the symbol 🕊 involve Helen in company with Karl or Helen alone, during the year 1949. She is the center (half of a double helix, if you will) around which Karl's life story turns in past-tense chapters between 1895 and 1919—a time that fascinates with similarities and differences even today when considered in the context of political, scientific, and historical developments. It is important to take note that television had not yet been invented. No maritime disaster of such colossal magnitude had occurred during the forty years previous to 1912. Hitler's Germany and World War II still loomed in the not-too-distant future.

A century has passed. Many books and movies have been made. But still there are a few missing pieces. Like a small object submerged in a sea of guilt, lost in the debris field that surrounded it, one man's life continued on for four decades after the tragedy. Because it was formed and tested early, his passion to save the endangered and oppressed could not be quelled. Against prejudice and self-doubt, he would come to influence the course of History.

At the Brink

I NO LONGER HAVE POWER *over what happens to me; I see every-thing differently now,* Karl thinks as he sits wrapped in a nest of coats. He tries to focus on the paper in his lap but looks, instead, at the pen in his hand, which seems to hover like an antenna waiting for a signal. He imagines it personified as a man anticipating an epipha-ny—the pen wavers and keels over, leaving a spot of ink. *My memoir will likely come to rest on a dusty shelf along with the rest of the ephemeral clues about me unless, someday, someone reads between the lines. What then?* He wonders: *Will Helen, will anyone see me as I was, or as someone else entirely?*

Behind him the house in East Hampton has emerged from early morning fog—feather-gray shingles and white trim lending it sem-blance of a seagull nestled into a knoll. At the bedroom window, Helen stands with an armload of laundry. She sees her husband on the terrace below, although locust tree limbs obscure her view. The morning has begun with hesitation—an early chill subdued the usual bustle of creatures awakening in late-summer heat. The night before, she and Karl had stood together, reveling in the pearly hues of sunset over the ocean's reach to a sky-blue rim as they peered at a scene that flowed backward, forward, and inward all at once. Perfume of beach plums had deflected a swirl of apprehension.

Above Karl the sky is magnificent—a passing storm has borne a cumulus cloud that swells voluminous as though bringing to cre-scendo the purpose of gathering attention to itself, whereas cirrus wisps arc in the distance. Beyond the clouds, shades of blue—

cerulean, cornflower, aquamarine—are sequestered; *as if I am peering through keyholes to see them,* Karl thinks.

His gaze turns inward. The doctor's pronouncement is even more menacing now than it was the first time he heard the words career toward him like boulders down a cliff: "You have cancer, I'm afraid. There's no way to stop it from spreading." Karl recalls the days preceding that sentence—*as though I'd been cantering along, flesh and blood running slipstream, when the reins slid from my fingers and everything gave way to some intention outside of me.*

He closes his eyes; the lids tremble. He envisions water dazzling with sequins of light. Reveling in the image, he considers the pulsing in his eyelids to be a coupling of sunshine with the force of his own heartbeat, and he muses that, at his age of sixty-four, *so much seems to teeter between anticipation and assessment.*

He pictures Helen—how she was at the doctor's office when he recaptured his sense of her and the undercurrents of worry she always kept hidden. The moment the doctor had finished speaking, she had squeezed the fabric of her skirt, gazed at the floor, looked up and then out the window. *She voiced the burning question as I could not—as if she were a mere conduit for the quandary contained in the air around us:* "How much longer will we have?"

Karl recalls having been given no answer—*time is always finally unfathomable*—as he had watched Helen take the first of many deep breaths while her unsteady hand moved to secure a hair pin and she rose from her chair as though she needed to awaken from a long sleep, or *to wrestle an impossible verdict.* Her skirt flowed like music—*andante, amoroso*—as she walked to the window. When she returned, lifting her eyes to him, he recognized her fear, as if it was the first time. *We smiled, although silence was wedged between us.*

A chorus of insects jostles like a pocketful of coins accompanied by a timpani of rings. *Reverie's my refuge now,* Karl reminds himself; his thoughts slide to a reservoir of scenes, conversations and ineffable desires. He is entranced by a faint murmur of ocean waves that seems to be synchronized with his breathing. *So much can be reduced to two little words—in* and *out.*

Karl senses undercurrents of urgency. Then he leans back, assessing his great fortune to have married Helen; to have had their three sons, Karl Jr., Peter, Jim, a daughter Sally, and now their extended families. The wicker chair creaks. He thinks of his brothers, Herman, Fritz, and Max; of his sisters, Margaret and Gertrude; and then of Charlie, his best friend. *Charlie, who could never be confined—if not by love.*

The summer of 1949 has disappeared. A return to New York City is only a day away and Karl is struggling to complete his memoir. One chapter has yet to be written. So far, he has welcomed every diversion in order to avoid reliving the anguish of the event that he must include, inserting it back into the middle of his chapters. He is convinced that the effort required, even to begin to explain this, will extend far beyond his capability, although he wishes he could record every detail—every gesture, utterance, and thought.

Helen had urged, "Tell it simply, Karl, just as you did when you submitted your testimony for the trial. Keep your dignity intact, darling. You did nothing to feel guilty about."

Days later, she reasserted, "Promise me you won't hide a secret confession in fine print or dishonor your legacy with doubts or second guesses if you believe your life is part of a divine plan, which it is, don't you think? …After all, you are my hero."

Karl whispers aloud as he considers her advice: "I guess I need to simplify." But his thoughts drift again and he is reminded of many other ship-board passages he experienced in his life—in particular when the oft-placid Caribbean surged wild as the mountains of Mexico. He was more seasick than he had ever been. He had crawled on his hands and knees to the captain's cabin to ask him if he thought the ship would make it through the storm intact.

Karl cringes now, recalling the look of hopelessness in the captain's blood-shot eyes when the response dribbled and sputtered off the end of his tongue: "We'll be fuckin' l-l-lucky if her sides hold!"

And lucky they were. But this was no rival to the episode Karl is trying to write about—the one that occurred when he was twenty-six. The one with far-reaching consequences that held him clamped in a vise between shame and jubilation to be alive.

Gazing without seeing the herringbone pattern of bricks underfoot, Karl thinks about waiting. He relives the day he'd hopped aboard a train to depart Gare St. Lazarre in Paris. How the train had reached Gare Maritime in Cherbourg-Octeville at 3:40 in the afternoon, a full two hours before the tender boat, *Nomadic,* was scheduled to ferry passengers to the ship Helen was on. How he had planned to leave Europe for America on the Hamburg-Amerika line, but decided at the last minute to take a chance to be with her.

He pictures himself running, *frantic as a madman* to purchase the transatlantic ticket, a sudden whirlwind snatching the hat off his head, flinging it behind him into a sideways skid down the street. "Oh, damn," he had uttered under his breath, "Just my luck!" He had had to let the hat go rather than risk losing his place in the line, which suddenly appeared impossibly long. He watched it getting crushed under the wheels of a passing carriage, then swung back around, impatient to detect some progress toward the ticket window; but there was none.

During those moments, caught in the context of innocence, Karl ponders—*how desperately I had wanted to be with my darling Helen.*

Once he had purchased the ticket, he stepped up on a rock and squinted across the English Channel, attempting to detect a speck on the horizon. Nothing appeared. Anticipation grew more palpable than any he had ever felt before, even when as a boy he had waited to see his first train. His imagination made manifest at the elusive horizon—at the meeting of sea and sky—a pinpoint ship that only he could see.

Karl remembers cupping his fingers to search the empty space, willing the great ship into existence. He envisions her approach and tries to relive the excitement he felt when it had seemed to him, as it still seems now, that she embodied everything he dreamed he might one day wake up to find had been real after all. He recalls how he'd worried: *What if following Helen is not a good idea? What if her mother continues to distrust me? I'll be doomed like Charlie was with Emily's parents.*

He had jumped off the rock to sit facing the other passengers. He had stretched forward to retie a loose shoelace…

Well, that's the beginning of the chapter I have yet to write, Karl muses: *The part where everything is still possible, because it all lies ahead.* Piercing the soft-coded chatter of birds gathering to fly south, a train's whistle interrupts Karl's musing. It hyphenates distance until the approaching rumble churns like a rush of floodwater, sublimating all other sound. Then as the train disappears, Karl finds himself straining to hear the last vestige of steel-rolled rhythm because he wants to hold on; he wants to will the hypnotic trance that the sound brings to inspire a stream of sentences for him to write. At the same time he yearns for the years he was too preoccupied to have taken such lengthy notice of a train. *Sound, a sorcerer of thought, veers into several parts and spins to its own conclusion, like eddies at sea,* he thinks.

Just the night before, having been awakened by the train, Karl had eased himself from his bed without disturbing Helen, to attempt to write that elusive chapter. The words he scribbled are in his lap:

We had no idea how many of us were out on the sea—only that we were reduced to paltry specks against a newly vacant sky—the same firmament we had scoured for eternity as we studied our ship's silhouette, praying that she might hold steady against the blazing stars behind her.

Now the massive cloud that was over Karl's head has moved toward the horizon. Across the lawn the dark sweep of a copper beech resembles the phantom ship. Karl drops his head, wondering: *Can anyone ever do enough? Can anyone ever be enough?*

Approaching the terrace, Helen draws a short breath as she peers through the glass panes alongside the door because she sees the thrust of Karl's torso bent forward and she is filled with trepidation that he is already gone.

The moment her foot reaches the bricks, she is relieved when she notices the pen move in his hand.

"How did you sneak out here without me?" She asks, looking beyond him—suspecting, knowing, dreading how her heart will break when he is gone. A coat slides from his shoulder. She lifts it back into place.

"Just the way I practiced in my youth," Karl answers. "One toe at a time—squeaky floorboard scrutiny in between. I have to admit though, I've been lonesome ever since I 'snuck' out here without you!"

"I see you're busy."

"Working on that chapter. You know…the one."

"Yes. Do you need me?"

"More than ever."

"I'll get us some tea and come right back," Helen says, kissing Karl's cheek and turning back to the house.

Karl presses his lips and drives wide-splayed fingers through his thick silver-brown hair to reclaim the wayward strands. His blue eyes shift as though searching for an answer. Across the yard a blackbird issues a raspy command. Underfoot, a shriveled leaf skitters and clicks across the bricks. Karl raises his head, closes his eyes, and begins to reach back.

PART ONE

Sea-breathing draws and heaves a knot of hands.

Herman Behr house, 1891
82 Pierrepont St., Brooklyn, New York.

2

A Stone's Throw

*I*N EARLY NOVEMBER, 1895, as the half-light of evening settled into darkness, Karl was riding in the family carriage with his three older brothers—Herman, Fritz, and Max—mesmerized by the clatter of horse hooves crossing the Brooklyn Bridge. He was returning from an excursion to New York City with his mother, Grace, who sat straight-backed in the front seat of the carriage next to her driver, Andrew. Having left her baby at home in the care of Sarah, she had ventured from Brooklyn Heights with all four of her boys in tow to buy warm clothes in preparation for winter and to replace the hat that Fritz, her second son, had lost in a street fight.

In the Heights, hats and caps were coveted enough to become catalysts for a ruckus between the gang that was known as the Micks, and the wealthier Remsen Street boys. The Micks were often in need, and they held a wicked grudge against anyone else who wasn't. Trouble originated from their having to walk through the well-to-do Heights neighborhood in order to get to public school. Whenever they spotted a "little rich boy" standing alone, the victim was robbed, no matter how he might have attempted to conceal his bounty, or how loudly he yelled to prevent their onslaught.

Sprawled limbs akimbo in the back seat of the carriage with his head bobbing contrary to the rest of his body, Karl gazed into small trails of fractured light that zigzagged across the river, remembering the first time the Micks had grabbed him:

On the way home from school Karl's shoelace had come loose, and when he bent over to retie it, the marbles deep in his knapsack burst from their bag. Scattering, they rolled, clinking and bumping for what seemed like *forever* down Henry Street—until they converged and plunked, one after the other, down a sewer drain. Karl

9

felt miserable losing them. The only good thing he could think of was that his precious German marbles had disappeared rather than get snatched into the claws of a Mick, which was what he had always feared and expected.

Without warning, Karl's optimism turned against itself. He was crouched, peering into the drain to see if he could spot a shiny orb in the black abyss, when the thrust of a boot shoved him forward and down flat. His chin hit the pavement, split open and stung like fire. He turned over, grasping it, lifted his hand to assess the blood, and peered into the faces of four giant Micks looming above him with their fists forced deep into their pockets. Their faces were contorted—glowering, nostrils flared—massive and angry as bulls. Although petrified, Karl glared back at them, wondering what weapons they might have concealed in their pockets.

Jiggling along in the back of the carriage, Karl cringed, remembering how he had lain on the street frozen with fear, holding his chin together; how he had taken the spittle that dribbled on him from the tallest of the Micks, because even though he had seen it coming, he hadn't moved out of the way quickly enough. The sticky glob had landed with a resounding splat on the corner of his mouth and trickled in. He felt a slither of nausea as he thought about it, and recalled what a grave mistake his feeble attempt at self-defense had been. After he jumped up and slammed his fist into the stomach of the Mick who spat on him, all four bullies took turns kicking, spitting, and calling him names.

Grasping his chin, Karl had gathered himself up in stages, extracting one appendage at a time as though he'd been a piece of putty trampled into the sidewalk. He peered around to see if there were any more Micks lurking, then limped home to tell Max and Herman about the fight. But he did not tell Fritz.

A few years older than Karl, Fritz would have added yet another and consummately more humiliating lesson in battle strategy just to toughen-up his "bitty" brother while reinforcing his own superiority.

Despite the constant barrage and razzing from Fritz (who always asserted that he was right about everything), Karl had believed his own less aggressive attitude proved more self-protective when it came to staving off a street fight. But after Karl was attacked for no reason, he had come to doubt the value of passivity, and Fritz's strong offense garnered new credibility.

Comparatively though, Fritz was aggressive beyond reason. During the last fracas, when Fritz had lost his hat, Karl considered the entangled Mick lucky to have come out alive. Karl heard Fritz explain the event to Max: "The scoundrel appeared from nowhere: P*ffff*...like a *ghost*!" Fritz said, swirling his arms in a giant circle and watching Max's eyes widen as he continued, "His fangs hung draggin' and slobberin' like the meanest mongrel I ever seen ... *saw*. But when he spat on the stone next to my foot, called me a 'puny Poly-Prep *bastard*' and asked 'where's your Mama?' I hauled off and let 'm have it...right 'n the kisser!"

Fritz had clocked that Mick over the head with a billy club that he kept in his back pocket. The boy collapsed backward and senseless on the street. Karl remembered the sight of his wild brother tearing down the block, bursting into the house and blasting everyone within earshot, yelling: "I've killed a Mick! I've killed a Mick! Come quick! I've killed a Mick!"

Andrew had followed Fritz out onto the street and helped to haul the boy's heavy, limp, bloody body into the house. Sarah laid baby Margaret down gently and worked to revive the boy. With Karl looking on, Andrew gave the flummoxed Mick some water before hoisting him into the family carriage and driving him, still delirious, to his wharf-side home.

Fritz losing his hat and nearly killing a Mick was a whole lot worse than me losing marbles, Karl thought, shifting in the carriage and peering out over shiny pathways in the river. He turned to see the glittery city diminish behind him, and twisted forward again to stare at the back of his dear mother's head, wondering how she had managed to keep her hair up like that all day. He strained to catch pieces of her conversation with Andrew about the pending election and the evening's festivities at their home at 82 Pierrepont at the corner of Henry Street. She was asking Andrew whether the cook, Mary Hamilton, had mentioned needing butter and curry for the night's dinner.

"No, Mum." Andrew responded.

"I suppose she'll have dispatched Louis for them by now. Mind checking when you get in?"

"Certainly," Andrew crooned: "I'll hitch up the horses and be right along. Louis'll fetch your packages, if he's at the door."

"We've only a small group joining us for dinner this evening, Andrew. Help yourself to a meal if Mary Hamilton's amenable. And bid Mary Walsh, our new laundress, do the same? We should have plenty for everyone."

Andrew nodded and drew in the reins.

Quick-as-a-thought, Grace turned to face her sons. Slivers of light stressed the stern intent in her dark-blue eyes as she spoke over the clopping hooves. "As soon as we arrive at home, you boys run upstairs, wash up and change your clothes for dinner. Herman, as the eldest, you take charge. Fritz! Don't look so gloomy. Max, watch out for Karl. I need you all to be on your best behavior tonight. Your father and I are expecting company for dinner. All agreed?"

No answer was forthcoming. When his mother had turned back around, Fritz directed a hand-slice signal across his neck at Max and Karl.

Max whispered to Fritz: "I'll run and check the stash. *You* take care of Mary Ham. We'll meet outside the bathroom, upstairs."

"No!" Fritz answered, rocking forward to cup his hand over Max's ear. "K and I'll check the yard first. You go with Herm to the kitchen and find out about supper!"

Herman, hanging limp, almost asleep, piped up to comfort his mother, if a bit pretentiously, "Right, Mother. Don't worry. We'll be scarce as a mad hen's teeth!"

Grace raised her brows and rolled her eyes so that Andrew, who had glanced at her, could surmise that she had not been fooled by Herm's slightly off-key and cavalier assurance.

The carriage approached a Romanesque mansion of stone, brick, terracotta and tile at the corner of Henry and Pierrepont streets. Grace's husband, Herman Behr, had had the home built for the family in 1890, only a few blocks from his mother Julie's house and his abrasives manufacturing business, Herman Behr & Company.

Karl looked up at the house, which appeared as alluring as a gift-wrapped shadow box. He saw reflections of silver light, strewn across the moist stone drive, turn golden on the glass panels by the heavy front door and merge with the glow of the entry hall. Then, after imagining them as eyebrows raised to acknowledge his arrival, he winked at two semi-circular windows high on the façade.

When Andrew opened the carriage door and Grace had stepped down, Fritz tried to push Karl out, but Karl dodged so that Fritz nearly fell instead. Ignoring the scuffle behind her, Grace walked forward, her boot heels striking percussion on the entry stones. She paused near the door, shaking her head at her husband's recently installed, and in her opinion, "excessively elaborate" burglar and fire alarm. Then she became engulfed in the reflective glaze of mirrors and chandeliers while running up the winding staircase. Karl stood watching her, marveling at the ease with which she extended her heels far out over the edge of every step.

Max hunched over in his attempt to replicate Herman's stride through the mansion. Firelight projected their amorphous shadow on the wall as they maneuvered toward the kitchen. At the opposite end of the house, first Fritz, then Karl, burst out the back door into the yard. Both were relieved to see that their cache of wooden barrels was still intact, stacked high against the eight-foot brick and stone perimeter wall.

It had taken weeks for the Remsen Street boys to stuff these barrels with hard coal to use as ammunition against the pilfering Micks. They had also filled other barrels with coveted combustibles that would soon be used to set their traditional election-night fire. Several boys, whose afternoon task had been to guard the stash, were still in the yard prepared to defend the precious bounty against a possible raid. Intermittently, they hoisted wooden clothes poles, which bobbed at the wall in a manner obliquely reminiscent of a medieval joust.

"Everything's been e-e-e-r-i-e since you left," one boy said, spelling out the word.

"Gives me the willies," another whispered. "How'd your shopping go?"

"Swell," Fritz said with a twisty smirk. "Like my new hat?"

Karl watched his brother lift the hat off his head, punch it a few times and shove it on backwards as they both looked up to see who had flung open a third-floor window.

Herman called down from there, through thick protective wire netting: "Supper in the pantry at seven boys! How's our depot holdin' up?"

"Good. Come take a gander!" Fritz called back.

Karl wondered how far away seven o'clock might be. His wool pants itched. He leaned over, scratching furiously. Apprehension about the impending night's activities competed with hunger. His stomach growled. Hunger was winning and the night was rapidly growing darker and colder. The trunk of an elm next to him loomed black and slimy. He thought he heard something stir outside the wall, stiffening as he strained to hear another sound.

Fritz drew a finger to his lips. "Shhh! Everybody! D'you hear that?"

"What?"

"Scratching?" Karl asked.

"I didn't mean you, *Mama's* boy," Fritz hissed.

They listened, but there was no threat, so they proceeded to Monroe Place with the barrels in order to set the fire ablaze, whereupon Karl stood spellbound by the conflagration as it flew up furiously against the darkness, noticing that as soon as he moved away, everything by comparison grew terribly cold and darker.

After abandoning the fire and happily heading home with just a few paces left toward the yard, he glanced down Henry Street and spotted a horde of Micks rushing toward him in a wicked stampede.

"Micks!" he yelled. Inside him, the warning sounded as if it had been uttered under water.

In two-company military formation, with lines extending from curb to curb that seemed to Karl like hundreds of boys, the Micks emerged en masse, roaring down the street toward the meager remnants of the Remsen Street boys.

"Close the yard door!" Fritz screamed at Herman, *"Move!"*

The heavy wooden door slammed shut but wouldn't lock. Herman continued fumbling with the latch while the rest of the Remsen Street boys hoisted their poles or gathered handfuls of coal in a mad-dash effort to beat back the first attack.

They heard a Mick shout, *"FIRE!"*

Caught vulnerable, still outside the yard, Karl suffered the impact of sharp-edged stones that stung his chest and face. He raised his arms in an attempt to deflect the barrage, then doubled over and collapsed with both hands cupped over his left eye. The pain was severe. He screamed and rolled from side to side as the Micks passed by; then he staggered to get up, but fell back to his knees.

Hearing the scream, Max grabbed Herman's sleeve and said, "I think K's in trouble." They opened the gate a crack, at first unable to see where Karl was, then spotting him, ran to help him up and into the yard.

From where she was standing by the third-floor window, Sarah heard shouts. She had gone there to see if the boys were up to something like their scheme the previous winter, which was to create a skating rink by flooding the floor with a hose from the bathroom sink while leaving the windows open in expectation that the water would freeze overnight. Closing the window that Herman had left open, she heard urgent noises coming from the yard and noticed that several boys were running hell-bent toward the wall so she raced downstairs to report to Mr. and Mrs. Behr that trouble was brewing.

In the yard, Max, Herman, and Fritz flailed at anything they imagined or feared—mostly hitting at nothing.

"Do you believe those idiots haven't just walked right through that door?" Max yelled to Fritz.

"Morons!" Fritz yelled back.

Curled up next to the tree with his hand clamped over his eye, Karl heard a Mick shout, "Scram boys!"

After a second or two, Max peeked out the yard door and said, "Get a load o' this!"

Karl approached and strained to make sense of a phalanx of white-shirted gentlemen in a jagged V formation with their coattails flapping and arms flailing as they charged up the street after the retreating Micks.

Herman recognized the group. "That's the old Crescent Club football team!" he said.

To save the Remsen Street boys, the elderly gents had abandoned their annual dinner and were running several yards ahead of two police wagons, swinging canes, cussing, and hurling epithets with derby hats poised to protect strategic body parts.

Once the Micks were some distance away, Fritz wanted to run after them, pounding the air and calling out, "Thumb suckers!"

Herman and Max grabbed Fritz's jacket and held him back.

Mission accomplished, the Crescent Club heroes swooped around in synch and waddled off into the darkness.

"Come on Karlos, we've got to get you inside!" Max said.

Karl welcomed Max's firm grip guiding him into the kitchen. Despite the pain in his eye, Karl worried about being punished for getting into trouble. At the same time, he hoped his brothers would deflect some of the blame.

As soon as Grace entered the kitchen, Max announced: "Mother, Karl's hurt!"

Fritz snitched a piece of bread and started gnawing at it.

"Sit here, dear. I'll call the Doctor," Grace said, guiding Karl into a ladder-backed chair before she vanished.

"Maybe it was the sight of the poles that provoked them." Karl's father's baritone conjecture had rounded the corner into the kitchen before he did. "However," he added, smoothing his mustache, "nothing as vicious as this has ever happened before."

"Yes it did!" Fritz corrected still chewing. "Remember when Charlie Engle lost…"

"Shut *up!*" Max yelled, angry with Fritz for mentioning Charlie, whom they all knew had lost his eye after he was injured in a street fight.

"Will I lose mine, too?" Karl spluttered.

"Nice goin' pal," Herman said, slapping Fritz on the back.

Fritz's shoulders hunched up near his ears.

"Hopefully not, son," their father said, turning back toward the dining room. Instead of proceeding, he changed his mind, reentered the kitchen, ran a cloth under cold water, and placed it over Karl's swollen eyelid. Then, after studying old bruises on Fritz's cheek, said, "You boys go sit by the fire and be kind to one another—if by any chance you are capable!"

Although Karl was relieved that his parents were too preoccupied to be furious, he thought that his injury was punishment for something he must have done wrong, even though he didn't know what that was exactly.

Within the hour, an optometrist arrived and examined Karl's eye. He gave no guarantee that it would heal without complication. "Only time will tell," he said as he glared through his monocle. He had attended to Charlie's injury as well and (as an aside to Grace in the hallway) mentioned the similarity of Charlie's wound to Karl's—adding, "In point of fact, this is the ninth such emergency from the bloody gang wars within the year!" Stifling a growl of frustration, he counted drops that he squeezed into Karl's eye and secured a large padded patch with a wrapping around Karl's head.

The doctor's demeanor grew more grim as he readied to depart. He reached for his valise in the hallway, and turning said, "Mrs. Behr, this could be critical I'm afraid. Sharp stones are lethal to the eye. Keep him quiet. Use the drops as specified. I'll be back tomorrow." He thrust one arm into his coat and doffed his hat in an undirected manner to Louis who was braced against the door.

Sarah herded the boys upstairs. Herman turned to Grace, laying his long-fingered hand on her shoulder. "We'll just have to wait, dear," he said. "Another trial is all this is. One day at a time, my darling. One day at a time."

Although Sarah brought biscuits and milk to Karl, he no longer felt like eating. All he craved was relief from the pain and the thought that he might lose his eye. When he lay back wondering how he could ever adjust, he was overwhelmed by compassion for his friend Charlie, whom he realized had never received adequate sympathy. The image of Charlie, standing with his eye-patch and a huge grin on his face, loomed iconic. *It must have been lonely and terrifying. I'll find him at Poly Prep and tell him how I know that now,* Karl thought, unable to imagine ever living up to the way Charlie had handled such a fate.

Empathy brimmed. Amber light seeped under the bedroom door. Floorboards creaked in high pitch. Voices of wind in the white pine outside lulled Karl to merciful sleep.

3

Traces

*H*ELEN WAITS FOR WATER TO BOIL so that she can brew the tea. She has filled the kettle too full for this to happen soon, so she leans forward to look out the kitchen window in East Hampton. Her gaze, passing over a late-blooming rose, travels to the center of the spiral where everything converges in darkness. Here, now, again, she recalls the ecstasy she felt when she discovered that Karl had joined her on board the *Titanic*.

She envisions him running toward her and relives her euphoria when he took hold of her hand as though he'd found gold. She remembers how they had stared at one another until they burst into laughter over the absurdity of their fixation. Passion begins this way, she thinks, swelling within the bud, replete with potential, at first closed tight to intrusion.

The rose wavers and she sees herself back in the ship's corridor, just outside her cabin door. She recalls how details contributing to the grandeur of the ship flooded her consciousness the instant she detected serious intent in Karl's emotion toward her. How her focus on aspects of minutiae—on the magnificence of the workmanship surrounding them—had helped her to deflect his intensity. How awkward and naïve she must have sounded when she resorted to superfluous chatter about the materials used to decorate her cabin: the fine linens, Jacobean moldings, touches of brocade.

It was all too much to assimilate—the fact, the sublime exaltation—that she was traveling First Class on the greatest ship ever built, with this exuberant, handsome man who seemed to find her desirable. She thought his attraction as preposterous as a practical joke played by God, not dissimilar to one of her brother Bud's little ruses to trap her into believing a convoluted notion to amuse himself with her gullibility when the truth emerged: Wasn't love a snare, set and hidden under leaves, just waiting for her leg to brush by?

What recourse is there against imposition of the immediate world?

Helen knows, but cannot realize that she is losing Karl. She feels that what she must do is hold still, fixate on him to enhance her memory and help him finish his writing, to bolster his sense of fulfillment.

It hadn't always been like this. There were times when she wasn't in love. But she detects that weakness doesn't matter anymore. There were myriad ways in which she had learned it was best for her not to feel that she could affect someone else's reasoning, only to try to understand it. The Great War had come and gone, but over every living thing its pall was cast. Helen had never stopped cowering underneath its shadow, which passed overhead with the deadly weight of unconscionable acts. That such cruelty can exist is beyond imagining; yet it is as real as it is shocking—a strident truth, unfathomable and inescapable.

She throws her head back, thinking again of how she felt when she and Karl embraced—how she had wondered then, at midnight on the ship, if she could believe in herself enough to convince her mother that she knew what she wanted. She was only nineteen and head-over-heels in love.

Now, after thirty-six years of marriage, having raised three sons and a daughter—the family she created with Karl—she sees that this has been her reason for living.

4

Train of Thought

"*D*ON'T STRAIN YOUR EYE TODAY, SON." Herman said, bending
to sit next to Karl. "You must stay here and rest, tough as it is for one
as *empfindlich* as you, my boy." Herman patted Karl's leg and handed him a means of distraction. "Here, I want you to be the keeper of
this Seth Thomas clock for a while. First it needs to be wound. Not
too tight. Exactly as I show you. During the day, study the roman
numerals from time to time. I'll help you learn them when I come
home tonight."

Karl fondled the sleeve of his father's coat, his fingers exploring—feeling the texture, measuring distances. He concentrated on
the contours of his father's profile, memorizing the way his high
forehead sloped down to the straight contour of his nose with its
protective mustache, full lips and rounded chin. A residue of factory
smells (wood, glue, dust, paper) lingered around him. Karl's gaze
scanned a pool of shadows under his father's eyes, which ineffably
evoked a sense of safe-haven engendered by his father's reliability—
evidence of his perseverance to a task.

"What is 'empfind...lich?' "

"A German word that describes someone who is easily hurt. Not
necessarily in a physical way, but who is too sensitive, driven to care
too much about what others think of him. I'm afraid you have inher-
ited this from your creaky old father, and I apologize. Often it is
better to be tough and filled with confidence—not arrogance, but
confidence." Herman cleared his throat and changed his tone: "By
the way, I had an eye injury once, so I know how you feel!"

Karl stretched up tall and touched his father's forehead.

"You did, Father? What happened?" He asked this, letting the
arrogance word pass by without inquiring what it meant in his
eagerness to keep his father talking so that he would stay.

21

"A pine needle stabbed my eye when I reached under a Christmas tree in the dark."

"Ooh, killer!" Karl commiserated.

"I remember it took several days for the pain to go away."

Karl stroked his father's hand. "What were you doing?"

"Doing?"

"Under the tree?"

"Oh…checking for mice. I mean biscuits…to see if mice were eating the biscuits!"

"But biscuits are put on the table for Saint Nick. You know that!"

Herman smiled and rose to leave for work. "You're a good boy," he said, patting the bed. "Stay in your room. Do not go out." Fastening his coat, Herman strode out the door and down the hall.

After straining to detect the last of his father's footsteps in the hallway, Karl reached out to hold and study the clock, regretting he hadn't delayed his father's departure by asking him what "arrogance" was. He turned the clock around, admiring the design on the face of it—a delicate splay of inlaid wood fanned like a scallop shell. The numerals were easy to identify at first, but then, what was IV? He placed the clock on the bedside table and attempted to actually see the minute hand move, but it was too hard to stare at it long enough. He sat back, wondering why paying close attention made time stop, whereas not watching made it disappear!

The tennis trophy—a little racquet and ball with his name on it, sitting on his wall-shelf—caught Karl's attention. Although puny compared to Max's golf trophies and Fritz's track ribbons, Karl remembered how his mother's eyes lit up on that sizzling summer day out in Boonton, New Jersey, when he had brought it home to her. Although the trophy was won in a local match (as Fritz had wasted no time pointing out), for Karl it was pure triumph.

Already innate in Karl and in his brothers, rivalry was reinforced by Herman and Grace, allegedly for the boys' benefit. Judgment resulting from their competitions (even if delivered by only a wink or a glare) always elicited some kind of sting. Whenever Karl was praised, if Fritz was jealous, Karl wished nothing nice had ever been said. The only time Karl dropped his fear of Fritz was during a tennis match when Karl's competitive spirit kicked-in regardless of the consequences.

Karl recalled the morning he and Fritz had been leaning out the third-floor window, arguing about which brother had gathered more wood for the stash in the yard: Fritz shouted, "I did!" When Karl claimed it was Max, Fritz couldn't tolerate insubordination from his little brother. "It was me!" he shrieked, slamming the window on Karl's fingers and stomping out of the room, leaving Karl to wallow in agony.

Later, at the dinner table, Fritz launched a series of offensive distractions to discourage Karl from spilling the beans about the incident to their mother: "By the way, Max, don't you think Karl's nose is too fat for the rest of his face?"

"Karl has a fine nose!" Grace swooped to intervene.

"Just look at the way he chews! Isn't it peculiar? You think so too, don't you Maxi!" Fritz kept prodding, ignoring his mother's defense.

Max remained silent. He had fetched ice-water for Karl's swollen fingers and knew Karl hadn't told anyone except him about the window-smashing, due to his dread of reprisal from Fritz, which was a mutual concern. Max had cultivated his middle-son position as a demilitarized zone. Meanwhile, Fritz whispered to Herman (just loud enough for Karl to hear), "What a floppy mop and puny upper lip he has!"

Despite his mother's deflections, Karl was mutilated by the relentless chiseling. "One day," he mumbled, still eyeing his tennis trophy, "One day, I'll prove to Fritz that I'm good for *some*thing." His sentence circled the room. As hard as he tried to muster confidence in projected wishful thinking, nothing ever erased the fact that when Fritz called him "a dumb, runty caboose," in his heart, he believed it.

Karl closed his eyes to pass the time by dwelling on summer days he and his family had recently spent on a farm out in the wild country around the Rockaway River—running naked with his brothers through the forest near the house until the noon bell, accompanied by his mother's call, triggered a scramble back into their clothes for lunch.

The place was teeming with creatures—dogs, ponies, sheep, chickens, cows, cats. Savory smells and succulent flavors abounded: sun-ripened tomatoes plucked and eaten straight off the vine; sweet carrots pulled from the dirt; grapes that were almost sweet; plums, strawberries, raspberries, peaches, and apples.

Each day renewed the challenge to conjure new adventures. Karl pictured the river as it appeared from the front porch of their big yellow house—bright as a quartz crystal set deep into the contoured hills. Then he envisioned himself and Fritz perched high over one of the streams, astraddle a gigantic tree trunk that had fallen across the river:

Fritz had hopped on first and made his way out over the water, chewing a stem of grass. Karl followed, nervously inching forward, trying not to look down. Sweaty palmed, he had lowered himself to a sitting position, unable to stop projecting the image of falling— turning over and over toward an ugly sprawl on the rocks below.

Karl remembered tossing bits of bark at pretend targets in an effort to appear nonchalant while wondering what Fritz was scheming. Staring down-river, Fritz had suggested forming a secret club. "Just the two of us," he said. "But, you know, Runty, we'll need an initiation ceremony, since you're the youngest member and I'm President, of course!"

"Like what?" Karl had asked, picking at the tree.

"Well, for starters, you'll have to walk barefoot in the stream when it's ice-cold. Hmm...and pee in a cup. Drink it. Then promise you'll do anything I say for a whole week. Uh...like hold still 'til I think of the next thing!"

"Oh *fine*," Karl consented, biting his lip. Being in cahoots with Fritz was worth just about any price, he figured.

As the clock struck eight, Karl sat up in bed, scratching his head, angry that he hadn't thought to ask Fritz what his end of the bargain would be. "I will never, ever be his fool again!" Karl announced, rising up, then flopping back.

His ruminations began to swirl as rapidly as water on the rock-strewn Rockaway. He pictured himself above the river, diving with his brothers from cliffs into tree-shaded pools, swimming through dark water pierced by shafts of light, then climbing up to dry on ledges as sun-dappled tree-trunks towered above. He recalled Herm say that Indians were watching them—that the jiggling sunlight reflecting off the water onto surrounding rocks and trees was really the spirits of their ancestors dancing.

Drawn to a thin line of light peeking at him from between the curtains, Karl slid from his bed across the floor to the window and pulled back the heavy damask to assess the various carriages passing by—a tally-ho, carrying almost a dozen people on top; then an old park drag painted black with gold trim wherein he imagined a mysterious passenger. Two men strutted along on the other side of the street, which was lined with brownstone buildings. Karl observed the people below, realizing they had no inkling that he—someone whose activities, unlike theirs, had come to a halt—was watching them.

He lifted a corner of the eye patch to see if...

"Morning my love!" his mother said, wafting in. "How do you feel?"

"Fine, Mum!"

"Can you see? Does it hurt?"

"Mmm…fuzzy… . Will I be all right?"

"I hope so. We won't know for some time. Promise me you'll stay quiet in your room today. You should not venture out where you might strain that eye or catch an infection. I've alerted the school. You've been excused. Do nothing, Karl, dear. Promise me?"

Karl nodded, pressing his lips together. "I've done pretty well so far."

"Get back into bed. Sarah will come with breakfast. I'll be in later to see you."

"Can I read?"

"No, darling. You mustn't. Not today."

When Grace kissed Karl's forehead, her skirt swooshed like reeds in a breeze. After she left the room, however, a trace of her stalwart demeanor overpowered the lingering scent of her sweet perfume.

Karl wrestled for a way to stay still and realized this was the first time he'd ever been eager to read. *Think*, he thought, letting his mind carry him. He lifted himself upright and crossed his legs, he considered whether that was *a tone of worry, or something else* he had detected in his mother's voice? To make himself feel better, he reminisced about a hot afternoon in Boonton when Grace and her friend, Mally Peabody, had gone rollicking up river, along with him, Fritz, and Max:

A local man had mentioned to his mother that fossils had occasionally (although rarely) been discovered in the riverbed, so she suggested going on an excursion to find one. She and Mally waded upstream with their skirts flowing in the water behind them. They picked up rocks, knocked them apart with makeshift rock-hammers, and tossed them back into the river with ever bigger splashes aimed at getting each other wet until—Karl laughed, thinking: *the activity hit rock-bottom.* Mally stumbled, dragging Grace along with her as they plunged into the water, shrieking with laughter.

Karl remembered how his mother's summoning had echoed from the riverbanks: "Come see what I've found!"

Cradled in the glistening palm of her hand was a clear and primitive impression of an ancient fish!

Several weeks afterward as Grace scanned the newspaper at breakfast, she drew the paper down, squinted at the boys over the top of it and said, "Remember that fossil we found in the river, boys?" Adjusting her glasses, she said, "Listen to this! Paleontologists attribute this specimen, *'one of the finest replicas of a prehistoric fish ever found'* to Mrs. Herman Behr!" Then, peering over at her sons added, "Who just happens to be your very own mother!"

"Do we get money?" Fritz asked.

"Fame?" Max added.

"Neither," Grace demurred. "Merely satisfaction from our luck!"

Continuing to pass time in his bed, Karl recalled the morning German friends of his father's, fresh from Hamburg, were seated at the Boonton breakfast table when Fritz and Max, proud as pirates, raced in and slammed the carcass of a skunk smack on the table to be admired by all. The slam/thump and noxious stink enhanced the boys' glee until a geyser of guttural German gushed from their father and they quickly removed the skunk. Then he remembered the moment his brother Herman dumped an entire bowl of butterballs on the bald head of their neighbor Harry Beecher. Herm was sent to his room for the rest of the day but emerged after only an hour without further retribution. This tacit leniency ignited fury in Fritz, who shouted that he'd never received a single "minuscule" reprieve from his penalties—"Never once!"

When Sarah knocked on the bedroom door, Karl was drawn back to focusing on his predicament, but she delivered the consummate panacea—Karl reached eagerly for the tray of food.

"You boys got into one heck of a row last night, didn't you!" she said.

"Mmm," Karl managed a mumble and a gulp of milk. "Sarah, I've been thinking..."

"Usually a positive sign, unless to devise a trick with sheets, slimy worms, or..."

Karl chewed but kept talking to delay her departure from the room. "Some people take over. I mean—take over other people in little ways or big ways, or any way they can get away with."

"You're quite a young lad to be so keen on socialization," Sarah said.

Not having any idea what she meant, slurping and wiping his mouth on his pajama sleeve, Karl said, "Well, I, I'm the youngest 'n all, and I'm s'posed to drink pee, keep still in achy water, wear my shirt backwards, be a slave—stuff like that—for no good reason. Fritz says so. If the Micks *pulp* anybody, it's always me. Herm isn't *really* helpful, 'though he tries. Margaret's a *girl*. Mum says she's *preoccupied*, whatever that means. Dad's always at work. Max is all right. But you're my best friend. Well, you and Mum. So can I ask you something?"

"Shoot now, or hold your fire."

"Since you are a *maid*, do you feel put-upon like I do when people tell you what to do all the time?"

"Well, I sure like to be on the other end of somebody's kindness toward me; but no matter what people do, they're serving something, or someone—even if only themselves. And this is the kind of work I'm good at: providing comfort. So, if you know the word, there's *dignity* in what I do. Whether queen, maid, captain, or crew, we all have reason to work, right? Even if it's just sweepin' the porch."

"Well, I heard Mum call you 'Angel.' Are you one? Because if angels are people who fly around helping, then you're an angel. That's for sure!"

Sarah leaned down. "Well, see what I mean! If you think it's true, then I feel like one! You hold on tight to your dignity no matter what happens. I'll be back in a while to fetch the tray after you've finished."

Karl sat back, listening to Sarah's airy footfall fade down the hallway. He sipped his milk, wishing he'd asked her what *dignity* was as his thoughts drifted back to Boonton—to their secret cabin in the woods. He had been standing by when his father answered Herm's request for wood to build it, agreeing to supply materials *if* the brothers could plan and build the cabin together with no outside help or fights. As soon as they began, arguments escalated, and Karl was convinced it would be impossible—until Sarah intervened to settle two disputes.

Gradually, a small one-room cabin with a tarpaper roof had been erected in the midst of a thicket on a creek, just far enough away from the farmhouse for privacy. The only way to reach it was by traversing tunnels that the boys had cut through the thorny under-growth—a maze of bramble passageways that wound for hundreds of yards, with false dead-end paths and a ceiling clearance so low no grown-up ever managed to make it all the way to the cabin. None but Sarah, who coaxed herself along by ringing out frustration in curse words from beginning to end, much to the boys' hilarity.

During their first night in the cabin together, the brothers con-jured ghost stories in macabre and grim detail. Herm was the master-mind. Candlelight sparred with shadows on his face. He lowered his bushy brows and brewed suspense, never wavering from his convic-tion about the legitimacy of every bloody embellishment regardless of the inevitably defiant fists that were swung at him.

When all was finally quiet inside the cabin, Karl listened to the forest creep with shadows and spooky little clicks. From somewhere in the darkness there was a slow discourse of owls, and Karl thought he had never heard a more spellbinding exchange. Early in the evening, the moon lifted above the stream like a juicy cantaloupe. And later, Karl saw it shine through the pine boughs, teasing him to think of it as a round white pillow flung at the stars.

In the morning, when Karl and Herman awoke, they noticed that Max and Fritz had gone. At the same moment, they heard a truculent though distant voice yelling in anger.

One heartbeat later, Max and Fritz burst through the door and fell to the floor, dropping the slippery watermelon they had carried through the thorny tunnels. They managed to slash it open and dive into the mouth-watering fruit—devouring everything (seeds and all) as fast as they could—so that if the farmer, whom Karl suspected had been yelling, was able to work his way to the cabin, he'd only have spotted a couple of skins in a puddle.

"Can we say we *borrowed* it?" Karl mused. He wasn't eating any. He didn't like watermelon.

"No, K, that baby was *stolen*. Go fill the bucket. We've got to wash away the evidence. ...*Now!*" Fritz snapped.

Although reminiscing was the only way to entertain himself, Karl's loneliness sharpened and restlessness tipped the equation, making it impossible for him to stay put; so he shoved his feet into the slippers by his bed and sneaked down the hall to the stairs where he stopped to stretch out his toe and lower himself onto the first step, willing it not to squeak.

Once in the library, he stopped to eye the portrait of a red-coated gentleman over the mantelpiece who resembled George Washington delicately holding a tri-cornered hat between his thumb and middle finger. The painting had never much concerned Karl until one wintry night when Fritz exclaimed, "No matter where you stand, he stares at you!" Karl had run around the room to verify that this was true.

Now "George" seemed to glare through Karl with stern accusations, all of which Karl shrugged off as he tiptoed into the kitchen, wiggled the lid off the cookie jar, stuffed four cookies into his pocket, and was just starting to nudge open the swinging door into the dining room when he immediately eased it back again—as s l o w l y as possible—because both of his parents were sitting at the table in their coats, engaged in conversation mere inches away.

Karl listened to his mother say: "Darling, it's imperative to do something. Intuition is all I have to go by, for better or worse. I know this may seem overly cautious to you, perhaps even frivolous or rash. Your world is all-consuming with so much to manage—your employees' health, sales, and salaries—whereas my concern is the well-being of the children. I'm convinced we have reached the end of peace and prosperity for them in this neighborhood. I desire a major change—one that will help them grow, learn languages, and meet new people. I want them to spend time in Europe as I did when I was young. It would be rewarding. Don't you agree?"

There was silence. A chair scraped against the floor. Karl turned to make a getaway, but heard his father reply, "You're right. I worry about the boys' safety and want to give them all we can. I often reminisce about my peaceful summers in Hamburg—the romance of the Elbe. It would be wise—*replenishing*—to return to Europe for a time. Things are running well enough here. I could see my way clear to visit. But won't this be too much for you to manage, especially with Margaret so young? I'm not surprised you have suggested this. I was thinking about it myself!"

"I'm glad you agree. We'll tell the boys. It will be fine to bring Margaret along. Meanwhile, pray for Karl's eye to heal, my darling."

Karl detected the bird-like sound of a kiss. He retreated backward through the kitchen and the library, turned to face forward when he had reached the stairs, tiptoed past his sister Margaret's room, sidled to his bedroom door, stretched his hand toward the knob, turned it soundlessly and slipped unseen into his room.

5

Reliance

*H*ELEN NOTICES A TINY REFLECTION of the kitchen window—a trapezoid of lemon light, a wisp of turquoise, a dash of indigo—on the side of the glass pitcher she will use for the tea. The shadow of a bird passes through the image; she sees a distortion of herself bent over in search of something amazing there.

When she was nine, Helen's father, Logan Newsom, did not return from a fishing trip. The anxious hours of waiting for him expanded ever outward like water rings to another universe. Her father had suffered a fatal heart attack as he was approaching the boat to begin his trip home.

Helen remembers managing, then, somehow through self-reliance, to get through the string of days and weeks following that terrible loss when her mother Sallie began leaving the house more and more often until she was rarely present; or if so, preoccupied with pressing concerns that catapulted over and above her ability to cope with them. Devoid of the advice and wherewithal from her dear Logan, upon whom she had relied for six blissful years, Sallie fell into despair. Papers were piled into towers on Logan's desk as if he might come back to deal with them; she neglected to assume responsibility. The lock on the door that he always fixed remained broken.

There was much to be concerned about. Their farm outside Columbus, Ohio, was part of an idyllic, interdependent patchwork that spread past the powder-blue hills visible from Helen's window. Quilted seams of fences, walls, and hedgerows protected and separated miles of crops, animals, gardens, forests, fields, hills, ponds, and streams. And the beads of a farmer's sweat anointed each and every detail.

With everything having frozen or turned brittle during the first winter after Logan's death, Helen's mother yearned for city life—for the company of people bustling between shops and businesses. She departed ever more frequently, leaving Helen and her brother Bud for extended days and nights with the housekeeper and the farmer, who took time from his chores to drive them by carriage to school.

In the fountain outside the kitchen window, Helen sees a reflection of dogwood leaves. She watches the leaves tremble. She listens to the cicadas' syncopated incantation. It reminds her of a night when she was thirteen, lying in her bed alone when her mother had gone to the city. The window panes were slick-black, but moonlight spilled in and blanched the room. She remembers how she envisioned the farmer's dark silhouette—his shadow climbing from the sill, creeping across the floor. The sudden shroud of smells: hay, cow-manure, engine oil.

She blinks at something beside the kitchen window and holds still, listening to the water churn inside the kettle. Pressure builds, growing louder until steam bursts out in an alarming whistle. As she lifts the kettle off the flame, she realizes how far she has come from that lengthy stretch of helplessness—especially from, worst of all, the look of shock and confusion that had welled in her mother's eyes over yet another problem she could not begin to handle.

Helen watches the tea infuser plunge. She places the lid on the pot and the pot on the tray next to the pitcher where the window reflection has disappeared. She takes two cups from the cabinet, sets them alongside the pitcher, opens a drawer, forages for spoons and gathers cream, sugar, napkins, then several biscuits to place on her favorite plate. She notices new prominence in the veins on the back of her hand and quickly lifts the tray to carry it out to Karl, eager for his company.

6

The Power of Trust

$\mathcal{K}$ARL RETURNED TO SCHOOL WEARING an eye patch. Although it was easy for him to understand his classmates' making light fun of it, he knew they had no idea what it was like to be on the inside. "Empfindlich"—he recalled the word—might describe me, but they are the ones who are blind.

Charlie tapped Karl on the shoulder from behind as they were climbing the stairs to class. Karl wheeled around. Expecting that someone was trying to play a joke on him, he was relieved to see just the person he wanted to find. He threw his arm around Charlie's shoulder.

"Now I know what you went through and I wish I'd said something about it!"

"I'm sure you do, K. Sorry you got hurt. But you're going to be fine. You have to be! It wouldn't be fair for both of us to have to wear one of these." Charlie raised his hand to touch his own eye patch. "I'm used to it, as long as I never have to move away from here—now that everybody knows what happened to me and I don't have to explain. Nothing's going to bring my eye back, but Dad says I'll get a glass one some day so I'll look almost normal. He says the best are made in Germany. We're already planning a trip. I hope you don't lose yours. But if you do, you can come with us!"

Karl smiled blankly, trying to avoid confiding in Charlie about his parents' plan to move to Europe.

Charlie and his sister, Charlotte, lived only one block south of Henry Street. Their family was part of a network of Karl's father's German friends who, through participation in a Brooklyn matrix of German establishments—the bakery, the church, the *Brooklyner Zeitung* (newspaper)—were able to compare notes on frequent trips back to *das Vaterland* (the Fatherland), which always inspired vigorous debates or sentimentality toward *alte Tagen* (olden days) in *Deutschland.* Karl's father's desire to give something back to Germany inspired his effort to translate classic English literature into German for people "back home" to appreciate. In these translations, he often said, he found nuances in German more aptly expressive than those in English.

Charlie's compromised vision never deterred him from excelling at goalie in the "shinny" street-hockey games with Karl and his brothers. Actually Charlie's deficit seemed to afford him a miraculous sixth sense, since he rarely failed to extend an agile limb in-the-nick-of-time. When Max and Karl stopped at his house after games, Charlie often spread his stamp collection out on the floor, touching the specimens as if they were butterfly wings while explaining the source, history, or peculiarity in the printing of each and details of philately, such as the fact that the value of a stamp depended upon the condition of the gum on its back. Once, when Max blared enthusiasm for Charlie's vermilion collection of bank notes with the three-dimensional busts that he referred to as those "floating heads," Charlie didn't skip a beat: "Take them," he said, "they're yours!" And then he handed the entire sleeve to Max.

Deception bothered Charlie above all other foibles. Maybe because, at times, he needed to second-guess a person whose sympathies might be purposefully hidden from him. Whenever Charlie detected blatant indiscretion, he pounced on it. Karl came upon him in the midst of chastising a classmate at school because the boy had lied to his girlfriend and Charlie called him on it. Charlie knew the boy had kissed another girl in the corner of the schoolyard and heard him deny it.

"You poor son of a *bitch*," Charlie said emphatically. "Doesn't *trust* mean anything to you?"

Since Charlie was admired by everyone, there was no recourse for his classmate but to apologize.

The more time Karl spent with Charlie, the more he began to identify with him, even to think that his own fate might be the same as far as his eye was concerned.

Days of wearing the patch accumulated along with Karl's internalized prayers, which were promises to God that turned into bribes: *If my eye heals, I'll do better in school. If my eye heals, I promise to become a better person. If my eye heals, I won't make another wish for a whole year.*

Before the doctor could finish his sentence declaring Karl's eye free of danger, Karl had heaved the patch into the waste bin. Gratitude rolled forward and broke in perfect waves. He was whole again and he swore he would never ever take his sight for granted. Waves of relief hit rock, however, as soon as he thought about facing Charlie. But the minute Charlie saw Karl without his eye patch, he whooped and danced so uproariously it would have seemed to an onlooker that Charlie must have won a prize or something.

After this great news, and since there had been only one other skirmish with the Micks since election night, Karl began to believe that his parents had rescinded their plan to go to Europe. They had continued to host lavish dinner parties, where, on one occasion, the world-famous Hungarian violinists, Albertini and Romani, performed for an audience of over a hundred friends, whirling to German waltzes in the glittering hall. At eleven o'clock, Romani announced his plan to complete the end of a rhapsody while sliding down the banister of the circular staircase, asking all the guests if they thought he could. Karl, Fritz, and Max wagered bets for and against this proposition from their spot at the top of the stairs. Romani charged up the staircase, two steps at a time, stood next to the boys, winked at Karl, straddled the banister, and proceeded to "polish" his entire way down while playing flawlessly, even adding a back-of-the-bow glance on the last sconce chandelier as he leapt off——*ding!*

"I win!" Fritz said, rapping Karl hard on the head and running away, his pajamas pants flapping.

Max, who had bet Spinner (the black and white bunny he kept in his room) that this could not be done, backed way, hoping no one would claim the prize.

In spite of having no further reason to think he would have to move from his beloved home, Karl was apprehensive whether or not to ask Sarah if she had heard mention of their going to Europe. "No, nothing," she answered without asking why he had inquired. Karl's ease about this was not to last, however. Not much past the day of the fire, anyway.

Some of the town's people theorized that mean-minded Micks must have started the devastating fire. On the other hand, those from South Brooklyn posited that it was likely the Remsen Street boys "on account of their bein' an idle-handed bunch who were fated to wrestle with the dangerous brew of boredom." Everyone agreed that only the most despicable of delinquents would consider setting waist-high grass ablaze on a breezy dry day in March amusing.

The second it sparked, the grass sizzled fast as a fuse to a firecracker. Before long the semi-vacant block where the fire began was entirely singed. Just as it needed fuel, wind obliged, nudging the fire to leap and burn a large factory near Tiffany Place, only a short distance from Herman Behr & Co.

One of a steady stream of three-horse fire engines galloped past the boys racing home after being dismissed early from school. Fritz was quickest to hop down the school steps on his way to check out the commotion. Herman, Max, and Karl followed directly behind him with smoke rushing up in giant black billows as they ran. Once home, Fritz leaped onto the front step, cupped a hand to the side of his mouth and yelled, "Hold on to your hats boys!" He reached up to grasp his own in the gale and pointed in the direction of the smoke, saying, "That could be Father's company!"

The sight of Fritz's silhouette—standing tall, legs splayed, looking skyward with one hand shielding his eyes—seared itself into

Karl's memory. It seemed to him as though Fritz's mere declaration could make a thing happen, even if it hadn't yet.

Herman suggested going to their grandmother's house on South Henry Street where they might have a better vantage point from which to see the blaze. So the four brothers dumped their books helter-skelter on the foyer floor and took off alongside the fire engines that thundered by—horses with blinders on, manes peaked.

As he raced into their grandmother's house, Karl was relieved as soon as he caught sight of his mother standing at the window, glancing in the direction of the smokestack next to her husband's factory only a block from where the fire was raging.

She turned to greet the boys; her wide skirt whispered at the floor. Furrows of concern lodged in shadows across her face. Karl ran to wrap his arms around her. She looked down, hugging him as she spoke to all her sons, "All we can do now is pray for your father and the people in and around the fire, boys. If you want to stay here with Gran and me, there will be no clashing, clowning or fighting. Agreed?"

The boys nodded and assumed their silent posts. Karl stared at a tower of smoke, directing his thoughts telepathically: *Stop wind. Stop. Please stop. Please God ... stop the wind,* he thought, over and over and over.

Max shut his eyes and placed a hand gently on his mother's back. Herm sat next to his grandmother, Julie, who looked at him and winked, although serenity was absent from her gray-blue eyes. Fritz pressed his hand on the windowpane and then immediately pulled down his sleeve to wipe away the greasy smudge with furious swirls.

"This is a day we won't forget," Grace said, her tone silencing even the innermost thoughts of her boys.

Waiting provided time to think. Time stood still as stone. Karl was transfixed by his mother's far-away look. It seemed to him that the fate of the world was suspended in her expression with the intensity of her stare leading him to imagine her thoughts traveling a thousand directions at once.

Although Karl had no notion of clairvoyance, his mother was indeed reaching into her memory—thinking of how her husband had started his business at the age of fourteen because *his* father, Eduard, after years of traveling back and forth to Germany to pay debts and to bring a hardware business to America, had suddenly died of consumption, leaving Julie and her six children obliged to find work.

Karl's father, Herman, a middle child, had spent some six months (which he once referred to as *eternity*) figuring out what to do before he settled on the idea of manufacturing "pouncing paper," or sandpaper, used widely by hat makers and other businesses in town.

First, over a bakery on Second Avenue, he constructed a brush by hand, drawing bristles through the holes he bored in order to facilitate spreading glue. Then, into many a wee morning hour, he crafted a faultless seven-foot-wide wooden wheel, upon which he wound his first finished paper, which was still in use at the factory.

Karl saw the slope of Grace's brows steepen. There was a subtle lowering of an eyelid, giving him the impression that her thoughts had shifted to something more distant. Indeed, she had begun to dwell on a time long before she met her husband when she had been consumed in a kind of fire, herself:

She was holding hands with her first love, Henry, while they stood marveling at a summer night's bonfire. People referred to Henry as "charming." He had a look—enticing as pollen to a bee. The spell of Grace's affection, enhanced by cities of fireflies and arpeggios of moonlight while they wandered the countryside for eight summers, was obliterated in a single afternoon when Grace bounded into his cabin by the pond, having come to surprise him—the moment he was busy making love to his friend, Jeremy.

Groveling for the reason she was standing in that doorway, Grace remembered she had wanted to discuss Transcendentalism. Instead, she stood transfixed, witnessing every hypothetical alibi twist into a Gordian knot. As time went by, she would learn that

Henry was driven to philander in order to satisfy his frequent need to express love by way of its inherent duplicity.

Karl looked from his mother—out over the rooftops—into furious thunderclouds of smoke, then peered back at the touchstone of her face to guess her thoughts again.

Suddenly, Fritz, with his shrewd eye trained on the branches near a street lamp, said, "Mother, look. Mother, look! The wind is shifting. It's dying down. See the tree's not moving!" He pointed toward the street, tugging at his mother's sleeve. "Neither is the banner over the grocery shop!"

Karl saw his mother's eyes settle into peacefulness, and he was convinced that Earth could continue to spin as she had told him it did. Grace tightened her grip on his shoulder, turned and swept her arm out wide as a wing. Gathering Fritz, Herman, Max, and Karl, she declared, "Oh my good Lord in Heaven; you're right Fritz! I think our prayers…"

"…have been answered?" whispered Herman.

Grace bid her boys hug their grandmother and return home immediately. Fritz was dead set on racing to the fire, but Grace was stern: "Fritz, some day you might want to be a fireman—such an honorable service—if so, you'll be grateful to every mother who keeps her children out of harm's way."

Fritz twisted his torso. He wound the cord of the lead weighted shade pull around his finger, launched it, and cringed when it came back crashing against the glass, bounced, and crashed again. Lunging forward to stop it, he said, "Well, then, Mother, how'm I ever going to know if being a fireman is something I'd like to do if I can't find out!"

"All in good time, dear." Grace moved to hug him.

Fritz pulled away, adding, "Then nobody else can either!"

"Herman may if he wishes."

"Not fair! That's not fair!"

"He's older than you are, Fritz."

"So? Age doesn't mean anything!" Fritz protested.

"Maybe not in some cases, but a sense of responsibility comes along with it."

"I'm not going anyway, Futzie, so don't be jealous," Herman said.

"Can I go?" Max asked for the sake of it.

"No, Max. Now, we're going home and leaving Gran in peace," Grace announced.

Fritz stuck his tongue out at Max, and shoved the curtain-pull hard at Karl when his mother had turned away.

"Bully!" Karl said under his breath.

7

A Signal

𝓗ELEN WALKS THROUGH THE HOUSE in East Hampton, carrying her tray of tea and biscuits to Karl. When she arrives on the terrace, she sees a leaf lift and whirl next to his foot. A memory lingers but does not manifest. She is relieved to be outside with her husband, thinking of subjects she might engage to raise his spirits.

She considers telling him something that happened to her, but thinks he won't know what to say about it, other than voicing skepticism. As she watches the leaf spin she sits to serve tea and decides to tell him about an event that she has never confided in him before.

"Something's on your mind," Karl says. He has been noticing Helen's fearfulness. *Why didn't I see it before,* he wonders.

"Yes—just popped in," Helen says, lightly.

"Might as well *pop* back out, then."

"Remember your grandmother's story about the poltergeist in Germany?"

"Yes, she swore it was true. Do you want to hear it again?"

"Yes, sure; later. But did I ever tell you mine?"

"Something tells me you're about to." Karl reaches for her hand, knowing that aside from the affection he had for his beloved mother, Helen is the only woman whom he has ever loved in the way of legend, of poetry. He sees that she wears her expectation heavily and he wonders: *Why was I never able to separate myself from my drive to perform?*

"If you're too busy, I can wait."

"No. No. I'm all ears." Karl welcomes the distraction from his efforts to write the difficult chapter.

"Well, when I was a little girl…"

"When were you *little?*" he kidded, testing her sense of humor.

"Oh, you remind me of Bud, you scalawag. When I was *young-er*, I felt and heard something I thought must have emanated from…"

"Tell me." He reached for her hand.

"It was a winter night," she said, grateful for his attention. "My mother was gone, as usual, and my backwoods brother Bud was out, likely stalking nocturnal creatures. There was no one in the house but me. We didn't have a dog then, as odd as that sounds. I was surrounded by an endless sea of countryside There was no living soul within shouting distance. I built and lit a fire, turned on the phonograph, and discovered my grandfather's albums that had been hidden for years in the cabinet right under my nose."

"I can't recall…had you known your grandfather when he was alive?"

"No. My father, Logan Newsom, was the ninth of my grandfather Junius Newsom's eleven children, and I was born during the year Junius died."

"How on earth did he bear up under the pressure of having all those children?"

"Well, I can't imagine, but I think he had *something* to do with creating the burden," Helen said with a hint of a grin. "He was a stalwart man, quite the adventure seeker, forever eager for fun though never far from home." She paused in thought and then continued, "Well now, in this bright morning light, the thing that happened seems inconsequential; although, for me at the time, it was not. I remember the event as having been real as real is *real*. Although subtle, it was quite a spectacular specter!"

"I'm hooked; reel me in."

"I put the albums back into their designated cabinet, spread the fire's embers, climbed the stairs to my bedroom, and placed my lamp next to a photograph of my grandfather that was on my desk. Then I stared at his face, longing to know him, wishing I could hear him—wanting him to say something to me from the other side, if you will.

Naturally this sounds a bit beyond the pale, but that's where the line of souls dwells. Does it not?"

"Yes, if at all. ...I've done that too—spoken to my mother's photograph, often in fact. And, as you know, I learned a lot from my sisters: Gertrude is an astrology aficionado and Margaret claims she can *communicate*, if you know what I mean." Karl attempted to wiggle his brows with little success.

"Yes, well, I never contemplated having psychic abilities. As a matter of fact, I would have shunned them, which is why what happened astounded me:

I walked across a small hallway and was on my way through Bud's bedroom when there was a sudden swirling of air behind my foot accompanied by a whirring sound like wind coming through a narrowly opened window. I felt and heard it behind me—my *left* foot in fact—and I turned around quickly to see what could have caused the vortex. But there was nothing visible and nothing consequential. I searched for a creature under the bed. Not a peep. Not a glowing eye. There was no source for a breeze, nor what I was looking for—*Bud!* hiding there, about to jump out and scare me. I know it seems a silly little nothing of a happening. I'm sure you might not believe me, but at the time it was…"

"Maybe when the fire was dying it drew cold wind in?"

"That's just it—I knew there was no apparent source. I wracked my brain for one! Once there was a wild raccoon hiding under the bed there, but that occurred many years later. There was nothing in the room. It was winter. No windows or doors were ajar. The flue in the upstairs chimney was closed tight and the one down in the living room fireplace was much too distant to have drawn such a whirlwind from out of the blue."

"Oh, it must have been him then—your grandfather's spirit!" Karl smiled and his eyes lit up. Something comforting settled his shoulders.

"At the time that's what I thought," Helen said, looking into the bottom of her teacup.

"Tell you what: after I go, I'll come back and send you a signal."

"A *signal?*"

"Sure. Well, you know—a sign, a scare, or a fright? Tickle your ankles?"

"Don't you dare! Just do something so I'll know you're all right."

"More wind?"

"How about sending a soft breeze—or money!" Helen laughs, bringing Karl's hand up to her lips.

8

Change

AFTER THE FIRE, KARL CAUGHT SIGHT of his father staggering into the foyer saturated in gray grime. He watched his mother embrace him and help remove his coat.

"We called for dynamite. Explosives were set to be detonated," Herman said. "We agreed to blow up the plant to prevent the fire from spreading. In fact we were kneeling, all set to go, when the wind deflated like a thief struck by conscience. Oh, *Geliebte,* my beloved, we were so narrowly spared! I've heard that this was the worst fire Brooklyn has ever had; it is still smoldering and could reignite."

Herman dropped his head into his hands and began to stoop. His English flowed naturally into the German word "schade," meaning pity, and then: "Gott sei Dank im Himmel, dass unsere Leben verschont geblieben sind" (thank God in Heaven our lives have been spared).

Grace suggested he go upstairs and rest a while as Max raced in and wrapped his arms around his father. "Mother told us to pray, Father," Max said. "Fritz saw that the wind stopped. I *whispered* it first; but he *said* it first!"

"By the grace of God our company was spared, but so many people have lost everything," Herman said.

Karl's father worked long hours during the subsequent months, attempting to double his production in order to relieve as many families of financial strain as possible. Signs of exhaustion pooled in mauve-gray depressions on his face, but he was content when Karl assisted him in reading letters of gratitude that were stacked high on his desk. In the process of meeting dire needs, Herman sacrificed most of his own profit. The over-exertion worried his mother enough to warn him not to repeat his father's history:

Herman's father, Eduard, first cousin to the Prime Minister of Saxony, was fifty-three when he died of "galloping consumption" after continuing to overwork despite a high fever.

Having achieved financial success through a hardware business, Eduard, at age thirty-one, and Julie, at age eighteen, fell in love and married in Hamburg on April 29th, 1843. But after Eduard's prosperous business was ruined by rust in the aftermath of a fire, and as a consequence of the liberal uprising during the Revolution of 1848, he left for America, "the land of unlimited possibilities," where he swiftly established and sold a profitable wallpaper business in Newark, New Jersey. Within a year and a half he had paid his creditors in Hamburg and brought his family on the steamer *Washington* to New York—an eighteen-day passage in the fall of 1850. (At the time, four of their seven children had been born. Herman was the third child, their second son.)

Eduard then traveled back to Hamburg (missing the birth of his fifth child) to establish supply and replenishments for a second hardware business in New York, which precipitated a move to Brooklyn. Providing him with resources to live well and the ability to take his family back to Germany often, the business thrived until it collapsed during the Civil War.

When Eduard died, Gustave, aged nineteen, the eldest child, was the only one able to earn a small income. Although merely sixteen, Henry, the fourth child (Herman's younger brother) had passed himself off as eighteen and was away fighting for the Union Army in the Civil War.

Incurring considerable debt, Julie opened a boarding house. Although her sons were eventually employed and promoted in various businesses of glue, metal, and piano manufacturing, it was Herman's abrasives company that provided the primary income for her family.

In Brooklyn, Julie enjoyed occasionally entertaining Karl and the rest of her grandchildren with recollections of her youth in Wandsbeck, near Hamburg, where she had grown up in a timber-framed Jägerhaus surrounded by tall fir trees. Her father (who also died early, when she was young) had been the forester for the estate there. When Eduard departed to seek his fortune in America, she returned to live in the same quaint cottage where her fourth child was born.

While his grandmother described that little Jägerhaus with wind whistling through the piney woods surrounding it, Karl was sleepily picturing her there, sewing by a fire in the "keeping" room. Then he sat straight up when she said, "It was an unforgettable occurrence when a poltergeist came shuffling down the stairs!" Julie continued: "The specter made a racquet in the vestibule and a commotion near the front door. But the moment I left my chair to see who or what was there, everything was silent. Then a few nights later, the ghost unpacked an enormous clothes closet in the center of the house while everyone slept—a most astonishing debacle that happened countless times and was so disconcerting to the farmhand who lived just on the other side of the closet that he demanded to move to other quarters. In spite of the mischievous spook, the Jägerhaus was a marvelously joyful place." Julie jested, "Just imagine how infuriating it would have been had I to rectify such a rumpus of linens in my boarding-house closet!"

Although Grace worried about Herman's health in the aftermath of the Brooklyn fire, it was Julie who was taken ill. The doctor's declaration was curt: "Her pneumonia appears to be irreversible. Provide comfort with as much warm moisture as possible."

Grace and Herman moved Julie into their house to be cared for. Karl kept a vigil at her door where he witnessed her transformation—he stood expecting angels, wondering if his grandmother could see them already, and noting that cannon fire could not have brought her attention back to him. On the afternoon she slipped away, her face seemed sculpted from sand, readied for a return to the sea. Everyone gathered around her, and in the silence, between prayers, Karl thought: *We must be the angels.*

Before the undertaker arrived to take his grandmother away, Karl was sent to rest in his room. He lifted his violin out of its case, nestled it under his chin and drew back the bow. Music flowed as though the instrument was playing itself.

Grace placed photographs of Julie strategically around the mansion and spoke about her often to reinforce memories. Then, on the day Karl's father's brother Robert moved in to occupy Julie's Brooklyn home, Karl noticed a map of Europe spread open across his mother's desk, accompanied by a scenic picture of the Alps.

The plan to move to Europe was announced by his father during dinner on Karl's eleventh birthday, May 30th, 1896. Karl attempted to ignore it by concentrating his attention on the candle flame that flickered, reflecting confusion in his eyes—its tip flared and intertwined, spitting a frenzy of sparks. Beyond the candle, in the scenic wallpaper, Karl spotted the man who had always smiled as he doffed his hat. Now he was smirking. Considering the inevitable, Karl could no longer tell which part of the news was worse—apprehension to leave his cherished home with summers at the river, or the pending misery of having to say good-bye to Charlie.

"Will Sarah come?" Karl heard Herm inquire from the peripheral fog.

"Andrew?" Max asked.

Fritz burst forth rapid-fire: "How 'bout Mary, Louis, Andrew, the horses, my bicycle, Herm's gerbils, Max's bunny, Pokey (the mouse) and..." He wailed after being kicked under the table.

"Of course, dears," said Grace, attempting to snuff-out the crackly reactions. "Margaret will come. And Sarah. Also any animals that can be easily transported: the gerbils; the rabbit, the mouse—if you must, unless you see reason to let them stay in Boonton along with the horses where they'd be better off. There are plenty of bicycles in Europe, but we could manage to bring some. Don't forget, we'll be coming back to America some day. What you must do is say farewell to all your friends and to this place. It is highly unlikely we will ever live here again. But your father will stay nearby in an apartment and he can send messages to you from your friends, or vice versa. We will not live abroad forever—just a few years."

"Years!" Fritz exclaimed, peering downward with such a look of doom that Karl wondered if his fearless brother felt in some way responsible for this fate—equating the word "years" with *forever* just as he was. Everyone at the table was of the opinion that boarding schools in Switzerland were stricter than at home. Karl had seen Herm gulp when his father mentioned the "boarding" part. Dread seized the air, thundering like a stone slab shutting a sarcophagus.

Conversely, Max grew more and more animated—swinging his legs, guzzling his milk and twisting at a dark eyebrow. "Well, I could jump Jupiter!" he declared. "This is gonna be some swell escapade!"

Max's enthusiasm broke the ice. Herm seemed to concur with a few, slow, thoughtful nods. Sarah cheered above Herm, squeezing his shoulders.

Everything at their Brooklyn Heights mansion—down to the last shoelace and pin—was packed, shipped, given or swept away. As it turned out, only Sarah was to accompany Grace to Switzerland—all the other servants readied to attend Mr. Behr's needs at a new apartment in New York City. Except for Andrew who returned to Boonton to find supplemental employment there.

On their final evening at the house, friends lured each Behr family member to an activity, with the exception of Sarah, who stayed with Margaret. When they returned home, cheers accompanied by a brass gutter band rang out from the shadows. Scores of friends in togas burst into song.

At the end of the evening, Karl stood next to Charlie and Charlotte, apprehension spiking like fever because he believed that his security and all his prized memories were tied to the place where he lived. Although impossible to rationalize, he regarded the house as a "being." When he glanced at its façade, he saw the windows glare sadly at him. But this paled in comparison to having to say good-bye to Charlie.

Charlie preempted good-bye with a promise: "The second you set your big toe back in America, I'll come visit you."

"Let's write letters," Karl added, attempting to be cheerful, tucking his lower lip under his teeth and directing a glance, which circled over Charlie, past Charlotte and landed near Charlie's shoes before glazing over. He reached around Charlie's shoulder with his free arm and whispered, "I'll miss you, pal." Then he stepped away, crouching down and pretending to retie his shoelace so that Charlie wouldn't have to see his tears.

The wind blew a slow moan outside when Karl entered his bedroom. He could hardly fathom that the change he prayed would never happen was coming to pass.

9

Empathy

*H*ER TEACUP CLINKS AGAINST THE SAUCER when she sets it down. Helen reaches for Karl's hand, takes hold, and sweeps her thumb back and forth across the back of it. Karl looks at her, tilting his head. He wants to know more about how she felt on the evening she was visited by the *ghost*. "That's quite a story; I must say! The more I think of it, the more I wonder—that little whirlwind; could it have been more imagined than real? Being alone in an empty house can be frightening."

"Well, I admit, noises in that house always made inanimate things like floors and bureaus seem to come alive, but on that night I did not feel alone," Helen says. She notices that Karl's hand is still cold even though the late summer heat is building again with insects clamoring like rusty-hinges and flocks of birds swarming chaotic at the edge of the lawn in an early onset of harvest season.

Helen is uplifted because she told Karl something she thought he would disparage. Instead he listened. He was even drawn in by his interest and his concern for her, which she had longed for—to feel loved by him. In contrast to his former preoccupations, his engaging question makes her realize that she has needed his attention for a very long time. She crosses her legs, uncrosses, and recrosses them. She takes a breath of silence.

Karl listens to the swish of her stockings, wondering, *is she thinking of something other than the spirit?* He longs for her to feel his almost unprecedented, superintendent love. He regrets his neglect, his absences and failures, wondering how to make this substantive enough to sweeten her memory of him.

Past the beech tree, the sky is a thin silk scarf of blue and white that pulls Helen back to her youth on the farm in Ohio, to the time when everything ceased overnight—apple picking, cider pressing, fence mending, sheep-shearing—when the magic of the place was mortally wounded.

Karl intuits the change in her, wondering if she is thinking about those days that she has told him about: How dogwoods drooped; lilacs were removed; vines strangled the boxwood. How magnificent trees that had once spread canopies of shade fell victim to disease and were cut down, limb by limb, soon after the farmer had been forcibly taken away from the farm.

10

Climbing Towers

*I*N 1896, THE IMPECCABLE STATURE OF Geneva's La Châtelaine school was legendary. The sprawling three-story building overlooked the Swiss city and its lake. Each of the one hundred and fifty boys in attendance had his own room. Half of the students were Swiss. The rest came from England, Germany, Greece, and a few other countries. Among approximately one dozen Americans were the Behrs: Herman, Max, and Karl. For disciplinary reasons Fritz was sent alone to another boarding school, La Villa, near Lausanne.

Karl was determined to adjust to the new school with ease. He planned to follow Max's advice: "Attack it like a dive into the Rockaway River—without thinking about the shock, then once you're in there keep kicking like blazes to warm up!" Together they figured that memorizing names, navigating the unfamiliar territory and learning the rules would keep them well occupied.

Although his mother rented a villa on the outskirts of Geneva, Karl would only be able to see her for a few days at Christmas. Hating to leave her, he clung to the comfort of knowing she would not be far away. After they hugged, he slung his new jacket over his shoulder, mimicking the nonchalance of Herman and Max and pivoted to wave good-bye before marching into the main building, well behind them.

The boys were due to convene in Center Hall, but not for over an hour. Upon entering his room, Karl was overjoyed to find that he liked it. Outside his window, Mont Blanc rose in the distant sky. He shut the door and jumped on his bed to check out the mattress. No matter that it was thin and lumpy; he lay prone with his legs splayed, happy to fill the rest time with recollections of what had just transpired.

The transatlantic voyage had distracted Karl and softened his loss. As he lay alone in his new room, a throng of hoary shadows, somehow inherent on the off-white surface of the wall next to him, brought to mind the wild bicycle ride he and his brothers had taken through London. Fritz had instigated the escapade while Sarah was fast asleep and Grace had gone out for tea.

With darkness descending, the boys had wound their way alongside the Thames, cruising past carriages from Northumberland Avenue to Trafalgar Square, pedaling top speed around Lord Nelson's Statue. Karl had kept the wheel of the bike ahead of him in sight at all times, until he heard an imperative whistle and looked into the face of a navy-blue-suited bobby with a spiked-helmet, chin to neck, gesticulating frantically to stop the boys from riding in the Strand. "Nary a fool's spun this roundabout before!" he insisted, "Let 'lone four at once!"

On his new old bed, Karl laughed to himself, and continued studying the subtle gray trails that shaded the wall's contour. The shadows appeared to be more than a remnant of history. They seemed to harbor a residue of the unwritten stories of every boy who had lived in this room before him. He wished he could know just a few of the things they had learned, so as not to make mistakes that would adversely affect his time at La Châtelaine—aware as he was of his status as a captive of sorts.

Early in September, Karl and Max were coaxed by two of the older Greek students—Nico, a Greek prince, almost twenty years old, one of the strongest boys Karl had ever known, and Ezani, Nico's friend—to inspect the strictly *off-limits* attic. "Each year," Ezani explained, "We pick two new students to share our dangerous exploit.

"Come on, Karlos!" Nico urged.

On the night in question, Max had already wedged himself through a thin opening in the wall at the back of the art studio in order to gain access to the attic. Karl lagged behind, desperate to ignore, hide, and deny the fact that his knees were quivering from fear of claustrophobia. Just as he had pictured falling from the tree over the Rockaway River, he visualized plummeting from the single-planked walkway, through the flimsy attic ceiling to land *shredded,* smack in Headmaster Thudichum's lap.

Professor Thudichum (pronounced Tudicome) was a fine elderly gentleman with a long white beard—not at all intimidating; on the contrary, he seemed eminently crushable. On the other hand, his son, the Assistant Head, about forty years of age, was much more imposing, having once been a burly Captain in the Swiss Army.

Through clenched teeth Karl mumbled, "Coming!" *Once having jumped from a cliff, landing is inevitable,* he reminded himself. Of course, there was no turning back. But he was glad to have proceeded with caution when his hand grazed a razor-sharp nail on the edge of the doorjamb.

"Come on K!" Max sounded impatient from somewhere in the shadows. Karl thought Max had been acting superior of late—as though he was trying to win a popularity contest.

Since one misstep off the narrow walkway would be sufficient for disaster, clammy fear closed in on Karl as he crept along the narrow boards above the entire length of the building, utterly disoriented and too scared to turn around. All he wanted to do was to hold perfectly still, but he kept putting one foot in front of the other, trusting the fact that Nico and Ezani had done this many times before.

Once they arrived at a trap door, they felt through cobwebs in the dark for the handle and pushed it up. Ezani hoisted himself through, then helped Max up into the belfry. When it was Karl's turn, he had difficulty getting up and stayed just long enough to ascertain that the view would have been impressive *during the day.* He was preoccupied by desperation to avoid touching the furry bats that hung wrapped within inches of his head while others flapped through open slats of the cupola.

By the time the boys made it back safely to the art studio, they had become fast friends. As they slinked to their rooms, Nico said to Max: "This must be kept secret so as not to spill the soup. Is that how you say…*Soup?*"

"*Beans.* We say beans. But soup works fine; makes less noise when it hits the floor," Max giggled as he veered off toward his room. "See you later—*today*," he said, since it was well past midnight. Nico hoisted Karl up on his shoulders, carried him down the hall, and tossed him on his bed where he fell asleep in the designated landing position, a grin plastered across his face.

The following morning, Nico and Ezani arrived at Karl's door, holding a peculiar leather harness that resembled a piece of Andrew's carriage equipment. Ezani announced that they had permission for Karl to accompany them on their senior division mountain-climbing tramp for three days. Freshmen were usually not invited, but Nico and Eze had convinced the Headmaster that they were prepared to carry Karl if need be. "We have this harness in case we must lift you over (or out of) a crevasse!" Nico said, laughing. Karl perused the rig, sensed wild enthusiasm in the plan they had devised, and sputtered guffaws along with them. He grabbed his hat, walking stick, and backpack to join their group.

The expedition—a long, arduous ascent into the Jura range—consisted of nine older boys keeping a steady pace as they sang French songs that rang out through the valleys, stopping occasionally to munch on cheese and chocolate. Although Karl kept up the pace, he was greatly amused when he caught sight of his reflection in a stream and saw what ridiculous, long-lurching, head-bobbing strides he was using to do so.

Beautiful vistas and charming scenes lined the trail—self-sufficient Swiss farms appeared in sudden clearings. Reaching the pinnacle on the afternoon of the second day, Karl experienced the full effect of the expression *breathtaking* when he looked beyond Queen Anne's lace the size of dinner plates over a sweeping view of peaks and valleys wreathed in ethereal-blue haze.

At the end of the last day, an incision of alpine light slid down above Karl's shoulder, extending his shadow across the trail in a projected silhouette that appeared to him almost as imposing as those of his senior friends. When he entered the school building, uncontrollable shaking from the fatigue in his legs prevented him from running to find Max or Herman to tell them about the excursion. He staggered to his room, shut the door, and sprawled gratefully on his bed, staring into space and then at the wall of shadows, realizing that he had done something that would never be entirely communicable to the rest of his family. *They will have their own climbs,* he thought.

Some weeks passed before Karl ambled through the Common Room tucked behind the grand Red Hall staircase. Several boys were there, listening to the conclusion of a rousing pep-rally from a young red-headed genius in the senior class by the name of Jack Farnel. "And so, my friends," he was saying, "we shall have a *unique* observance of Thanksgiving! I am well aware that the Swiss do not celebrate the day. But this year, they will have a chance to observe us, as we do!" Word sped through school that an impending mass "escape" had been organized with mandatory attendance.

Immediately following breakfast on Thanksgiving, the entire student body gathered outside the main entrance to the school, just as Jack had planned. In spite of the fact that Professor Thudichum was standing on the steps, calling after the boys and threatening to expel each and every student who dared to leave campus, they proceeded to march right on by him, down hill, into the center of Geneva where they enjoyed a fine romp until they meandered back, in unison, late that afternoon.

Fully expecting some kind of punishment, Karl was stunned when there was none—except that dinner was not served.

Two nights after the Thanksgiving romp, Karl was sitting on his bed studying a list of vocabulary words. A goat's neck-bell rang below his window. A train rumbled on the mountainside. The door-knob began a slow turn.

The second that space between the door and the doorjamb grew wide enough to accommodate his slim body, Jack Farnel slipped into the room, breathless, his eyes darting around.

"Hey," he said, "can we talk?"

"Sure," Karl said, raising himself. "Have a seat." He patted the bed for Jack to sit next to him.

"There's going to be *trouble* the day after tomorrow."

"Why?"

"A lock-up!"

"Who's getting locked up?"

"The masters."

"Which ones?"

"All the ones who live on the third floor," Jack said.

"How?"

"By me."

"When?"

"Sometime before dawn."

Jack shifted himself around on the bed, smoothing it with a stroke of his fingers. Karl saw his brown eyes sweep the room with another furtive glance, wondering why he had come to him—if there was something he wanted, as Jack continued, "With help from an iron gate—the flexible kind between train cars, or, you know, in banks. There's one that stretches across the hallway on the third floor. Nobody seems to know what it was used for. I checked it out; it works and…"

Jack struggled for something in his pant's pocket, finally lifting out a lock and key and dangling it in front of Karl. "I bought this in town the other day, so I may as well put it to good use!"

"Oh, you aren't kidding. This is *serious* trouble!" Karl said, giggling nervously. "You're planning to lock them in?"

"Right," Jack said with a grin-span the width of Lake Geneva. He reached forward and tousled Karl's hair.

"But we just came back from busting out on Thanksgiving, Jack! We were lucky not to have been expelled. What if…"

"The *whole* school can't be expelled, my boy. There would be…*nobody* left and therefore no school! So that means the whole school will just have to go on another trip into town! If you ask me, we deserve our freedom after being cooped up like a bunch o' lifers for two whole months already!"

"Right, but how will they unlock the gate without finding out which one of us had the key?"

"Karl, my friend," Jack leaned forward, hugging him. "You're a smart kid. That's why I like you. See, here's the plan: I'm going to hide the key and leave an anonymous note explaining where to find it—smack-dab on Professor Thudichum's desk—which he'll see as soon as he comes into his office, but not until we've already headed *down hill* again on our way to *All-Gone-to-Geneva!*"

Jack crawled up from the bottom of the bed, placed his head on the pillow and crossed his arms. "There's just one little thing," he added.

"What's that?"

"A dummy."

"Huh?"

"Someone has to make a dummy. You know—the kind that you see around at Halloween. Max and Nico are planning to hoist it up the flagpole in place of the usual flag, right after I lock the gate and give them the high sign. It'll be a wee bonus, which, when added to the Masters' morning, will inspire them with a sense of *humor?*"

"Or make them mad as hornets."

"Not totally out of the question! Let's see, all we need is a spare pair of pants and a shirt. Got something flesh-colored?"

"Oh, my shirt—the one Sarah calls peachy." Karl jumped down and pulled out an old shirt from his bureau drawer.

"Yeah, that'll work! Max said you'd manage it! The dummy has to be made by tomorrow, carried unseen to Nico's room and put under his bed by nine so he can figure out how to tie it onto the flagpole pulley."

"Hmm. I'll make it. *But,*" Karl said, surprised that Max was in cahoots with the plan, "I won't move it. You need to get someone else to pick it up from here."

"Deal," Jack said and reached for Karl's hand, which he kept holding as he blinked and hugged Karl for a while—a long while—until Karl pulled away and Jack slid off the bed and disappeared.

11

Hanging the Dummy

*L*ATE IN THE AFTERNOON KARL NOTICED that someone had re-moved the dummy from under his bed when he returned to his room. Then after a nearly sleepless night, he heard predawn shuffling and whispering outside his door. After he peeked out and saw students trickle from their doorways, he dressed and left his room to merge with the steady stream.

Outside the school building, several boys were looking up and pointing at the dummy that flapped indolently at the top of the flag-pole. Max mocked a small salute and ran to catch up to Karl and Herman. Everything was executed according to plan.

Once in town, however, they soon realized that the morning was bitter cold. They had spent most of their money during the previous "escape," and it was so early that hardly a living soul was in evi-dence. So they sauntered through town, sidled up to the lake, skipped stones, watched the sun rise, and waited for inspiration. Comparative complaints about hunger, thirst, and discomfort worsened exponen-tially. Gumption on the wane, the boys headed back to the warm school-building, albeit reluctantly.

Upon approach, they saw several gendarmes gesticulating toward the dummy, then back to Professor Thudichum, stopping when they spotted the students who could not beg to blend in to the panorama. Thudichum was being issued a fine for hanging a figure on the flagpole after some of the townsfolk, believing it was real, had lodged a complaint to register their "terrible anguish" caused by the dummy, which constituted a "disturbance of the peace!"

Careful to omit the fact that his faculty had been effectively locked away, thus rendered incapable of preventing the caper, Pro-fessor Thudichum apologized profusely, saying that he would see to the problem with "utmost expedience." The boys were summoned inside the school as the police withdrew.

Center Hall assumed an unprecedented source of fascination as Karl braced for a lowering of the boom. He tried to lose himself in his vision of artisans at work carving the scrolls and leafy designs in the ornate escutcheons on the ceiling. Although the entire student body surrounded him, he felt utterly alone.

The Professor finally appeared on the landing. Mustering an air of pomp and circumstance, he bellowed, "Gentlemen, you shall contact your parents in writing to inform them as to the reason they will receive a summons for their percent of this fine! I expect your letters on my desk by noon." Each syllable was a sharp, wet projectile followed by an extended pause during which the Professor gazed out over the boys as they readied themselves for further punishment. But the professor simply tugged at the edges of his Tyrolean jacket in a vain attempt to stretch it down, clicked his heels curtly, swiveled, and walked away, leaning on his cane as though his life depended on it.

Recovery from the sardonic tone of the day lingered incomplete that evening as the boys exited the dark-paneled dining hall and Professor Thudichum's son, Ruben, accosted Max.

Watching this from the opposite end of the hallway with Herman, Karl noticed that Ruben was apparently pointing out something amiss with one hand pressing into Max's chest while the other waved about, until the exchange culminated in his slapping Max hard across the face.

Herman roared like a cargo train to rescue his brother, knocking the ex-officer flat onto the floor. Karl gathered around Max in a tight circle of boys, but inexplicably, Ruben just stood up, dusted his jacket and extended his hand to shake Herman's in a gesture of conciliation. Then Ruben stood rubbing his sides, scratching his chest nervously, and apologized for having lost his temper. "A fine job! You did a *fine* job of defending your little brother," he said, complimenting Herman while he nodded and backed away slowly.

On retreat from the scene down the corridor with Max and Karl toward their rooms, Herman said, "How do they expect us to respect them? This behavior may seem amusing, but it's pathetic. There's no one in charge here!"

Karl took Herman's disparaging comment to heart. Several times, growing up with his eldest brother, Karl had wished Herm would ease away from the serious role he assumed. He rarely exhibited pure enjoyment since he was expected to be responsible for the welfare of his younger siblings. But no one was more fun than he, or could be better relied upon in times of trauma or need. His was the voice of authority, however stern. Whenever Herman spoke, Max and Karl paid attention.

Back in his room, Karl was wondering if Herman had any clue that both he and Max had helped mastermind the morning's escapade when Jack bounded through the door, swigging a bottle of apple schnapps that he had pulled from his jacket pocket.

"Guess what? We're about to hit the jackpot! Here, have a taste."

Karl took a gulp of the contraband, feeling it burn the back of his throat. "Mm, smooth," he faked. "What jackpot?"

"The stash of coins in Ruben's desk! I inspected it during the time when the man in question lay flat on his back in the hall, thanks to your brother. I decided to take advantage of the opportunity. Good word, *opportunity*, don't ya think? A few coins just happened to jump into my pocket."

Jack's shoulders rose up. He held his breath. Curly wisps of hair escaped from his cap. He showed Karl some of the money. "There's just one shot at the top, my friend," he said, "Got to keep one foot 'n front o' the other with your head down and grab what you can along the way. It's you or the other guy. Hear me? Chances only come around once. Then they're gone!"

Jack's chest swelled with every new emphasis, as though he was sucking every ounce of air from the room, leaving Karl to fade into the wall of spirits. While Jack spoke, Karl thought of the Micks—of their me-first-and-only attitudes.

"Jack, taking only for yourself might get you to the top, but without a single friend by your side, and chances are you'll have to watch your back every minute to see who's coming to push you down."

"Yeah, well, I'll *share* then. How 'bout that?" Jack said, deflating a bit. "We needed some coins today when we didn't have any. I only swiped a few. He won't notice."

"Wrong, Jack. He will. You could get the boot."

"We'll see. If so, I'd go home and my father might have to talk to me for once." Jack shoved his glasses up the bridge of his nose, took another deep breath and hugged Karl, this time laying his head on Karl's shoulder before running out.

Confused by Jack's behavior, Karl pondered the difference between having a good time and crossing the line. He stared at the wall, then decided to write:

Dear Charlie,

Thanks for your letter. Bought any new stamps lately? I've been too busy to write. That's why you haven't heard from me for so long. I wish you were here to meet all these guys and go hiking with me. It's the most beautiful place I've ever seen.

I have to be honest about not really missing Brooklyn like I thought I would, just you and our hockey games.

Lately, things have gotten confusing. I'm breaking rules, which is easy, but I don't really want to. We're getting away with murder all the time. Today we went into town for larks, and we just did that last week! I wonder whether I should sit back and enjoy the ride, or jump off the train and roll until I hit my head on a rock. Either way I lose.

Know what I mean?

Your friend,
Karl

12

Gift of Absolution

$\mathcal{M}$OONLIGHT INTENSIFIED KARL'S INSOMNIA. His imagination conjured images that veered from shape to shadow on the wall, over the door, behind the chair. He thought he heard the sound of faint singing as Jack slid into his room again and approached the bed.

"Pssst! You asleep?"

"No, just trying to be."

"Can we talk?"

"Sure."

Jack lay down next to Karl and draped his arm over Karl's chest. After a minute he asked, "Have you ever had sex?"

"Nope. Well, not with anybody else, anyway."

"Me neither, but I figure it's got to be…" Jack's hand traveled along Karl's torso.

Karl turned over, remembering what his mother told him about steering clear of this. He wondered if Jack was drunk.

"Hey, Jack, you're a clever guy. I like you, so let's talk."

"Tell me a story. I'll rub your back."

"Once there was a man who wanted to be famous."

"Hmm, and…?"

"Well, he wasn't sure how he'd manage it since he had no outstanding skills, but he thought if he chose something and worked at it every day, or every chance he could, eventually he'd get better; better would turn into good, and sooner or later—best!"

Jack rubbed Karl's thigh. Karl shifted away from him and sensed Jack's frustration.

"Jack, I've got to get some sleep. Sorry you're having trouble settling, but I'm tired."

"Yeah, okay, sorry," Jack said, stood up and left the room.

At mid-year break, all the boys had plans to leave school, except for Jack. Without hesitation, Karl invited Jack to join him and his brothers. "My father's coming to Geneva. We're going to hike and eat tons. Max wants to learn to yodel. And Fritz will be there. Wait 'til you meet him. You won't believe how smart he is!" Jack accepted.

Karl ran ahead of the others into the villa, plunked his suitcase on the foyer tiles, wrapped his arms around his mother, and stayed glued to her. She was brimming with levity, reporting to the boys once they gathered around her: "Mally Peabody visited for weeks! We went to Venice, then to Paris where I revived my French by shopping!" She paused, noticing Jack and asked, "Who's this?"

Sweeping Margaret into his arms, Karl held his sister's chubby hand as he introduced Jack to his mother.

The smell of vanilla and freshly baked shortbread permeating the villa transported Karl back to Brooklyn and he caught sight of the trophies his mother displayed on a shelf in the dining room. One was Fritz's high hurdles victory at La Villa. Two came from Max's triumphant "football" (soccer) team.

"All right, you scarecrows and scalawags," Sarah said to the boys when she saw them. "Come on over here and let me take a gander at ya! ...Hmm, scruffy as ever!" She surveyed them intensely. "What a motley lot. I expected better. Aren't they feedin' ya?"

No longer banished from the kitchen (once Mary's exclusive domain), Sarah had improved her cooking skills. Mixed in with bits of news to garnish her runaway and run-on sentences, she reported her culinary escapades by drizzling sweeteners to entice the boys' appetites. Then she added a final dollop—the fact that she had a new friend who was "bright 'n cute as a Swiss franc." She asked the boys to guess his name without waiting for an answer, giggling: "Frank!"

Herman, Max, and Karl rolled their eyes, but Jack laughed and Sarah took an immediate liking to him. Everyone did, except Fritz.

Initially, Jack and Fritz struck up a propitious rapport, which took some pressure off of Fritz's usual grating interactions with his brothers. But then something happened that was never disclosed and they began to circle each other's territory like two young bucks.

Karl's father arrived with great fanfare to travel with the boys to Lucerne and Interlaken. Except Fritz had been wallowing so morosely in his own dark shadow that it was "suggested" he stay home to help Grace and Sarah with Margaret. As it turned out, this was a welcome relief for him. He planned to explore on his own, he said.

At Interlaken, Herm, Max, Karl, and Jack were eager to climb the Schynige Platte. Karl's father announced that he would ride the funicular railroad to an inn at the summit where he could enjoy the view of the Jungfrau until the boys arrived to meet him for lunch. But when the boys finally reached the inn, it was late enough for supper, and Herman, after having been roundly reprimanded by men at the inn for allowing his boys to attempt such a climb without a guide, directions, or water, was gaunt with guilt and worry. There had been real danger in their crossing an area of snow near the summit where crevasses cascaded at sheer drops from the trail. At the sight of Karl shivering, his father could not refrain from biting at the ends of his mustache.

"We're all right Pop," Max said, wiggling his toes inside soggy black boots.

Herm spoke hardly a word. His dark brows sank low; he felt at fault for having said the climb would be easy.

Invigorated, Jack's cheeks were bright red. He asked what there might be to eat.

After dinner the following night in Lucerne, Karl walked outside alone and absentmindedly trailed a military band and a column of Swiss troops returning from maneuvers to their barracks on the outskirts of town. Like a lemming behind a pied piper, the lure of the music and the rhythm of the march held him utterly enthralled.

When the troops finally disappeared behind a gate, Karl realized he had no idea how to get back to the hotel since he had paid scant attention to where he had been walking. During the two hours it took to find his way back, his poor father was frantic again. The only saving grace, Karl realized, was that he was spared an additional dressing down from Fritz.

The next morning, eager to return to Grace and to Geneva, Karl's father raised his juice glass over the breakfast table as though proposing a toast: "Well, there are some experiences we can omit telling your Mother, boys. All agreed?" He had pressed his luck far enough. Running a business was one thing—having responsibility for young boys was quite another.

Being back at school was welcome. Nico and Ezani, exuberant as always, hoisted Karl between their shoulders and jogged with him around the hallways. Nico was thrilled to be "home" at La Châtelaine—"back to freedom!" he declared. "Life as a prince in Greece is *fatal*. I never saw a single human my age. Father was away in Crete 'busy with diplomacy' the entire time."

Jack settled into a routine—fencing with a French master, while Karl took riding lessons with a French Cavalry officer. Max played "football" since there was no golf. Herman pursued an extended climbing course. Escapades into town ceased. Weather warmed. The end of the school year grew near.

Karl decided to participate in the school tennis championship and was elated each time he won a match along the way to the finals, which, as it turned out, was to be played against Ezani (four years his senior) on the dirt court outside the school.

Many came to watch—a few spectators dangled precariously from the window ledges. Dust swirled as Karl and Ezani rallied to warm up. A lanky, part-time tennis instructor from Geneva served as an umpire. Professor and Ruben Thudichum were strategically positioned near the umpire in case they were called to stave off a controversy. Neighbors and townspeople arrived with hats and parasols in tow. Aside from the wind, it was a fine clear day. Karl was adequately dressed in a long-sleeved white shirt and trousers.

Ezani took an expected lead, 3-1, as Karl struggled to gauge the wind. He knew he needed to make adjustments, but the more he analyzed, the more difficult this became. Then he began to play *with* the wind—taking the ball early—and each time he hit a winning shot, he stopped to ponder where it came from. The score tipped more and more in Karl's favor, until he won in a climax of cheers and hurdled the net to shake his friend's hand.

Nico and Ezani hoisted Karl up on their shoulders, paraded around the school grounds, and redelivered him to the court for his trophy presentation.

Karl's mother emerged from the middle of the spectators where she had tucked herself into the crowd, not knowing if her presence would be a distraction for Karl during the match. When he handed her his trophy to take home for her shelf, he felt as if he would burst with pride.

With only one week left before the end of the school year, Karl was looking forward to spending the summer traveling through Europe with his mother. Dawn painted the sky with streaks of pink and mauve. Streams of birds had arrived. Accents of spring-green enlivened undergrowth. Windows were flung wide to draw in fresh air. But as Jack's fencing teacher walked past the basement window, he took hesitant strides backward retracing his steps and peered inside with his hands cupped to the glass. A sunbeam shot through the window on what appeared to be … a body, hanging limp.

Professor Thudichum was summoned. He dispatched his assistant to call the coroner with an urgent request that the coroner arrive immediately in silence, wanting to have the body removed to spare the boys from such a vision. Then he summoned everyone to convene in Center Hall.

As the boys and faculty assembled, Professor Thudichum stood rigid. He held up his hands and waited for silence until everyone realized he would wait forever. Then, softly, he began the short speech that he had delivered once before:

At times, we are dealt inexplicable and tragic blows. When someone decides to take his own life, the rest of us are left to try and make sense of it, but we can never know or fully comprehend the unbearable torment and pain that that person suffered.

Although suicide should not be condoned because life is a sacred gift with reason to choose hope over despair, we come to understand that having the ability to sustain optimism is not always achievable in the hearts of the desperate.

I stress to each one of you gathered here that no one shall assume fault, or believe that he might have prevented such a tragic occurrence. I hope you will come to accept that certain aspects of fate fall under the exclusive jurisdiction of the Almighty. Therefore, even an abhorrent act such as this one deserves a gift of absolution.

Last night, Jack Farnel took his own life. His body has been removed. His parents and family will come for him and his possessions. At this time, his room is strictly off limits—as is his cubicle. If any of you know of his property outside of those two places, please report to me.

God bless us all. Let us bow our heads and pray for Jack's eternal peace.

Everyone stood paralyzed by the fact that life could end as abruptly as a snap of a stick. Karl heard someone behind him whisper, *"Why?"* as murmurs broke out through the congregation. Herman, Max, and Karl found one another to commiserate. Karl was already wearing a heart of guilt on his sleeve. Everything Jack had ever said or done—his advances, his traces of despair—intertwined.

Shouldn't I have known? Karl wondered. He dropped his face into his hands.

13

Eight Bells and Shoelaces

$\mathcal{M}$AKING CONVERSATION HAS NEVER been difficult, but now a specter of apprehension needs to be exorcised. Karl returns to his morning repartee with Helen. "So when I get to Heaven, you don't want me to tickle you, just to send money?" He says, half asking, half smiling.

Helen scans the tree above Karl for the oriole she had seen earlier. "Yes," she says blithely, "to grow on trees outside my window. And I'd like to live in the country again. Can you arrange that?"

"I'll see what I can do. Should have some clout from above, don't you think?"

"Assuming you're *up* rather than down, my dear. Shame we have to leave tomorrow," Helen mutters, changing the subject, pouring more tea.

"Oh, you're a love," Karl says as he takes a cup.

"How's your writing coming along?" she asks, settling into the chair next to him. "Mind if I join—interrupt, *interpret* you for a bit? I'm tired of organizing."

"It would be a pleasure and a relief. We're on the same trolley," Karl says. His hand shakes; the cup clangs against its saucer.

"Shall we get to know each other then?"

"Might just try our best to! We've only been married for a thousand years."

"Hmm, think I'll let the implication slide. Where are you in the memoir?"

"In a muddle, actually."

"How so?"

"I've tied the writing in knots by trying to tell about all my sporting activities."

"Hmm?"

"I remember every game and almost every teammate, but who would care to read all of that egotistical mish-mash?"

"I would."

"Are you sure?"

"Yes. And so would our children—Karl, Pete, Jim, and of course little Sally who says she's the historian in the family. You know our Sal! And how about the future grandchildren?"

"Prepare for them to claim I was cracked. They're going to lavish pity on you."

"No doubt about that!" Helen smiles.

Silence locks Helen and Karl into the scene as though they are in a photograph, as though time could stop just for an instant. They stare in the same direction—into days gone by.

The summer has been deliciously fecund, beginning with Helen's discovery of a wood duck nesting in a thick clump of ivy near the house. A once endearing fiddlehead unfurled to grow thigh high. The rose of Sharon brims white with raspberry-centered blooms at the far side of the yard. Buds of Montauk daisies swell. Salvia leans to catch the sun, attracting hummingbirds and myriad butterflies. Throughout July, hydrangea has thrived in astonishing tinctures of blue and ivory. One extraordinarily hot night, Helen had seen a Luna Moth circle the lamplight.

Every fair-weather evening, venturing to the beach to see light cast across the breaking waves, Karl and Helen had scanned the margins of blue-on-blue and wrestled speculations that pivot around the constant and constantly evasive horizon.

"Where did the summer go?" Karl asks, expecting no answer.

Between them, silence insinuates separation to come.

"So how about that memoir-muddle, darling? Can you fix it?"

"I'm afraid not. All I can do is braid it."

"Sorry?"

"Like shoelaces. Weaving ends up, over, then back under."

"Lacing your shoes, you mean?"

"Do you remember when I was—did I mention to you that I was—voted best athlete by my class at Yale?"

"Mmm, a *few* times."

"Well, it is necessary for me to substantiate that honor in my memoir, don't you think? After all the truly great athletes there were in my class? So, in my writing, I jump from tennis to football, back to tennis, to baseball, and then to hockey. Today I thought of our one and only loss, senior year, in hockey. Harvard beat us in the fifth overtime after I pushed the puck over to my good friend Cornell who was only fifteen feet in front of the cage. All he had to do was shoot it into the net to win the championship, but he was so utterly done-in by exhaustion that all he could muster was a weak wave of his stick with one tired arm, looking pitifully helpless, while a defenseman skated along and knocked him flat. Harvard's defenseman ended up scoring off a long shot that bounced and curved (believe it or not, I can still envision every gyration) into the goal. See, there I go, overloading with details. But memories of that game and others remind me that I need to tell the boys and Sally about the game of hockey as it used to be—with few substitutions and seven skaters, which required, in my opinion, much greater skill and stamina than the game does now. Remember how Hobey Baker could carry the puck from one end of the rink to the other without even watching it?"

Looking up from his interior view of rink dynamics, Karl searches in vain for stars in Helen's eyes. "But of course, you had to have seen that for yourself, I know. It's just so damn amazing—interesting—to me." Karl leaned forward to lift his tea cup.

"Right!" Helen says, although her concentration is centered more precisely on the flavor of her tea.

"And then," Karl takes a sip, "I have to put in *everything* about baseball, which was really in many ways my best sport. I gave it up when there was no place for me with Barnes, Coté, and Huiskaup in the outfield. They were simply better. But that provided the twist of fate that started my real tennis in the spring—how I came alive there. But do you find this all terribly boring?"

"Absolutely…"

"What?"

"Not!"

"You've pulled my good-for-nothing leg once again, Mrs. Behr."

"Mmm. I did get you there, didn't I."

"It's all such a weak literary effort, like shoelaces intertwined in the wrong holes, I'm afraid. Plus the writing suffers from a whopping overdose of vitamin "I" to boot. But the biggest problem is—as you may recall your brother Bud claiming that he never thought I was the slightest bit enamored of females—well, I hate to admit this, but so far I've omitted mentioning anything whatsoever in regard to either of my two beloved sisters! This is shocking even to *me*. Granted they existed separately from the rest of us boys. That's my only excuse. I'll have to find something to include about them!"

"How about the fact that your little sister, my best friend Gertie, introduced us to each other!"

"Yes. And I should say Margaret was a very fine tennis player. I have tried not to be overly sports-oriented by inserting other things here and there, like my trip during the spring of Junior year to Puerto Rico."

"Oh? Which one was that?" Helen put her teacup on its saucer and sat back, noticing how Karl retreated from the subject of his sisters.

"When Max and I went to visit Captain and Mimie Walling."

"Tell me again."

"U.S. Navy Captain Burns T. Walling was a friend of my father's. I was a page boy in his wedding when I was four or five."

"Oh, let me see if I remember…that was the time when the ceremony had already begun, and you obstinately refused to go down the aisle under any circumstance, threat or bribe?"

"Until my clever mother promised me a tennis racquet—my very own brand *new* tennis racquet. So I stumbled out of the pew, picked up the pillow-nested ring, and carried it as though it was about to hatch."

"And what about Puerto Rico?"

"I had been invited to go on the Easter-vacation Varsity Baseball trip, but once again my mother held sway. Can't remember what she said—must have been persuasive or decisive—most likely both. It was 1905, the year of my first trip to the tropics. I chiefly remember swooning over heavy perfume worn by the dark-haired belle of San Juan who charmed us with her dancing, under those deliciously moon-bathed palms."

"Try not to trip on your laces now, dear."

"Oh, my funny girl." Karl turned away, then quickly picked up his story. "Max and I explored every inch of that fascinating island, then went to Culebra on the USS *Lancaster*, a square-rigged, picturesque Civil War ship that was being used to train the sailors, partly—believe it or not—to swim."

"Really?"

"And the water was infested with sharks!"

"Oh!"

"Extremely unattractive sharks."

"*Harmless* sharks?"

"Yes. Well, I was asked by Captain Walling to prove this *harmlessness* for the benefit of the sailors by diving from one of the masts. Not too high—just thirty to thirty-five feet or so—from where I looked down and saw that the cute, teensy-weensy sharks had formed what appeared to be a solid mass. And I thought I would surely land on one—in which case the outcome might not have proven so innocuous after all."

"Luckily you didn't consider that a cute shark attacking might be female. Things could have taken a turn for the worse!"

"I dove, and I wasn't bitten, nibbled or even kissed. But do you think our kids would like to know about that? Should I include it?"

"Of course! …I imagined being up there with you on that mast, my darling, and there is no possible chance in hell I could have ever let go!"

"But then, you're a *girl*."

"Oh, you're incorrigible. If you want encouragement you'd better be sweet to me."

"Now that I think of it—on the day I met you in 1911, when Gertrude returned from picking you up at the train, Margaret and I were sitting under a tree with our old dog Shirley at the farm in Boonton where we had gone to take care of Mother's horses. I remember the moment you walked toward us as though it was yesterday. I got up to shake your hand and beheld the loveliest girl I had ever laid eyes on. It was the luckiest moment of my whole life. How does that sound?"

"That'll do, dear. That'll do. I hear violins."

"Don't you mean bells? Oh, remind me to tell you my violin story." Karl takes a sip of tea and clicks his cup back onto the saucer. "Do you remember our first carriage ride to Split Rock Lake?"

"Sure. Did you devote a whole entire paragraph to it?"

"Not yet."

"Well, don't forget that you need to make me sound terribly alluring and important. Don't claim all the glory for yourself."

"But it wasn't just your beauty that captivated me."

"My wit?"

"The fact that you were so unaware of it—your natural lack of vanity."

"They say opposites attract!"

"There you go again, stepping on my toes."

"Someone needs to!"

"Well, I guess you're right about that."

"Can you finish telling me about Puerto Rico?"

"If I had to relive it all over again, I'd be dead within the first five minutes, I'm afraid. As a matter fact I almost kicked the bucket twice then. First, from a fatal case of humiliation, which occurred during my first night out after a marine dressed in full regalia saluted the Captain with his white-gloved hand, and in a snappy voice asked, 'May we ring eight bells, Sir?' The Captain, in the same stiff tone replied, 'You may tell the Quarter-master he may ring eight bells.' As the marine saluted, made his about-face and retired, I laughed and snickered like a fool, asking the Captain what sense there was to all that useless formality. Captain Walling wheeled around—turning on me with lightning speed—and bellowed, 'You have just witnessed a naval custom, which is over one hundred years old. You are fresh and disrespectful. If you can't be more tolerant of naval tradition and its crucial protocol, you may pack up and get off this ship immediately!' "

"Oh. You never admitted that one to me. Death by mortification!"

"It was a lesson I always remembered. I apologized, and was so embarrassed that I never forgot the importance of naval protocol again. But subsequent to this egregious mistake was another even more threatening event."

"Neptune exacting revenge for impertinence?"

"I hopped on a small freight-steamer back to New York with only a dozen passengers, leaving Max behind, since he decided to extend his visit. Two days into the trip we were struck by a hurricane with 110-mile-per-hour winds. The sailors could barely crawl. On my foray below to meet with the whiskery Scottish Captain, I found him chugging whiskey in his cabin. When I asked him how things looked from his perspective, he answered in a somber tone, 'We'll pull through all right if the old lady's ribs can only stand fast. She's getting the worst pounding of her too long life.' The ship trembled from stem to stern every time its propeller surfaced on pitches and troughs of the enormous waves—like mountains, only much more menacing. I can still hear the straining of the ship's sides against her rivets. For three days it was like battling for sanity against a drunken stupor, although I hadn't touched a drop of alcohol. Finally, the wind died down and the Captain admitted that Gulf Stream conditions, added to the severe wind, had made it his closest shave in over thirty years at sea."

"Now I do remember you mentioned something about this when the *Titanic* hit the iceberg. You said the impact was miniscule compared to the wicked jarring on your way home from Puerto Rico. Well, that's another experience I'm happy not to have shared with you," Helen adds. "Are you going to chronicle all the tennis matches or just a smattering?"

"Bits and pieces, I guess; just try to tie a few raggedy ends together."

"When you're done, take off your shoes and dance with me?" Helen says. She leans to kiss her husband's forehead and lifts the tray to leave.

For a few seconds Karl notices a hummingbird suspended in evening light on a stem of red salvia. After the bird flies away, the stem waves, and waves, and continues to wave for an unusually long time. As he watches, a shiver seizes Karl and he wonders—*is this some kind of sign?*

14

Dresden

$\mathcal{A}$FTER A YEAR IN SWITZERLAND, the boys had not acquired a whisper of the language skills Karl's mother had hoped for. Nor did separating Fritz from his brothers mitigate the difficulties between them. Furthermore, Jack's suicide fueled Grace's decision to move from Geneva to Dresden, placing all four boys at the same school in her husband's beloved Germany.

It was Frank Purcell—Sarah's Frank—who first suggested Dresden. He was going there to study architecture and he heard that Franklin College had a fine reputation. Grace's cable to the school to inquire about available spaces for the boys received a prompt and positive response: They would be pleased and able to accommodate all four of her sons. Hoping the school's smaller size would improve her boys' focus on learning, Grace forged ahead. She shut the villa door behind her and journeyed north by train with Sarah, Frank, Margaret, her four boys, and all their accoutrements, including Spinner, the pet rabbit Max had acquired without consulting her.

At first glance, Franklin College, owned and run by an Englishman, with English masters, appeared a sizeable building on exceptionally adequate grounds at the outskirts of Dresden. Most of the forty students were either English or American. Karl doubted he would be as content there as he had been at La Châtelaine. The urban atmosphere was not conducive to hiking or riding. He watched his mother sign the necessary papers before they proceeded to Paris and the Netherlands to fill the ensuing summer weeks with sightseeing.

On the first night at Franklin College, Herman and Fritz became embroiled in a bloody battle over a pillow. In retaliation for Fritz's having stolen the pillow from Herm's bed, Herm set an alarm clock to ring at three in the morning and hid it under Fritz's bed.

The following evening, Fritz grabbed the pudding off Herman's dinner tray and their wicked skirmish escalated until black marks against them had accumulated as fast as bruises. Augmenting the misery, a cold, teary rain dripped continuously down the small-paned windows. For the first time, Karl envied Charlie for having been able to stay in Brooklyn at one school. He hadn't heard from Charlie in over three months—since telling him about Jack's suicide—so he wrote him a long letter:

Dear Charlie,

Well, here's a day to tell you about! I don't know what started Fritz's fight with Master Smith. I walked into the classroom where Fritz was working off some of his black marks. Smith was standing with ink all over his suit, screaming at my brother, whose shot with the ink well was spot-on, as they say. Fritz took one look at me and rushed out the back door to the playground, shouting for Max at the top of his lungs (which didn't make me feel too valued I have to admit). Master Smith nabbed Fritz not far from the door and proceeded to punch him as hard as he could. Fritz fought back frantically, all the while yelling for Max. Luckily, before I could reach the battle zone, Herman had raced to the rescue.

Fortunately for Master Smith, the Headmaster and two other teachers dove in and had already pulled him off of Fritz before Herman could get into the fray.

As soon as the fight was over, Fritz jumped on his bicycle with a black eye and a swollen and bleeding mouth, and rode to the Albertshoff Hotel where my mother is spending the winter.

Mother was furious. She telephoned the Headmaster, outraged about Fritz's beating.

Herman followed Fritz to the hotel where he heard Mother say she was withdrawing her sons from the school at once. The Headmaster must have calmed her down because she agreed to speak with him that evening. Herman told Max and me that he was going to join Mother in the Headmaster's Study. He said the rest of us should wait outside the door and listen. If we heard any insult to Mother's womanhood, or if there was any distress in her voice, we were to run in with our baseball bats and "clean up" the masters right then and there. At one point we almost did, but then we heard Herman say something soothing, so we waited. The rest of the meeting was calm. Master Smith apologized to Mother and her "dear, little son."

Can you believe that? I guess this is like Jack's gallivanting with the whole student body at La Châtelaine. When you think of it, if all four of us left here, well—there would go one tenth of the school! It was fun listening to the Headmaster sprinkle sugar all over my mother like that. But to be honest, I wish she had taken us away.

Your friend,

KARL

15

Vicarious Wisdom

*H*ELEN WATCHES WATER FALL from the kitchen faucet and spill over the rim of a cup onto the porcelain sink. Apprehensive about soon being alone, she pictures resolve as resignation akin to compromise, like a once-shiny anchor encrusted from scraping the bottom of the sea in search of something to cling to. Then, thinking of her grandfather, she wishes he was still alive to answer her questions as she considers that Karl's loyalty to grand causes is so much like his was.

Water disappears down the drain. The boundlessness of nature—the interaction of forces, attractions, and purposes that drive mechanisms to assume changes of form—leads her to wonder how adaptability relates to personal manifestations of desire. Even as thoughts wander, are they not also circular, perhaps, or spiraled? If the invisible seems to be nothing but is really something responding to unseen forces, then might spirits of the departed abide in air, in light, or even in thought?

Drawing her shoulders back, Helen remembers hearing her father speak about *his* affable father, Junius Newsom, describing his life of business, necessary to meet the imperative needs of eleven children. Then she thinks of finding the albums that he had hidden away, and how this initial window into his past that she told Karl about served to breathe life into him.

Looking at the scrapbooks soon after she had first found them, Helen had been in the process of closing one of the covers when she felt something underneath the cover lining, which was loosely bound with rudimentary stitches. She cut the threads, slipped out an undated, raggedy missive written by her grandfather and began to read:

> *It behooves me to record a confession about my participation in unspeakable horror. For decades I have held the truth fast from the perception of my loved ones, even as I tried to negate it from my own. I lived in the shadow of self denial for the majority of my days. But you who are reading this will learn the truth.*
>
> *No one knows me as other than a hard workingman from Ohio, father of eleven children. But Truth is contained in a War within my heart. For I saw fit to join an invasion of the Creek Indians when I was a young man.*
>
> *The bulk of us frontier riders accompanied Major Gibson and Davy Crockett across the Tennessee. The river was high and raging. The horses balked. We waited days before crossing. Eventually we reconnoitered through the wilderness of Creek County, encamped for several days armed with rifles and what we thought was sagacity, but which amounted to not much other than foolhardiness.*
>
> *When the Creeks crossed the Coosa River, we gathered that the Indians were set to attack. Crockett never backed down to any man and always got what he wanted. We followed him without much regard for consequences.*
>
> *We split up in the moonlight, single file...*

Here, the pages were torn, corners charred, and stains rendered them mostly illegible. Helen thought Junius must have considered their content too wretched to leave intact, because what followed was indicative of the horrific nature of the event:

> *What I have reported brought me utter despair due to my part in the bloody mayhem of the slaughter. I stood in the midst of it and kept firing my rifle, knowing I was wounded, grazed at least, but far worse off than the Indians I was*

killing because I saw myself as a murderous madman. Although I'd gone to invade under the guise of protecting my people by preempting an Indian attack, I could not reconcile any part of what was happening. Nothing of it made sense to me. The commandment "Thou shalt not kill" resounded in my mind over and over until I lost my bearing completely. I could neither run away nor cease shooting. A different version of the man I was took possession of the man I would become for the rest of my days.

One hundred and eighty-six Indians were killed. And five of our men. I was wounded in my left calf, and pretty nearly starved to death in the days that followed, but I survived.

I confused something I thought I wanted, an adventure in the wilderness, for I loved the woods more than any town, with my desire to do right. But ever after when I beheld a child, I was filled with self-loathing for what I had done to the Creeks. I had no desire to enter wild country ever again. And I never told Elizabeth for fear she would shun my touch.

Hung on the rack over a door at the cabin we used for fishing by the lake at Gallipolis, my rifle never had a hand placed on it again. But every time I laid my eyes on that weapon, a ghost of the memory gained on me, and I spent the rest of my life running from it, knowing that on the day of reckoning, I would not escape being eaten alive by guilt and remorse.

Helen realized that by hiding the letter, although saving it, her grandfather expected someone to see it, eventually.

Some months later, on a mid-November night when the farm bowed under bone-chilling wind and she was curled up by the fire, reading Wilkie Collins's *The Woman in White* while Bud appeared to be lost in Jack London's *The Call of the Wild*, Helen got up from her chair, walked over to the cabinet, took out the album, slipped Junius Newsom's letter from the back, and handed it to Bud without a word.

"What's this?"

"Our grandfather's hidden confession," she said.

The fire snapped. Sparks flew up. Helen waited for Bud to read the letter that had so astounded her. When she saw him press away tears she knew that he had sympathized with his grandfather's misery and must have discovered a kindred spirit for his passion for life outdoors.

Bud gnawed at the inside of his cheek, looked aside, then at Helen and asked, "When, where, did you find this?"

"It was sewn into the cover here," she answered, handing him the album. "I discovered it when you were out and I was sauntering through olden days."

That was the only time Helen ever saw Bud with tears in his eyes. The need for space between him and any other human being was imperative. He was at one with himself, only in Nature. "Give me a compass and point me toward the trees," he would say with longing and a faraway look. He amused people, especially his sister, as a way of living well. But despite the fact that trouble and water seemed to roll off his back, he didn't fool Helen. Bud was never complacent. Not about a miniscule thing.

Out the kitchen window, Helen watches a bird defend its branch with squawks and fury. She realizes she can only imagine what her grandfather must have endured in terms of guilt, and she understands how a person can be trapped in circumstance that leads to inevitable consequences. Guilt was integral to her. Although she had never been to blame for what the farmer did, somehow she always felt at fault for it.

16

Élan

*E*XCURSIONS TO EXPLORE the countryside had become one of Grace's favorite pastimes after she returned to America and resettled her family at 11 Elm Street in Morristown, New Jersey.

Karl watched clouds floating like soap foam in a china-blue bowl as he rocked alongside his mother in a carriage pulled by a pair of sorrel ponies with Andrew at the reins. Familiar smells—livestock, floribunda roses, orchard grass, and wild strawberries—filled him with ecstasy as the carriage moved through a canopy of shadows and intermittent dashes of sunlight. He closed his eyes, then popped them open to take in details of each vista, reclining to languish in the sentience of it all. The percussion of hooves beneath the horses' plum-shaped rumps lulled him. And he reveled in the pantomime of his mother's hands that pointed to a marvel one minute, then folded like wings in her lap the next. He was euphoric to be reacquainted with senses he had missed for two years.

When the carriage swerved to pull up alongside their small white house, Karl hopped down, ready to guide Grace if she needed him. His brothers were all away. Herm had taken a factory job, along with part-time work at his father's abrasives company. Fritz and Max attended the Lawrenceville School in central New Jersey. Although peaceful, their new home was far from empty. Margaret was there, and so was Max's bunny, Spinner, an English Spaniel pup named Shirley, and Fritz's new mouse, Pokey II, who frequently needed to be chased, caught, and returned to his cage. In addition, Karl's mother had announced that they would be welcoming a new baby.

As promised, Charlie had come to visit Karl by train from the city. Charlie had grown to become a lanky track-sprinter with a baritone voice that complemented his natural assertiveness and keen acumen. He had an impressive new eye, which had been crafted and fitted for him in New York City by a visiting German ocularist. When the tone of Karl's letters from Europe changed from exuberant to miserable, Charlie had come to appreciate having been able to stay in Brooklyn. He and Karl resumed their easy rapport as though there had been no hiatus at all.

"Tell me about Jack," Charlie said on their way to the soda shop.

Karl expressed his regret and tried to describe Jack as they slid into a corner booth.

"Well, what else could you have done? You weren't really with him for very long." Charlie said. "Maybe God has a plan for us. Already mapped out, I mean."

Speculation intervened. At their shoulders, cold window glass expressed a barrier. Resting his chin on his fist to stare at a tall man strolling by, Karl said, "Do you think Jack was supposed to die?"

"Well, the possibility that everything is all laid out for us like shoes in a closet...I don't know. What do you think?"

"I guess it's possible, but..." Karl didn't finish his sentence; he was watching an elm sway like a feather duster across the street. "I mean, *maybe*. I remember that time when my brothers and I begged—prayed—for wind to quit fanning the fire in Brooklyn, and when the wind stopped, it seemed like we had had power—as though we were suspended in it. Like we were being watched or something."

"You were. You were a kid!"

"Expecting miracles—and thinking we could control them with our minds."

"Not yet caught up in harsh reality. But what about now?" Charlie asked, chomping down on a straw.

Karl intuited that Charlie was thinking about something else—his girlfriend, Emily, most likely—so he said, "Well, my feeling about control changes all the time. But my faith in God is tied to natural things I can see, you know, like Nature, with humans being just a small part of the picture. There might be some force that drives the world. But people hardly matter compared to whatever *that* is— so far above and beyond—there's no way to fathom it."

"Even though everyone tries to decide what they think it is! I sure can't see a man in the sky working controls," Charlie said.

"Must be a *wo*man, then!"

Charlie laughed, gulped his cream soda and held a hard blink. "What I'd really like to believe is that we'll find out some day, but mostly I doubt that, too. Consider all the religions of the world—they each have their own opinion, right? Well, if men are supposedly created equal, then which belief is right and which is wrong?"

"None and all. Or all and none!" Karl answered.

Charlie twisted the straw. "I try not to pray for favors; just to accept what happens, hoping that being humble might work in my favor. I'm saving my special request for a time when I'll really need it. No crying wolf. Know what I mean?"

"Sure. Good for you. I could never stick to that! I look up, coaxing God for every little thing—to help me figure out the rights and wrongs—which I can't."

Charlie brushed crumbs off his shirt with the back of his fingers, reinspected his mangled straw, and said, "At least I can't see being forced to die settling somebody else's score. I would pray out loud, *loudly*, to be spared from that Hell; although I know I could sure benefit from learning how to shoot straight!"

"Hope we never have to," Karl said.

Walking home with Charlie, who was planning to catch the evening train back to New York, Karl realized that although he had begun to make new acquaintances at Morristown School, Charlie was by far his closest friend.

After the carriage ride with his mother, Karl was missing Charlie as he walked into the kitchen. So he was elated to see three of his new buddies from school attacking waffles they had conned the new cook, Marley Ellis, into making for them while they waited for Karl.

The boys' plan to play doubles at the Field Club dribbled out between chewing and slurping.

Karl ran upstairs, changed clothes, grabbed his racquet, and strode out the door to the tennis court with them. Shirley the pup pattered along behind until Grace called her back to the house.

Once Grace was back in the kitchen and had turned on the tap to replenish the water in the sink full of flowers, she shouted to Marley, "When Karl goes to Lawrenceville next year he'll have a bit of catching up to do with his brothers!"

"Oh, I don't think much, Mum. Somethin' tells me he'll have no trouble a t'all," Marley countered. "That boy has the mind of a wizard and the heart of a lamb. Not to mention those good looks!"

Grace lifted one of the flowers.

17

Red and Black

*D*URING THE FALL OF 1901, after discussing the day's meal plan with Marley and placing her flower arrangement on the black marble-topped table under the mirror in the hall, Grace crouched to search for a pair of black athletic shoes at the back of Karl's closet because she had just received his request:

Dear Mother,

Outside my window there was a parade with roman candles, blazing lights, gongs, drums and dinner bells ringing while the six shooters were being reloaded. Lawrenceville is much more fun than I thought it would be!

By the way, I sprained my ankle playing football and the doctor has put me in a plaster cast to rest it, as you might have already heard? A chap named Colson wants me to play with him in the tennis doubles championship anyway, with my foot in the cast. So would you mind sending the black shoes that I left at home? Or just the left one? Thanks.

Love,

KARL

Later that year, Grace received another letter from Karl brimming with details about how he had managed to win the National Interscholastic Tennis Tournament, although she had already heard about this from his brother, Herman, who provided an eye-witness account. Karl had learned to avoid writing anything that might upset his mother. Instead, he included the sordid details in his letters to Charlie:

Dear Charlie,

My first night at Griswold House when I leaned out the window and spotted Fritz clad in white pajamas, torch in one hand, red and black banner in the other, I couldn't believe he had school spirit! Now I have a hunch why.

Yesterday, I was in the room of two boys who live on the ground floor of Griswold. They were cutting classes and smoking. Just as I walked in, a buzzer went off. They rigged it by concealed wire to the assistant housemaster's door on the floor above them so that whenever his door opens they are forewarned that he, Mr. Breed, is on the move, at which time they run around frantically stubbing out their cigarettes, opening the window, and fanning the air.

Fritz has explained to me how they manage to stay in school. They sneak in and carefully erase the ink figures recorded in the weekly demerits and cut log, then write in more moderate ones. How about that!

Oh, remember my friend, "Butter Ball," the tenor in my Sunday chapel quartet? When we sang our hymns so loud at one of the Sunday evening Bible classes at the old village church that we were asked to leave and never come back? Well, just last Sunday at chapel, Butter Ball watched the tardy arrival of one of our best-dressed masters who looked around the chapel and cleared his throat before finally taking his seat. No sooner had our "beau Brummell" master seated himself than Butter Ball stood up, cleared his throat, and adjusted his collar and necktie in perfect mimicry. Although this brought hysterical laughter, when added to his demerit record, it proved too much. They called it "flagrant impudence." So Butter Ball's been kicked out, and the worst part is that that's the end of our quartet.

By the way, I'm going to Yale next year, to the Sheffield Scientific School.

Yours truly,

KARL

One Sunday afternoon, Karl stepped into the Lawrenceville Chapel because it was his habit to listen to Mr. Van Dyke's organ practice, letting his thoughts coalesce in the pensive atmosphere. He had brought along a letter from Charlie:

Dear Karl,

Emily is going to the University of Chicago next year. I overheard my parents say they hope that the separation will end our relationship since I'm not Jewish and her parents don't want to accept me. But how could it? Emily is every-thing to me. I'm torn in pieces about this. Worst of all, what if my parents are right? What do you think?

Your chum,

Charlie

Karl lowered the letter, wondering whether he would ever find someone he cared for even half as much as Charlie loved Emily. He didn't doubt it, but at the same time there seemed such an immense variable of luck involved, combined with a heap of fairy dust. Love, he had noticed, rendered normal, committed, ambitious men semi-conscious. His reading of Keats had lately reinforced his awareness about the power of love.

This poem, which Karl had chosen to write an essay on, was in his hand along with Charlie's letter. Organ music eloped with the red stone walls. Karl read the poem again and thought about what he might write.

The word "unreflecting" confused him, although he knew it was important to consider: Unselfishness versus egocentricity—the essay was beginning to form in his mind. *Synchronicity? Simpatico?* Karl wondered which, if either, was the word he needed to describe the kind of love he'd be looking for.

WHEN I HAVE FEARS

When I have fears that I may cease to be
Before my pen has glean'd my teeming brain,
Before high-piled books, in charactery,
Hold like rich garners the full ripen'd grain;
When I behold, upon the night's starr'd face,
Huge cloudy symbols of a high romance,
And think that I may never live to trace
Their shadows, with the magic hand of chance;
And when I feel, fair creature of an hour,
That I shall never look upon thee more,
Never have relish in the faery power
Of unreflecting love;—then on the shore
  Of the wide world I stand alone, and think
  Till Love and Fame to nothingness do sink.

Tones in the organ music softened, evoking intimacy, reminding Karl of the first time he had attended a concert with his grandmother; how she had taught him to listen for the composer's message. "Or close your eyes and imagine," she suggested, "a forest, a battle, the moon like a velvet hat, a street hockey game!"

Like a contrapuntal fugue, the tone of the organ changed again. Listening to music was one of the few ways Karl could transport himself from haunting visions in the aftershock of the sudden death of Oscar Raynor.

The accident had been inscrutable, a horrific tragedy—impossible to reconcile. On their return to Lawrenceville from Thanksgiving vacation, friends of Oscar's had hopped aboard a trolley car in Trenton at the corner of Warren and State streets. As the trolley started to move, everyone jumped inside. Everyone except Oscar. He was left outside when the door shut. At the same time another trolley came along fast from the opposite direction. With only six inches between the two, Oscar was dragged along the tracks. He died before reaching the hospital.

Karl compared the manner in which Oscar was snatched away to Jack's suicide. Oscar was hailed for his faithfulness, modesty, and courage: *"A noble life having both his moral and his physical sides already well developed with strength and athletic ability as well as unusual powers of mind and heart."*

In collaboration with other members of the Calliopean Society to which he belonged, Karl had helped write an addendum to honor Oscar that was printed in *The Lawrence Ledger,* November 1902: *"We pledge ourselves today in devotion to those ideals that our beloved classmate realized to such an extent that his memory will be treasured and preserved."*

Pieces of Karl's conversation with Charlie came to mind: *How much control do we have over our lives, or just think we have?*

Unexpected staccato notes along with lighter concerns lifted Karl from his pensiveness. He rose to exit through the chapel vestibule, associating the resonant ring of his heels on the stone with that of his mother's on her way into their house in Brooklyn. Immediately stunned by sunshine, but able to recognize his friend Bummy Ritter crossing the lawn on the other side of the green, Karl pressed his papers to his chest and ran to catch up. Music slipped through the open chapel doors behind him and swirled up into the treetops.

18

Confidence

*M*AX'S GOLF GAME *is consummately superior to mine,* Karl contemplated as he walked toward his next shot, laughing to himself: *the word calamity could be a euphemism for my game compared to his.* Karl's talent for golf was paltry, although he never gave up trying—too hard. *Maybe,* Karl thought, *if I'd been able to talk him into giving me more strokes, I could be somewhat optimistic about the outcome. But, in golf, does winning really matter? Aren't I really playing against myself? Or against the course?*—a conundrum he had yet to reconcile.

Max had conjured the idea of a golf game to appease Karl's angst over leaving Lawrenceville. Graduation day, June, 1903, manifested the usual bitter-sweet oxymoron. The ceremony had taken place in Lawrenceville's brand new auditorium.

Close to the end of Commencement, after clearing his throat (a bit too close to the microphone) Mr. Green leaned over to confer with Dr. McPherson. Their mysterious exchange resulted in summoning Karl's classmate Frederick William Ritter to the platform.

Bummy Ritter was one of the most revered students at the school. Karl had written a letter to his mother, describing a baseball game during which Bummy refused to stop playing after some of his front teeth had been knocked out. This was only a fragment of Bummy's legendary gumption. His school spirit was unmatched.

At the mention of his name the entire student body began to clap until applause sounded as loud as torrential rain on a tin roof. People in the audience shifted and shuffled. Programs fell to the floor as they swiveled in their seats, searching for a glimpse of Bummy, who, white as a sheet, ambled to the platform in personal silence thunderous as the applause.

Once on the platform, Bummy stood like a guard at Buckingham Palace while Mr. Green announced with booming decibels:

"Frederick William Ritter, this school for the first time in its long history has determined to present to you a special diploma in recognition of your outstanding character, leadership, and loyalty to Lawrenceville!"

When Henry Green finished the final word of this surprise honor, every able-bodied person in the auditorium stood, many with tears in their eyes. Cheers and stomps reverberated—a freight train might just as well have roared through the already burgeoning storm.

Overwhelmed by emotion, Bummy collapsed off the edge of the platform. He would have hit the floor if not for the rush of several people in the front row who caught him on his way down. Accompanied by the crescendo, they carried Bummy out of the auditorium. The exodus abruptly ended the ceremony, leaving the chaplain to rue the omission of his benediction.

Karl found his family. Although content to be with them, he felt lost in the mêlée of the moment along with experiencing a powerful urge to be back with his friends on a routine school day. The only thing left for him to do was return to his room to round up his haberdashery, suitcases, valises, violin, and tennis racquet. He walked out of Upper, passing the freshly painted (yellow) smoking room—*through one haze into another*, he thought, trying to be cheerful.

"Hey, brother," Max said, walking alongside Karl, "I know how you feel right now. I had a great time here too. And, all-in-all, you've been to five schools. But if you think this is tough, wait 'til we get home and I clean your clock on the golf course!"

Max's tease was just what the doctor ordered. Before they had left campus, Karl's strategy-wheels were working to devise a plan: *How can I get Max to give me enough strokes?*

Karl and Max were playing as a twosome because Fritz was "gallivanting" in Europe and Herm had declined their invitation to join the game, saying he needed to accompany Sarah on an errand. Sarah had fallen into the doldrums since Frank Purcell (as Grace had predicted in confidence to Karl) ended his relationship with her after he moved to Chicago—distance providing apt leeway for him to commence his inevitable dalliance with other "lovers."

"Do you think they're having a fling?" Max asked Karl as they approached the second green.

"Who?" Karl was suspicious of Max's distraction tactics.

"Herman and Sarah!"

"A *fling*? You mean...oh, come on Maxi, that's preposterous. What? Hmm...well, that would be quite an upset...of the apple cart. But Hermie has been moony-eyed lately, hasn't he! Sarah received that farewell letter from Frank, and she's..."

"Vulnerable."

"Extremely so."

"Reason for Herm to feel a need to take care of her."

"Naturally."

"Your shot!"

After waggling his club three or four times, Karl swung but failed to follow through his chip shot with enough club speed; so the ball (a fifty-six-sided Park Royal he had snitched from his father's bag) advanced only a few feet and stuck in a clump of long grass in the fringe off the green.

"Damn!" Karl said, hurrying to whack it again after guzzling the Zoolak he had stuffed in his bag. (Sarah insisted that fermented milk was good for him.) His next attempt was another fluff. "Max, what makes you like this game, anyway?"

"Self-control," Max answered smugly, sinking his lengthy putt for par as the ball landed in the hole with a pleasing kerplunk.

Near the end of the 17th hole, thunderclouds darkened the western sky, providing just the excuse Karl needed to call it quits. "No sense incurring the wrath of Mother Nature here, Maxi! Let's make a run for the clubhouse." Karl hoisted his bag, jogging ahead in a brain-rattling dash. When he turned around, he spotted Max, lagging way behind, preparing to hit his second shot up the 18th fairway.

Accompanied by a clap of thunder in the downpour, Max finally emerged from the course with a splashing leap onto the clubhouse porch where Karl was already ensconced, toasting him with lemonade. "Here's to the difference between devotion and desperation," Karl said, laughing at Max's soaked shirt. "You're a winner. You've got dedication all sown up. What d'ya have on the last hole?"

"A bogey. Putting was a little tough."

"Not bad, Maximum. Not bad at all."

PART TWO

Expecting will not make it so;
Climb! Climb!

Theodore Roosevelt reviewing the Rough Riders before World War I.

19

Fractious Influences

*I*T WAS A DARK DECEMBER EVENING in 1905 when Karl, as a member of the Debating Society and the City Government Club at Yale, filed into a well-lit second-story room at the White House in Washington along with thirty-three finely attired students from Harvard, Princeton, Columbia, and nine other colleges.

Dressed in a dinner jacket, President Roosevelt (the "Colonel" as Karl and his friends enjoyed referring to him) stood at the door, greeting each young man individually. Once introduced, the visitors sat on small chairs that lined the room, until there were no more available. The President, finding there were not enough chairs to accommodate everyone, walked to the end of the room and sat on a large table, suggesting that some of the students join him there. Karl seized the opportunity and planted himself next to Roosevelt where he proceeded to listen intently, memorizing everything Roosevelt said as well as he could:

"I want you to suspend thinking of me as President of the United States tonight," Roosevelt said. "Consider me simply as Theodore Roosevelt, Harvard, 1880." He then said he was anxious to talk as a college man, [and] without too much reservation, laughingly referred to recent criticism in the press of his having too wide an interest in matters not pertaining to the running of the government. In a more serious vein, he asked everyone present for a pledge that nothing he discussed be repeated so as to get into the hands of the newspapers.

The object of this meeting, he said, was to endeavor to interest college men in future public and political service. He dwelt on the necessity for greater activity in local politics by college graduates. Then warming to his subject, he remarked that perhaps the best way to explain how this might be done was to outline his own early

101

experiences in Ward politics in lower New York fighting Tammany. This he did in fascinating detail, finally bringing his story up to his present position as President. Here he paused, and looking around the room, again reminding [them] *of* [their] *pledge of secrecy, saying that he wished to tell* [them] *something of the present condition of the country. Quite suddenly he said, "Certain big business people and certain big politicians have come to consider themselves more powerful than the Government of the United States. I shall shortly start to fight this menace without gloves. There will be a great storm over this country before I am done, but my successor in office will calm the rough seas created by the impetuous Roosevelt. I am now, as shown by election results, a popular President. When my term expires—mark my words—I shall leave the White House the most, certainly one of the most unpopular Presidents ever to leave office. However, young men, we shall have a better country."*

Karl's impression of Roosevelt's virility and fiery strength of character was informed firsthand from a casual position on the table. Framed by magnetism and receptiveness, Roosevelt's responses to various questions exuded passion—*as though the questions them-selves were savory*, Karl thought. Most of all, Karl felt compelled by Roosevelt's zeal for his vision of integrity, which embraced a life of action and self-sacrifice. Although of different ages, like-mindedness between Karl and his mentor was forged that night and would be-come a vital camaraderie in ten years' time.

Since mid-winter Yale hockey games were played at the St. Nicholas rink in New York City, Karl could combine these events with spending as much time as possible at the 74th Street apartment of his parents where, much to his chagrin, he became an intermediary in a skirmish between them.

Karl's mother was obsessed by her need to clear away posses-sions she considered extraneous from the apartment—all of which, she explained to Karl, had become a burden to her and to the family. Herman refused to recognize the urgency of her mission. In his opinion, nothing ever qualified as superfluous. Nevertheless, Grace assumed a one-woman crusade to "raus mit dem," as she would say, rolling the "r", meaning "throw away" whatever she deemed unworthy of having around regardless of her husband's reluctance. Herman's disgruntlement advanced to anger. He valued every inch of leftover string and Grace's pseudo-German did not amuse him.

In his small room, Karl could hear his father tramp along the hallway grumbling: "Lieber einen Spatz in der Hand als eine Taube auf dem Dach" (A bird in the hand is worth two in the bush.) At his desk, Karl shoved back his chair, entered the hall, and endeavored to express his mother's point of view. At first, Herman whispered back to Karl to prevent Grace from hearing: "Seit ich mit ihr diskutiere, hat sie mir die kalte Schulter gegeben" (Since I argued with her, she has given me the cold shoulder). But when Karl cajoled, his father countered with gusto: "Sie bekommt alles was sie will!" (She gets everything she wants!)

In theory, Karl's sensibility about saving things tipped toward that of his father; nevertheless, he needed to communicate his mother's position in order to quiet the burgeoning rancor between them. He even pitched in to help her pitch out a few things, realizing that her responsibility to divest Julie's house of several decades worth of collectibles and keepsakes had convinced her that paring down was not only beneficial but mandatory in order to spare others from the daunting task.

Late on a Sunday afternoon in February, hoping that his father had softened, Karl suspected that Herman's new diplomacy was a ruse to prevent disruption to the tranquility of their on-going chess match in the solarium. Sunlight glinted on the tips of Shirley's fur where she lay curled with her nose resting in the valley of Herman's boot. And it highlighted the lengthy contour of Herman's index finger as it circled the tip of Karl's rook and arced back to stroke his chin and smooth his mustache before reaching into his vest to lift out a pocket watch and check the time. Karl was lulled to complacency, until—swift as a lizard's tongue—his father grasped his own knight, tucking it into the palm of his hand, and scooped up Karl's bishop in a swap of the former for the latter to assume the square. The captured bishop was plummeted into exile at the edge of the table where it was lifted and dropped with defiant little clicks against the wooden surface.

"Your knight is in jeopardy there, Father," Karl warned, his tongue pressing against his cheek. Having won the first game, Karl was buoyed by a sense of security.

"Oh," Herman said, only mildly concerned—*click, click,* "I'll take my chances!"

While calculating the next move, Karl's thoughts wandered back to details that he and his father had discussed earlier in the day concerning the introduction of garnet to improve the process of manufacturing sandpaper, and then to a serious power struggle between partners at the company.

Suddenly, in juxtaposition with these thoughts, Karl was startled by the sight of Fritz who, after having been absent for several weeks, appeared to be lurking in the shadow of the doorway with his arms crossed taking stock of the chess game without a word or a greeting.

Karl imagined his brother stalking the game like a carnivore eyeing a slab of meat as Fritz walked in and stood over the table.

"Oh, baby brother—still can't take the old man, can you!" he said, pawing Karl's shoulder.

Karl moved his queen.

"Check king!" Herman bellowed.

Karl scowled at Fritz: "How 'bout scrounging up another feeding ground, Blitzer!"

"Oh, but you're the perfect target for a razz, my boy. How could I resist? Buck up, old pal. Don't blame me for losing. I'm not playing the game!" Fritz circled the table and winked at his father.

Intent on the game and disinclined to dignify Fritz's treatment of Karl, Herman did not respond.

Karl opted for the one-time move, castling to protect his king. But this did not prevent the inevitable next move.

"Checkmate!" Herman said, shoving back, his chair growling against the floor. "Ausgezeichnet" (Excellent)! "Excellent game, son. Better luck next time!" he declared, thrusting his fist into the sunny spotlight.

Fritz moved to help his father up. They strode arm in arm from the parlor, leaving Karl to gnaw on his thumbnail.

Karl called after them: "Come back! It's a draw!" But hearing his father's contented giggle, he rested his chin in his hand, wondering why he had never been able to fathom the ease with which Fritz got under his skin.

Releasing his bottom lip from the pressure of his top teeth, Karl mumbled "Schadenfreude," as he realized how much he cared about Fritz's opinion.

20

To Keep in Mind

*W*IND RATTLED THE WINDOW PANES, whistling *arioso* through a space between sash and sill while rain tapped code on the gutter. Karl opened his eyes to a summer Sunday morning in New York City, initially forgetting that he was in the little room he occupied at his parents' apartment.

Once he had established his location, a conjecture popped into his consciousness: *Either William Clothier will come up against the great Bill Larned, or I might.* In just a few days, Karl would be playing in the 1906 Eastern Tennis Championships at Longwood Cricket Club in Boston. *With so many Bills and Williams, my name should have been Big Bill Behr, or Wild Will Wooly-Behr;* he chuckled at the silly alliterations.

Karl admired Bill Larned, who had returned from the Spanish-American War in 1901 to win the first of his championship matches. He considered Larned fortunate to have had the honor of being one of Teddy Roosevelt's "Rough Riders." Already a legend, Larned was the number one tennis player in the country—referred to as a daring attacker with a backhand bullet. It was going to be tough to give him a game. But first, Karl would have to beat Clothier, and that would be challenge enough. Ranked among the top ten, William Jackson Clothier was a Harvard man known as the right-handed net-rusher. He had won the intercollegiate championship in 1902 and had given Larned many a run for his victories.

Karl got up to shut the window and saw that the storm was dramatic. Rain crisscrossed and cascaded, undulating a vast curtain down the street. He watched a pedestrian hurdle a small river almost to safety, only to be drenched by the splash of a passing carriage; then he dove back under his covers, pulling them up to his chin, and thinking about the fact that out at the end of Long Island where this kind of northeaster spawned lakes in the flat terrain, Max would, nevertheless, have to continue playing in the golf tournament at Shinnecock Hills.

Max and Karl had kept close tabs on one another since their mother had died in December. Although blizzard conditions descended the day before Fritz's wedding and Grace had fallen ill, it was unthinkable that she would not attend. Fritz was marrying a "nifty gal" who had been a darling friend of the family for many years. Herman tried to dissuade Grace from enduring the train-ride to Morristown, but he knew she would travel regardless. Once on the train, Karl helped to wrap her in blankets in an effort to keep her warm; but upon arrival, she was suffering violent chills and had to go to bed. The pneumonia, already advanced, spread quickly. During her last clear moments, she called for Karl. They were alone when she lost consciousness.

His mother's death caused the deepest sorrow Karl had ever suffered. Grief continued to inundate him with a feeling of emptiness that he could not alleviate. He realized he had done everything, literally *everything*, with her in mind—always needing her reaction to feel complete. Now that she was gone, his intentions had lost their aim; his opinion had no final analysis or sounding-board from which to resonate.

He turned to scan the photograph of her on the bedside table next to him. The image seemed suspended in space. Memories of her sincerity, her great loyalty and affection, flowed through him as though integral to him. *If the scope of a person's worth could be measured by the manner in which that person is kept "alive" in the mind of another, then my mother will be supremely honored for as long as I live*, he intuited. Cloud-gray shadows by her eyes abstracted his thoughts of her. When he looked away—back at the rain-streaked window—he heard her bidding: *have faith in yourself.*

After Grace died, Marley Ellis found a position with another family. "Missing your mother is too much for me," she said. But

Sarah stayed on, much to the benefit of everyone. She had become an accomplished cook and the smell of her bacon wafted to Karl's room where he sat up in his bed, glancing at his desk, which was piled high with Columbia Law School journals. *Fodder for brinkmanship and brouhaha,* he thought, considering he should get up to read, but instead sinking deeper under his covers, glad that it was Sunday. He was tired.

On days without classes, Karl had honored his decision to learn his father's business by immersing himself in physical work at the factory where the adhesion of abrasives by glue to either paper or cloth was accomplished in a complex process on a "making machine." During this stage, the product could be easily ruined when the material passed through large steel rollers, because the rollers were often forced out of kilter by variations of thickness in the glue or bad spots in the paper or cloth. If the man operating the rollers was not a vigilant expert, thousands of yards of worthless product would result. There were only three expert "makers" at Herman Behr & Co. After a series of ten-hour days from October to May, Karl had succeeded in becoming the fourth. Along the way, he had become acquainted with the employees and machinations of the company while augmenting his efforts to help his father whose usual stalwart demeanor had begun to slump—first in posture, then in belabored expressions as he suffered from the desolation of losing Grace.

On Karl's bedside table next to the photograph of his mother, a once colorful corsage from Fritz's wedding lay next to an unopened Moxie soda and Upton Sinclair's *Manassas.* The Moxie reminded Karl of the lengthy conversation he had had with his father the night before:

After dinner they had retired to the library, firelight teasing the old General's portrait above the mantel. Karl slipped out a thin book from between two fat novels. Embossed on the cover were the words: *Illustrations by Herman Behr.* As he turned the pages, Karl was impressed by the quality of the drawings. Subtle shading and delicate detail rendered each more elegant than its predecessor. An intricate interior gave way to an exquisite portrait of a dark-eyed woman.

"These are masterful," Karl said, looking for his father's reaction.

Herman responded, "Oh, that's a portrait of my sister, Jennie. I drew it many years ago—during a summer in Hamburg with Mother, who taught me to imagine that I was touching my subject as I drew. What great pleasure it was to wile away those hours. I can't draw any more; my hand shakes too much."

"Well, these are achievement enough!" Karl added, wide-eyed.

Herman propped himself up in his wing chair and said, "Son, have I mentioned to you that my friend Edward Beech and I are taking on a modest mining project in Mexico; most likely, next year?"

"Really Dad? How would that be possible given all you have to do here?"

"Oh, I'll provide funding. Someone else will have to travel."

"What makes you think it's promising?"

"A prospector by the name of Paul something-or-other recently brought up samples of silver ore from a group of workings he's gained title to. They've shown so rich that Ed claims there's bound to be a winner amongst them. But Paul needs a supervisor for the project."

With little forethought, Karl jumped into the river. "How about me?"

"Can't imagine anyone better," was his father's reply.

Up and away, in synch as a pair of birds, Karl and his father soared to the plan. Karl threw another log on the fire and retrieved a Moxie from the icebox—the one that was now on his bedside table since he'd been too preoccupied to drink it during their lengthy chat about mining.

Enthralled by the prospect of going to Mexico, Karl weighed his obligations to law, tennis, and the abrasives business where orders and projects accumulated the need for a steady response. The three corridors converged. And now there was Mexico. Since Grace had passed away, Karl's father seemed to be folding inward, and Karl was reluctant to leave him.

Eager to continue discussing prospecting with his father at breakfast, Karl got out of bed, dressed, and stooped to comb his hair at the bureau. Lingering there, he stared at a face he had come to know from the inside, but which remained enigmatic to him vis-à-vis the world at large. Approaching the end of the tennis season was daunting. There was always a chance of winning. Then again, he could easily lose, in which case he would consider the extensive time he had spent practicing as having amounted to little more than folly. Karl remembered the anecdote he invented for Jack about practicing to become better, then best at something, realizing that he had followed through with the story he'd invented to protect himself. Older now, however, he realized that notoriety would be secondary to merely having met each new challenge as it came along. He glanced at his reflection again, curious to know the future of that young man staring back.

Rain trickled down the window. Droplets zigzagged, hesitated, then veered off on their individual pathways before rejoining the main channels once again.

21

Filling with Emptiness

*I*N HER BEDROOM, PREPARING to leave East Hampton, Helen inspects the hat she wore on the night *Titanic* went down. Although faded after thirty-seven years (almost all spent in the box), she still wouldn't part with it. Somehow, it had stayed with her the entire night in the lifeboat with Karl. Not the greatest help in terms of warmth, she recalls. Nothing could have prevented the shivering, which had sources in fear as well as in the cold.

She had held that hat with one hand while grasping the edge of the lifeboat with the other when the lifeboat tilted drastically on descent from the ship. If Karl's arm hadn't reached around her waist for added support she would have had to let the hat go.

"You were better than nothing," she says to the hat, dusting it off and placing it back in the dilapidated, hexagonal box.

She traverses the room to pause at her dressing table, where she sits to catch sight of her reflection, wondering at the design of aging—a gradual fading to less and less favorable regard that has assumed an etched expression divergent from how she feels or wants to appear. She riles against the passing of her beauty—against this overlay of history, like a crinkled film, a map laden with traces of impediments and channels of concern.

She leans forward, rests her chin on her hand, and looks into space—far beyond any Heaven. There is resignation in her eyes. She senses that flaws provide a preamble, a protective gauntlet; so that only those willing to brave defective trappings will gain access to the heart beneath. Some claim that all one needs to know is within. Simultaneously, she intuits that answers and reasons, if they exist, lie beyond what she can perceive. Acceptance of this unknowing seems the greatest truth of all.

She looks in the mirror again, sighs, and goes to retrieve two large suitcases from the back of the closet—placing them on opposite sides of the bed, opening first one, then the other, tossing the restraining ties outside of their compartments. She walks to Karl's bureau, opens the drawer, lifts a pile of his white shirts, and brushes them gently against her cheek before laying them into the suitcase. She is startled, suddenly, by the sound of something clicking outside. There is a small, unidentifiable tapping noise, then a thump. She hears fluttering—wings of a hummingbird? In the honey locust something feathery is being carried forward from years ago—a feeling of assurance that she will manage, somehow.

Smoothing the pile of shirts, she surveys the bedroom, which is already evincing impending emptiness. She listens for the sound of the ocean she had heard the night before, but hears nothing. Growing up in virtual solitude, she realizes, has formed her into a vessel of containment. Unspoken, her thoughts have often been insubstantial by lack of decibel, or credence given them by others. Instead, they flow back upon themselves like smoke in a glass jar. Her dream from the night before begins to return—that she had awoken from a dream with the sound of glass breaking on stone, but reentered the dream as she picked up an indigo vase she had accidentally knocked over. At first thinking it intact, she turns it over and sees that a piece of it is missing.

She stares. The room blanches as though swathed in white muslin—semitransparent, gauzy as a winter sky, then opaque—a question without answer. Her lips quiver. She lies down, prone between the suitcases. Everything and nothing is manifest in the ceiling above her.

22

Winning and Losing

$\mathcal{A}$T THE EASTERN TENNIS CHAMPIONSHIP in Boston, the players have taken time to sit and sip water. Karl leaned over to retie his shoelaces. He toweled off his arms and surveyed the crowd without distracting himself from his inner focus. His white headband has proved effective at keeping the sweat out of his eyes; but he dabbed at them gently and wiped the back of his neck. Then he dropped the towel, stood up and walked toward the baseline of his deuce court while checking and rechecking the tension of his racquet strings. He glanced up briefly at his brothers in the stands. Max waved. Karl nodded and grinned.

In the middle of the first set, a woman had fainted and play had been suspended until she was adequately cared for. Up in the stands, Max released his death-grip on the oversized binoculars he had been using to report details of the dramatic resuscitation. Straightening up, he asked Fritz, sitting next to him, "What do you suppose Karl's strategy will be now?"

"Haven't the foggiest. Our tennis crack's likely whispering prayers right about now," Fritz said. "Lucky little bro's lookin' limper by the minute. 'Fraid he's licked. Let's leave," Fritz kidded, pretending to stand up.

"Don't write him off, Futzy. You might covet his notoriety some day," Max said.

The hiatus caused by the lady's fainting had given Bill Clothier an advantage over what had been an early surge of energetic accuracy from Karl. Clothier flipped Karl's 3–1 lead to 4 all.

Taking up the binoculars again, Max said, "Uh, oh, Karl is peering skyward, appealing to the powers above. That's not a good sign."

"Told you! …Ooh…Get a load a' the beauty over there, Maximus! She's a stunner, no?"

Max checked out Fritz's new sexational belle—a long-legged, low-lidded blonde who was rolling her delicate ankle to admire her red high-heel.

"You're happily hitched. Remember, Beelzebub? While you were waxing moony over the blitzy blonde, your brother won another game."

"Hmm, 5–4. Great! I'll be right back," Fritz said, as he hopped down to talk to the girl.

Max watched Karl and Fritz at the same time. They were both winning. Fritz, who apparently knew someone in the group around the girl, was being treated as if he were her new best friend, and Karl's effective timing had returned—his shots faster, stronger, closer to the tape. He didn't need to scrutinize his opponent as much and was more connected to his own rhythm—a rapport with speed and spin. Rallies lengthened. Karl's mistakes became infrequent. He won the first set, and then the second.

During the third set, at three games all, Karl was serving at 15–30. In answer to Clothier's low center-court return, he threw up a perfect lob that landed just inside the baseline. His confidence surged along with the applause. The next shot clipped the top of the net with a resounding smack as the ball kicked forward and landed two feet on Clothier's side, giving Karl the advantage.

"Karlos is winning!" Max said when Fritz returned to his seat.

"Oh, right. 4–3, third set. Miracles never cease. When did that happen?" Lifting his hat, Fritz gave his head a vigorous scratching.

"While you were down scraping up the swish dish," Max answered with a tone of disdain.

"Give me the glasses. I promise to pay attention from this moment on!"

"Impossible," Max muttered, handing the binoculars to his brother. "Matter o' fact, Futzer, if you didn't have that hat, you wouldn't know what to use your head *for*," Max said.

Fritz stared at the court.

Scanning rapt concentration on faces of the spectators, Max felt a burst of pride in his brother and could hardly stay seated.

The match progressed to 5–6 in the third set, with Karl returning Clothier's serve at love–30 in what could become the last game if he could break Clothier and win the final set by the prerequisite two-game advantage. Clothier played a smart drop shot to stave off the potential break, bringing the score to 15–30. Then he double-faulted, giving Karl the advantage. Clothier's next serve landed hard and fast, but kicked up high in center court—right into Karl's forehand. Karl went for broke. He hit an all-out, flat, cross-court winner and ran forward for a victory leap over the net. Clothier, who had been heavily favored to win, offered his hand graciously. People in the stands jumped out of their seats cheering, clapping, raising and tossing their hats for the underdog.

"How's that for triumph!" Max said, pounding Fritz's back; launching the binoculars off his brother's chest.

"Wait 'til Pop hears about this one!"

"*Fantastic,*" Fritz added as he jumped down to carouse with his new friends before accompanying Max to congratulate Karl on his way to the locker room.

Tempering Max's enthusiasm as they walked alongside Karl, Fritz said, "Well, it's not exactly a strategic science this tennis game. Men who need accolades for breakfast, lunch, and dinner have a general lack of acceptance of things as they are—hung out for hang-ing's sake!"

"Thanks a lot for coming," Karl said, spinning his racquet and staring down at his worn-out black shoes.

After Karl's boost from beating Clothier at Longwood, anticipation churned around the traditional match to follow, known as a "challenge" match. Awareness that Charlie and Karl's father were among the spectators aggravated Karl's disappointment when he lost this match to the "meteoric" William Augustus Larned. But later in the season, Charlie, Max, and Herm watched Karl's triumphant final in Southampton, New York. Afterward, Karl lost a second "challenge" match to Larned. This time after five well-played sets.

Consequentially, at the national championships known as the All-Comers Tournament in Newport, Rhode Island, few, if anyone, would have predicted the results:

Although merely the second round, the stands were teeming with spectators—always the case wherever Larned played. None of Karl's family or friends were in attendance. During the warm-up rally, Karl noticed a book lying open near the court; its pages were being flipped back and forth in the wind.

A lady coughed as Karl tossed up his first serve. The rest was a blur.

When Karl's senses returned to him, he saw the crowd on its feet. Benevolence from the ether was shining down on him.

Hats dotted the sky.

Karl had beaten Larned in go-for-broke sets: 6–4, 6–4, 7–5.

Someone had taken the book away.

During the next match at this same championship, Karl played his friend, Raymond Little: 2–6, 6–2, 6–8, 11–9, 6–4. Due to rain, the marathon, interrupted intermittently, was a battle of endurance that started at 11:15 and ended sometime after 2:30, with rallies almost exclusively from the baseline. Little had had eight match-points in the fourth set, but Karl eked out the win.

Max tapped Karl's shoulder in jest with a rolled up program as they walked toward the court before Karl's final match, "Well, I guess you'll have a field day with old Clothier now!" he said.

"Winning's never a sure bet," Karl countered, "unless Herm's playing Acey Deucy!"

Clothier was victorious in three decisive sets. Although Karl had beaten Larned and Little along the way, he finished the tournament as runner-up.

After playing singles exclusively, Karl's rank jumped from 35th to 11th to 5th in 1905, and then to 3rd in 1907. He had gained confidence in his control over deep backcourt strokes and retained his New England States title. Playing daily and trying to live up to being lauded by reporters as having "the most exciting record of any youngster the country had ever seen," he lost thirty pounds.

In early spring of 1907, a letter addressed to Karl arrived at 74th Street from the headquarters of the United States National Lawn Tennis Association in Boston, inviting him to play with Beals Wright as part of America's team to recover the Davis Cup. The matches were scheduled to take place in England in July.

You're *going*, Karlos!" Max said, reading over Karl's shoulder in the front hall of the apartment. "This is the chance of a lifetime!"

"Guess it is," Karl muttered, perplexed. He stared at the letter signed by James Dwight. "But..."

"But what?" Herman interjected, coming into the hall.

"Karl's been asked to play for the Davis Cup with Beals Wright," Max said to Herman, flipping thumbs up behind his back.

"Who?"

"One of our best players," Karl said. "He lost a finger in an accident just before last year's matches so he couldn't play and we failed to get the Cup back. It'd be an honor to be his partner. But I don't understand why someone else isn't going—someone who's already played with him. We've never been paired together; he's a lefty. Guess I'll find out." Karl left the letter on the hall table.

"What is the Davis Cup, exactly?" Herman asked.

"*Ignoramus*," Max whispered, under his breath.

Karl happily filled in: "A rivalry that started at Longwood where the trophy was first introduced. M. D. Whitman, Dwight Davis (that's Dwight F. Davis, I think) and Holcombe Ward defeated the English trio: A. W. Gore, H. Roper Barrett, and E. D. Black."

"How do you remember all those names and initials?" Herm asked.

"It's the people that make the game great—similar to golf. Right Maxi?" Karl said.

"Almost. The only name that matters in golf, these days, is Jerome Travers—Jerome G. D. Travers. He wins *every* time, *every* where."

"You could take Jerry, Max. Matter of fact, the U.S. Amateur is coming up in September and we're expecting you to win, aren't we Herm?"

"*Absolument*. My brothers the chimps—champs, I mean." Herm said.

"Davis Cup's a three-point tournament." Karl continued his history lesson: "First there are two singles matches, then a doubles match, then two more singles matches between the pairs that haven't played yet. The second contest of the Cup took place at the Crescent Athletic Club in 1902 when the Doherty brothers, along with Dr. Pim, represented England and won. They absconded with our Cup. I think Larned replaced Davis for that match. The Doherty brothers aren't competing this year, but the Australasian team is, and is heavily favored—A. F. Wilding and Norman E. Brookes. If they win, the Cup goes to Australia. Heaven forbid!"

"So the reason no one wants to play is that they're sure to be shellacked!"

"Maybe. But Clothier has a knee injury, and I think Bill Larned believes that playing doubles might weaken his backcourt game."

"I'll bet he just can't stand the idea of losing," Herman said.

When Karl's father returned home that night and read the letter on the hall table, he carried it with him to speak to Karl who was at the desk in his room with the door open, smiling in anticipation.

"What do you think, Father? Can you spare me?"

"No. I mean, yes. Yes, of course you have to go. What an honor. As a matter of fact, I read in the *Times* today that President Roosevelt is furious about the paltry zeal for this tournament to date. Even his Rough Riders, Bob Wrenn and Billy Larned, aren't planning to participate. Roosevelt is quoted as saying that following the call to compete for the Davis Cup is a patriotic duty—'a sacrifice in nation against nation' in which an unenthusiastic player is just 'afraid of defeat.' Apparently, while Roosevelt and his 'tennis cabinet' switch sides of the net, or sit to rest, they refer to this lack of ardor as 'mollycoddle tactics of some of the experts at the game.' "

"I saw that article too. And, if it's all right with you, I'll go fight like hell—with every ounce of energy I've got—for Wright, Roosevelt, the Cup, Country, and the honor of it!"

"I believe you will, son," Herman said. "You know, I've lived in this country for many years, and although my father arrived before the Civil War and his brother fought in it, he told me never to lose heart for where we came from. And I never have. But I see that the time has come for our family to have a dedicated *American*. I hope you win that trophy and bring it home where it belongs!"

On Tuesday, June 11, 1907, Charlie rang and reported to Karl's father: "I've just seen a headline in *The Boston Herald*:

> TENNIS CRACKS WRIGHT AND BEHR ON THE SAXONIA;
> EX-MAYOR THOMAS N. HART DEPARTS FOR A REST."

He had to shout over the poor connection: "Underneath the headline is a picture of Supreme Court Justice Oliver Wendell Holmes, Jr. in a Panama hat and gray suit. Says he plans to begin an aimless sojourn aboard. Maybe Karl will rub elbows with him. Hey, best of luck!" Charlie said, ringing off without waiting for a reply.

The *Saxonia* resembled a giant duck spewing a mass of downy feathers as she departed from Boston in a fanfare of confetti and white handkerchiefs. Her departure was delayed an hour due to the late arrival of baggage from disorganized ferries undergoing repair. The ship was carrying an unusual number of tourists—nearly a thousand in steerage alone.

Karl had achieved a measure of success, but he was still a virtual unknown in the tennis world, his doubles play sorely in question. He blithely boarded the ship, however, and stood under the torrent of confetti with new confidence because he had recently won a round-robin singles tournament at The Crescent Athletic Club in Bay Ridge, Pennsylvania, which included Little, Dewhurst, Clothier, Larned, and Beals Wright. Above all, Karl looked forward to becoming acquainted with Beals as a friend. Beals's father accompanied them, and Karl's brother Herman planned to join him in England.

During the first afternoon at sea, a rowdy bunch of gentlemen rallied on deck, wagering bets as to who could jump the highest. They held a rope taut across the walkway and snapped pictures of each other. "You'd better practice your victory leap," they shouted as Karl got ready to give it a go.

At dinner that evening, Karl felt apprehensive because he had been seated next to Justice Holmes at the Captain's table. He pulled out his chair blurting, "Regular stunt men, we were today!"

"You took quite a risk, don't you think?" Justice Holmes retorted. "There is considerable probability of spraining an ankle when jumping like a kangaroo on shipboard. Just like that," he snapped his fingers, "you could be splinted and ridiculed for irresponsible behavior. I can see the headlines now: U.S. bereft—jolted from Davis Cup due to asinine frivolity aboard *Saxonia.*"

Holmes winked at the Captain, who winked back *obviously* for Karl's benefit.

"Well sir, now that I think of it, you're absolutely right," Karl said, rolling his eyes, pressing his lips, and drawing the napkin down to his lap. "But did you, by chance, place any bets on my behalf?"

"I did not," Justice Holmes said. "Had I known we would be dining together tonight, I might have. *Should* have, I gather?"

"*Could* have made a killing, sir!" Karl said with a grin and a swish of his napkin.

"Slim chance you'll win next time Behr," Beals teased from across the table.

"Betting is fool's folly," an elderly man at the table interjected, chin to chest.

As soon as the gentleman was distracted in conversation with the Captain, Karl whispered to Beals, "Who's he?"

"A prominent British steel merchant by the name of Balfour," Beals said. "Confident John Bull," he added in a whisper.

The Captain, a young and handsome ex-Royal Navy officer, began telling Karl how much he admired Napoleon. They found themselves comparing the numerical losses at some of Napoleon's great battles with those of the Civil War, with Karl quoting casualty figures of the battles at Antietam and Gettysburg.

Abruptly, Mr. Balfour interrupted Karl. "Your figures are positively bogus and absurd," he claimed. "Furthermore," he added with indignation, "it is nonsense to compare the fights of your un-trained Civil War mobs with the battles of the trained armies of Napoleon!"

"Poppycock!" Justice Holmes interjected, rising from his chair, enraged to the hue of a plum. "Rubbish, Balfour; young Behr's figures are astonishingly accurate. I ought to know. I was carried off the field of Antietam seriously wounded." Without a further glance or word to Balfour, Justice Holmes turned to the Captain, excused himself and left the dining room.

Each night thereafter, Karl and Beals kept a running tally of points in regard to Justice Holmes's repartee vis-à-vis Mr. Balfour.

After putting in a week's practice, Beals and Karl entered the British Championship at Wimbledon. Reporters touted Wimbledon as a warm-up for the Davis Cup. Norman Brookes defeated Wright in straight sets, and Wilding in four sets. Then he played Karl in the last and most exciting match:

Karl was two sets down. He changed from his flat serve to a low bounce-twist and won the next two sets. The usually quiet, well-controlled Wimbledon crowd was stirred to froth. When Karl won the fourth set and the score was posted at 2–2, the spectators threw their straw-cushioned seats all over the court. An American woman fainted, and after a prolonged delay was carried across the court to the clubhouse. The full ten-minute hiatus to quiet the crowd was unfortunate. With Karl's momentum broken, Brookes, "the better player," as Karl admitted to Herm that evening, gathered his strength to win a close fifth-set climax.

Teamed together for the doubles matches afterwards, Karl and Beals beat the English champions Gore and Barrett in the semi-finals, but lost in the final match against Brookes and Wilding.

In New York, Max picked up the July 1st edition of the *New York Times* for a penny and ran into the corner restaurant to meet Fritz for breakfast and read about how the Davis Cup tournament was progressing.

"Let's see," Max thumbed through the paper toward the sports section while Fritz set his hat down on the table. "Hm, gee, here's a story," Slowing momentum to get to the sports page, Max read, "Captain Mulford caught a nine-hundred-pound, man-eating, whip-tail shark five miles offshore at Amagansett."

"*Pfft*, that's something," Fritz said, studying the breakfast menu.

"Oh boy, two columns covering the disappearance of John D. Rockefeller. *Pandemonium!* Do you think he's trying to avoid a subpoena?"

"What for?"

"A supposed infraction of the 1887 Interstate Commerce Law." Max continued flipping toward the sports page. "Oh, here is some news: Ship skippers are now *wiring* each other to warn about icebergs."

"Get to the tennis, would you!"

Max continued to torment Fritz: "A dog named Casey (natch) rescued a waif under the Dreamland Pier by tearing off a piece of the kid's coat and bringing it to Peter O'Hagan, head of the Coney Island Dreamland police force."

"Ah, *Dreamland!* What a filler-fluffy t'ing is 't? What 're you dallyin' for? Afraid to find out what's happen'd in England?" Fritz cajoled.

The waitress arrived. Fritz grinned at her, then went on and on with his order. "I'll have two eggs over easy—lightly that is—and scones, with a touch of Tabasco on the side. Could you make the eggs *slightly* runny? Where is the salt! Oh, here it is, right in front of me! ...Coffee? Yes, thanks. Black with sugar." He folded his menu, refolded it, and handed it to the waitress with a wink.

"Scrambled eggs, two rolls, coffee with milk, and orange juice, please," Max said as soon as the waitress had had a chance to extract her attention from Fritz. Max returned to his reading, adding, "You know, Fritzel, the waitress is *not* the cook... Oh! Here it is! You won't believe this!"

"Spill it, Maximum!"

Max read: "Fine tennis by Americans—Wright and Behr rally after losing two sets and win match." Max looked up at Fritz and back to the paper: "They beat Gore and Barrett 3–2. The scores were 8–10, 4–6, 6–1, 6–4, and 6–2."

"So? Who's that? And what's next?"

"They've beaten England's best. This is about Wimbledon. It says that these four players are to meet in the contest for the Davis Cup. Guess we'll have to wait and see."

"*Torture*," Fritz said, scratching his head.

"Oh, and Fritz, there's one more little thing," Max added.

"Tell me," said Fritz, leaning his head on his hand.

"I'm getting married," Max said.

Max found his father, a few evenings later, to talk to him about the engagement and to broach the subject of a burgeoning problem at the company. Herman noticed the worried look on his son's face, but preemptively said, "Did you see the paper today?"

"Not yet. You?" Max asked.

"It appears…that Karl and Beals won their Davis Cup doubles match today."

"They must be ecstatic."

"And exhausted. Both of them lost their singles matches. Beals was beaten decisively by Brookes. And although Karl gave Wilding a good fight, he lost too, which means that now they both have to win their pending singles matches."

"What was the score of the doubles match?"

"It went five sets: 3–6, 12–10, 4–6, 6–2, 6–3. The Australasia team took the first set with comparative ease. The reporter wrote that it was 'only after the most strenuous play that the Americans were able to place the second set to their credit.' "

"I should say; it took some stamina—12–10!"

Herman continued reading: " 'When the Australasia team won the third set, it looked as though the match was out of reach for the Americans. Wright and Behr, however, made a great effort and, tiring out their competitors, had all the best of it in the concluding sets.' " Herman folded the paper. "So, what are you worried about?" he remembered to ask.

"Nothing, Dad. It's nothing, really," Max said, deciding not to ruin the moment by telling his father that the works manager at the Company was stirring up trouble.

The moment Beals Wright won his singles match against Wilding, everything would rest on the pending outcome of Karl's contest with Brookes. Karl was unaware of this at the time; he had been playing his match on the side court while Wilding and Wright were competing at Center Court. Karl had won the first set. His serving was smooth and accurate. He heard a great burst of applause come from Center Court. Someone in the audience flashed him a smile, confirming what he had hoped—Beals won.

Karl's match was then moved to Center Court and he struggled valiantly in the second set, getting to 4–5 before he began to lose ground. His volleying became erratic. His cross-court shots were dropping a hair wide. During the third set he only scored eleven aces. Then, sadly, it was over.

"Beals, I could *shoot* myself," Karl said. "This is a moment I'll never be able to forget. Letting you down is even worse than losing for America and disappointing my family." He thought of his father's words and his heart sank.

"Hey, listen my friend," Beals said, "Norman Brookes has the best serve of anyone we've ever played. He clobbered me. I know. I used to beat him, but he's improved. I doubt if anyone could take him now. It's just that simple. You gave him a better run than I did. Furthermore, this isn't about us as partners. We won our match. So don't feel bad on my account, Karl."

Once the tournament had ended and the sting of defeat had begun to abate, Karl traveled from London up to Cambridge with Herm to absorb the beauty of the English countryside in an attempt to bury his disappointment. The magnitude of his loss was subdued as he strolled through Caius College quadrangle. Antiquity—the history infused by centuries into hallowed stone—diminished the disappointment of momentary events.

Although considering it maudlin, Karl wanted to hear the sound of his violin in the King's Chapel's famed acoustics, so he carried it in. He lifted the violin from its case and pulled back the bow. He followed the sound's reverberation as if tendrils of a vine were growing—*around pillars, through archways, along the nave, soaring up the wall*—in smooth, ascending intervals: C to E, then up to G, A–B–C, high D, and back to middle C again. He stopped. It was enough. The wistful tone soothed him and he placed the violin back in its case, afraid that his playing might disturb the tranquility of someone he could not see. As he held still in the silence, he heard birds sing unconcerned about any listener, and he reconsidered the lines from Rudyard Kipling's poem that were engraved over Center Court at Wimbledon—*the true standard by which mettle is measured*, he thought:

If you can meet with Triumph and Disaster
And treat those two Imposters just the same...

Karl saw himself as a miniscule dot beneath the fan-vaulted arches eighty feet above him. He raised himself upright in the pew, then bowed to pray, the way he remembered Charlie had said—*not for favors, but for humility.*

Karl and Herm, along with a few of Karl's Yale friends who had joined them in London, traveled to Brussels, then to Paris where Karl's classmate, Louis de Mores, arrived at the hotel in a white motor car to take him and his entourage out on the town. Although exciting, the evening could not stave off Karl's dread of the disappointment he would see in his father's eyes when he arrived home. He would soon leave Europe in response to a number of cables from Dwight Davis urging him home to prepare for the National Championship at Newport.

"I'm struggling with a general lack of keenness; something's missing," Karl said to his father once he had returned to New York, having not performed particularly well in Newport.

"What you might do is take some time to rejuvenate, to be re-inspired," his father said without any hint of judgment, only pride in his manner. "Be aware that President Roosevelt has lauded your great effort. We received a letter from him, praising you for playing valiantly." Herman reached to squeeze his son's shoulder and continued: "At your age, no matter how many times you hear that life is fleeting, it is both merciful and unfortunate that you are unable to assimilate the fact. Young people perform in the moment. Failure lurks inevitable as success. A man my age knows that finding fulfillment from any small triumph—without self-abnegation—is paramount. Much of the pleasure in life is derived from a long look at experience. Keep in mind Milton's adage: *The mind is its own place, and in itself can make a heaven of hell [or] a hell of heaven....* Now, after that pontification, I have wonderful news to report. Max plans to marry. He realized the certainty of his love while you were away."

"Evelyn."

"Such a sweet gal—beautiful, enthusiastic about golf. She seems to be wild about him."

"Great! ...let's watch him play the U.S. Amateur this fall," Karl said, grateful for his father's sensitivity.

"Excellent idea!"

On September 19th, 1908, the fairways of the Garden City Golf Links were lined with spectators. "Must be more than a couple thousand people here," Karl said to his father as they leaned around people to catch a glimpse of Max. It was a warm, muggy, windless day. The course had been finely groomed in preparation for the 36-hole final round.

"*Smoky*, isn't it." Karl's father said, referring to the haze.

"I suppose, but I doubt it is bothering Max. The visibility's good enough. Isn't that Henry Taft over there?" Karl pointed toward the brother of the notable Republican presidential candidate.

"Looks like him.... *Yes*," his father affirmed.

Karl blinked in quiet empathy, admiring Max's ability to have come this far against the best of the best, because time after time the skill of Travers on the putting green was nothing short of masterful.

"Look, he's right out with Jerry," Karl's father said, referring to Max's drive. "Let's advance to the next green," he continued, striding forward.

Max's ball rimmed the cup before falling in as he sank a twenty-foot putt to win the 3rd hole.

At the 11th green, Travers ran in a forty-foot putt. Then he rolled in a curly thirty-footer on the 14th. "Can't beat precision putting," Karl said. "Jerry's simply too good."

Max lost to the defending champion Travers, eight down with seven holes left to play.

Once the Award Ceremony ended, Max and Karl traveled home with their father, both gazing at the scenic panorama and taking some comfort in their simpatico.

"Are superlative achievers born, or honed, do you think?" Max asked Karl.

"A rare combination of both," Karl said.

At the apartment later that evening, Karl's father asked Karl if he still wanted to go to Mexico in the spring after Max's wedding.

23
Adventure Mexico

"ADDED TO THE LIKELIHOOD OF injury, there's slim chance you'll come back alive, little brother. I have no idea what our father was thinking when he proposed this harebrained scheme. Heavens to Betsy, he must be daft. What's going to happen to your tennis? You're practically on top, ranked number three! After taking so much time off, you'll slide to the bottom of the list. The premise of this trip is ridiculous. Haven't you heard that gringos are scum in Mexico? You know as well as I do, they get shot for no reason. Do you have even the remotest clue how dangerous those mines are? Not to mention landslides on the treacherous cliff-trails, which are the only snake-ridden means to reach those rat-holes in the ground! Mules careen into chasms one-per-hour. You know you can't speak a spit of Spanish. Swindlers will salivate at the chance to snooker a fella like you! Don't go, K. I swear, this plan is monkeyshines. Furthermore, it's Sisyphean."

Karl's brother Herman spouted all this at the beginning of the summer of 1908 from his aerie command post—a rickety chair in the corner of Karl's room overlooking 74th Street. Seeing no response coming from Karl, he leaned forward and buried his head in his hands, desperate to come up with another more dissuasive point.

"Bah, don't think that way, big guy," Karl said, folding a shirt under his chin in the process of packing. "Chalk this up to Adventure with a capital A. You know I can shoot straight, and you have to admit there's a good chance we could strike it rich; in which case, I promise to share so you'd never have to lift a finger again! After all, all you have to do is stay here and take care of Pop (plus whatever else crops up) 'til I get back. Be optimistic! Should I take this shirt? What the hell is Sissy-peon, anyway?"

"Not that one, Karl. It doesn't hold up well," Sarah volunteered from the doorway. "Don't forget you'll be washin' all your clothes by hand in the streams." Her arms were tightly wound around a pile of towels. She noticed Herman's twisted face. "Take the sleeveless shirt there, and the khaki one under it."

Herman didn't say any more. He stood up and followed Sarah down the hall. Karl lifted the Winchester out of his closet, put it in its case, and placed it into the center of the duffle, relieved that it fit in end to end. Then he heard the triple-bell of the telephone down the hallway and Sarah's shout, "Karl, Charlie's on the line!"

Karl had left Charlie a message about his mining expedition and was happy not to leave without speaking to him. He took hold of the phone eagerly and mumbled, "Hola muchacho!"

"Eso era terrible. Usted necesita practicar su Español…and you'd better get back home in one piece, pal," Charlie said, "because I need you to be my best man 'long about December. Emily and I are getting hitched, and you've got to hold me up!"

"I'll be standing next to you with nuggets of silver, or maybe gold, bulging from my pockets! God *damn*, Charlie, that's the best news I could have ever asked for. You and Emily are a match made in Heaven. We've known that forever, haven't we, in spite of a few snags along the way. How'd you win approval?"

"Landed a job at the bank, so although I wasn't raised in the bosom of Judaism, Emily's parents have been worn down some after all these years. Or maybe they figured I wasn't going to go away no matter how hard they wished for it."

"As soon as I get back, having struck it filthy rich, I'll blow us both to a pair of gold cufflinks. Not that you'll need any help from me with that lucrative paycheck of yours!"

"Karl, take care. Watch your back. I'll be worrying about you."

"No need. I'll be fine. Grimy around the ears, I suspect, but healthy as a horse. You'll see. Take care, chum. Best to Emily."

"Good-bye and good luck," Charlie's voice faded. The telephone rang off.

"Paul's at the door," Sarah said. "Ready, Karl?"

Karl tucked an extra bandana into the side of his duffel bag, which he quickly fastened and slung over his shoulder. He surveyed the room for any item he might have forgotten and glanced one last time at the photograph of his mother. He had already said farewell to his father over their morning grape nuts.

Max expressed enthusiasm about the prospect of Karl's trip despite agreeing with Herm that the hiatus would jeopardize Karl's tennis standing. Fritz, with predictably less interest, also called Karl to say, "Don't be anybody's cat's paw," just as a female voice called him away from the phone.

Karl and Paul climbed aboard the first of many trains to El Paso where they planned to meet Karl's Yale classmate, Waldo Sheldon, who was to be their mining engineer. Karl kept half an ear open to Paul's embellishments about the wild country they were heading toward as he leaned over to scan the vast expanse of countryside they were passing by—aware that space was increasing between him and all of the ineffable forces that had held him captive in New York.

Once in Kansas City, Karl and Paul hopped off the train to take advantage of an afternoon's layover. Paul announced that he was "bent on seeing something of this rapidly growing town."

Just as they set off to roam the streets, they heard a voice calling, "Karl? Karl Behr? Is that *you*?" Karl turned to see a man running down the bank steps toward him and recognized Blatchford Downing, a fellow athlete with whom he had played football at Yale.

Blatchford took it upon himself to show Paul and Karl all he could of Kansas City, until he stopped short in the midst of a most impressive neighborhood and sputtered, "Oh, I almost forgot! We've got to get to the Athletic Club, pronto! The Missouri Valley Tennis Championship is underway. You'll be the guest of honor!"

At the Club, members of the tennis fraternity surrounded Karl the moment he arrived. Paul was pulled aside by a man who extolled Karl's achievements. He explained that Karl had been accredited for eliminating the old method of having a "standing out" champion so a tournament's previous year's winner would participate in the tournament from the beginning, along with the other players, instead of only playing the final match. "This new and fairer test of athleticism came about solely through Karl's strenuous advocacy," he added, not noticing that Paul was stifling a yawn.

Placing an avuncular hand on Karl's shoulder, a frosty-mustachioed gentleman looked him in the eye and said, "You shall honor us by playing an exhibition match as soon as you can change into the clothes, and take up the racquet we have provided for you. No dilly-dally! We'll be waiting!" he said, tapping Karl on the back.

"I'm afraid you'll be sorely disappointed. I haven't played since August. I'm out of synch, and out of shape," Karl protested, but he was escorted to the changing room then ushered to the grandstand court to perform an exhibition doubles match. Before a large cheering crowd, he wilted in the face of the florid introduction:

"From his phenomenal record of last year and his amazing racquet work in the internationals, a man who has a host of followers—even a visit from Prince William of Sweden—here is one of our country's most exciting players: Karl Behr!"

"An unimpressive performance," Karl said, slurping soup at Blatchford's house that evening before being taken back to the train.

"Not even a tad rusty, Karl," Blatch said. "Your agility was evident, I assure you."

Paul ate heartily. He hardly blinked, unaffected by his companion's celebrity. *Undoubtedly*, Karl thought, *Paul would much rather have seen more of Kansas City.*

By the time the train reached El Paso, Karl was permanently slouched in sun-soaked contemplation, but the soporific comfort vanished when, after several hours of waiting, Waldo Sheldon hadn't shown up. Karl and Paul were obliged to board the next train to Mexico without him, and this train, which had begun to roll forward, suddenly stopped with a raucous screech. Frenzy whirled up like tumbleweed. The Rurales, in the guise of border guards, riding their horses alongside the train, dismounted, hopped on board, and began a brazen search for guns.

Paul had been half expecting them because as he had mentioned, Porfirio Diaz, the President of Mexico, was instituting tough restrictions against the importation of firearms since many Mexicans, restive under his decades-long rule, were beginning to lean toward the use of violence.

"Quick, Karl—your Winchester—here, with the revolvers and ammo," Paul said.

"Where?"

"Here—behind the Pullman seats." Paul lifted five or six pillows from the unmade berths and tossed them haphazardly over Karl's gun, then added his own. At the same moment, Waldo Sheldon burst through the door and approached Karl with a guilt-assuaging grin on his face.

"Waldo, throw your guns in here!" Karl said foregoing a greeting, yanking up the pillows.

They sat stonily, then pretended nonchalance in pseudo chatter as the guards stormed through the car, missing their stash, but finding two other guns and seizing them. A woman gasped.

"Got delayed by my Uncle," Sheldon said, tugging at the scarf around his neck. "He wanted to spend the entire day lecturing me about the dangers 'I was blindly jumping into.' He wouldn't stop. By the looks of those guys, I guess he had a point!"

Still on the lookout for more guards, Karl said, "I have to admit that Paul and I gave up on you temporarily, but I was sure you'd make it to Chihuahua sooner or later. I understand what you went through. My brother rattled at me, relentless as a sidewinder."

Shots were fired outside the train. The Rurales rode off with inimical bravado, which Karl would soon discover was the only way they ever did anything. During his first night in Chihuahua City, he watched them, intrigued by their courtship hubris as they glided, or practically levitated, around the square in tight corduroy pants, be-silvered coats, long spurs and high sombreros while they ogled the finely dressed señoritas who strode with equal allure in an opposing direction.

During the next four days, Paul, Waldo, and Karl set about the task of gathering supplies to express west to Minaca, the terminus of the Mexican Kansas City & Orient RR, a one-track line running to the edge of the Sierra Madres. Finding and packaging drill steel, sledge hammers, picks, powder, fuses, shovels, canned goods, and condensed milk among other multiple necessities, was a feat of engineering unto itself.

Karl opened a bank account at Banco de Sonora. Then, as he walked out onto the streets of Chihuahua hoping his Spanish had been accurate, a man approaching from behind him, urgently pleaded for him to stop.

"Mr. Behr," he said, "Escusa, Mr. Behr, "May I have word with you?"

"Did I make a mistake?"

"No. No. Señor. I heard you are to Urique." He shook his head vehemently. "Mr. Behr, I no like that you go there. The last two gringos did not come back. The *only* gringos who were in Urique last year are dead. One was a young American, same as you—an engineer—stabbed to death on Christmas at dancing. The other, German—an older man—was shot on the trail a few miles outside of town, together with his Mexican mozo. No esplain. No esplain. You are not safe. Do not go to Urique! Mining there is nothing. Not worth the risk."

"Gracias," Karl said and could think of nothing else; so he repeated himself and bowed, "Gracias Señor—for the warning."

Three strikes, Karl thought on his way to find Sheldon. *Should we change course? This last warning screams louder than all the rest.*

After Karl finished reporting the gruesome news to Sheldon, Sheldon slapped him on the back and exclaimed, "This trip is just loaded with Zane Grey possibilities. We're pretty much already committed, wouldn't you say?"

"Adventure with a capital A," Karl answered.

24

Eagles in Urique

*T*HE TRAIN'S STEADY CLACK, like a pair of hands rubbing together, both soothed and excited Karl. Beyond the window, a tableau of endlessly sublime terrain rolled by like backdrop scenery in a play for the gods. Within a few hours they traveled through dry hills, past spindly ocotillos and century plants, into fertile valleys of natural fecundity where yuccas in blossom mingled with measured-out cattle ranches still thousands of feet above sea level. Water flowed into riverscapes from streams in the surrounding hills. The multifarious hills—some velvet as new antlers, others treed and angular or shaped in stony profile—grew steadily more dynamic. Their slopes reflected the color and contour of wind-sculpted sand turned at times to the indigo of a whale's neck, or into a mosaic of terra cotta, ochre, dun, and sienna. From a distance, they appeared to stoop in angled submission like camels waiting for riders to mount.

There were a few settlements. No towns. Karl was reminded of the self-sufficient farms of Switzerland. At a ranch station, the train screeched and exhaled to a stop. It was met by groups of Mexican cowboys in bright-banded sombreros, mounted on horses with heads that were smaller and shaped differently from any Karl had ever seen. Karl and Sheldon got off the train to watch the cowboys haul a recently killed black bear into the baggage car.

As they continued through the foothills of the Sierras, deer were a frequent sight, along with pronghorn antelope. Bald eagles, sacred as cattle in India, stood undaunted as the train roared past them on tracks that zigzagged upward. When the train entered a densely wooded forest of big tooth maples, quaking aspens, and Douglas fir, its windows articulated the sylvan setting with spatters of jade, pewter, and cinnamon overlaid by splays of feathery light. The train seemed quieter then, sibilant, slowing into shade and enchantment.

Then reentering the open countryside, it was taunted by sunlight as it roared to define the valley with clouds of smoke.

The train arrived at Minaca, a town of a few dozen adobe dwellings. Paul, who had become mercurial and phlegmatic since Waldo Sheldon arrived, was greeted outside the train by an associate, Señor Hermosio and also by Francisco, who had come as their assistant, or "mozo." Señor Hermosio had ridden up from Urique to hire their pack train of twenty-five mules with three mule drivers, and to oversee the special purchase of three saddle mules.

From Minaca, pack trains fanned out—traveling along the ancient Indian and Spanish trails that reached deep into Canyon country where loose rock, dense catclaw, prickly pear, and horse crippler cactus made navigation rough and dangerous. About the size of polo ponies, the saddle mules were bred at elevations of five thousand feet or more and were tough, fast, well-trained, and sure-footed enough to maneuver along the steep stony cliffs where a sheer drop was often only inches away.

Although more than an hour had been spent roping supplies to the pack mules, it was still in the dim light of early morning when the pack train set off on its four-day trek to Urique. Mist enhanced the margins between hills and stirred an awareness of mythical proportions in Karl. Moisture, clinging to spider webs and to the looping intricacy of gossamer strands, revealed their architecture of entrapment. A kangaroo rat scurried across the trail. Holdups occurred on the trails from time to time, so Francisco carried a Winchester across his lap. Everyone else had a revolver strapped to his hip. Steadily they climbed, descended, and climbed again; their caravan draped the passes like a strand of black pearls.

During the four-day ride, they saw only two adobe houses, each with small corn patches nearby. The rugged country, conjured by wild winds, could bend a piñon tree almost ninety degrees, chisel a rocky ledge into thin-layered wedges, or carve ground rock into a helter-skelter labyrinth of crevices. Nature radiated a vast quintessence, dwarfing the transient mule train as it swayed in its self-important meander through the hills.

Near the end of the day, Paul broke from his self-imposed seclusion to announce their location. He swiveled in the saddle and used his black hat as a sounding board to yell out, "We'll be setting up camp after we stop at the edge of Baranca de Cobre."

Following Paul, both Sheldon and Karl dismounted. Karl would have wagered that his legs had permanently forgotten how to hold him up. He leaned over to rub his thighs and calves, attempting to stretch partway toward his feet. Then he and Sheldon lay flat at the edge of the six-thousand-foot-deep canyon to take in the sunset.

"I saw the Grand Canyon six months ago," Sheldon said. "This 'canyon of copper' is even more astounding."

"I've never been to either, but I can't imagine anything topping the spectacle here!" Karl reaffirmed.

As the kaleidoscope turned, Karl and Sheldon pointed out various vicissitudes—shades of salmon, mauve, dusty pink—until the exchange waxed prosaic and they resorted to silence.

The night-sky was spun from glory. Moths the size of small birds gathered around the lanterns. Orion's bow and the head of Taurus were outlined in nearly countless stars. Karl climbed under a blanket, contemplating the constellations, wondering how the image-outlines had first been identified. Eventually, he fell asleep with an eye half open to beasts and gods swirling above, and an ear attuned for slithering or footsteps.

At the beginning of the fifth day, Paul revived. Discussing the history of several abandoned shafts and tunnels along the way, he explained that, several years before, Urique had been a boomtown with thousands of prospectors when the Rosario mine, just across the river, was still being worked. Now the population had dwindled to a few hundred. Thinking they were still some distance away, and lulled by the continuous motion of the mule, Karl was elated when Paul suddenly turned and pointed downward into a canyon where a refulgent river wound itself into a luminous *S*.

"Urique," Paul announced. "There she is!"

Five hours later, after a series of switchbacks, they slowly loped through the few scattered buildings in town to the place where they would live—a small white adobe with a walled patio only fifteen feet from the river.

"Well," Sheldon said, "eyeing the water."

"A very deep subject?" Paul joked.

"Time for a swim!" Karl said.

"Last man in gets KP!" Paul said facetiously. He couldn't swim. Whenever their journey had intersected with a river, he had had to cling to a log while the men pushed him across.

Karl walked up-river, stripped down and waded out to wash himself. The current, with water clear as glass, was moving at a good clip, which made bathing quick and easy, but getting back to where he'd left his clothes more of a challenge.

Sheldon had unloaded the supplies by the time Karl returned. They gathered on the patio, hungry for Francisco's covered pot of beans that was steaming next to the soothing trickle of the river. With little warning, light dimmed and rain began to fall—at first in huge, intermittent droplets, then suddenly, sidelong in glossy-grey sheets. Almost instantaneously, hundreds of little waterfalls cascaded from the multiple cliffs above the other side of the river and all across the valley, raising the water level ten feet closer to the house. Then, just as quickly, lizards and red-legged centipedes emerged as the sun poured out and countless rainbows, projected through the prismatic falls, shimmered in clouds of mist across the mountainside.

"Ahh, would ya look at that!" Paul uttered as he emerged squinting from the doorway.

One by one, day by day, week by week, each new promising mining prospect dwindled or disappeared like another mirage. First the Guadalupe, about a mile from the village, with its three-hundred-foot tunnel and one-hundred-foot deep shaft where the ore was rich in silver-bearing galena. Samples assayed ran up to three-hundred ounces of silver and ten percent lead to the ton. Two-dozen men worked there, opening the vein in the shaft and the tunnel. But the vein remained only three inches wide at the working points and was even beginning to show smaller values. Consecutive properties proved just as disappointing, with narrow veins and long barren intervals, while the money to explore kept flowing out.

Paul appeared deflated. He took to the village early some evenings and often did not come back. Once he stayed away for four days. Even Hermosio and Francisco couldn't find him, so Sheldon built his own assaying furnace. Thinking they would never see Paul again, he and Karl took off to examine some other properties.

Arriving at one mine, Sheldon secured the mules while Karl assessed the tunnel leading inside to be in solid condition, although the project appeared to have been abandoned for some time. Venturing about a hundred feet or so into the tunnel, it became much smaller—most likely due to a cave-in, they thought. The space continued to shrink; they dropped to their hands and knees and crawled deeper inside.

Karl was ahead, holding a candle, when they heard a rushing roar.

"Oh, my God, a cave-in!" Sheldon yelled, turning.

The first creature flapped by Karl's head: "Bats!" he said.

Thousands were bursting out in a fluttering mania. Then there were more!

"Lie flat," Karl said, smashing his hat down over his face with his elbows low.

The flying rush was not much louder than the wails and groans from Karl and Waldo who were pressed in to the ground.

When the siege was finally over, the floor of the cave was slippery with bat excretions. Karl crawled through the guano. Once outside, he perused the pieces of his hat and said, "Pulverized."

"Guess we can knock that mine off our list,' Sheldon said, checking out the sad state of his pants. "My knees are flappin' like a couple o' trout."

Karl stood up.

A trigger clicked next to the back of his head.

He froze.

Sheldon fired an arsenal of sharp Spanish.

A hand reached around from behind Karl—down his shirt and into his pockets searching for—*silver?—gold?—a gun?* Finding nothing, the hand receded.

Sheldon's banter continued clipped and caustic.

The bandit kicked up dust and shouted, "¡Quedate!", then side-stepped from Karl to Sheldon to frisk him next.

There was nothing to take—no money, ore, or weapons. Karl didn't know if he should be grateful or terrified, having neither defense nor collateral to negotiate a release. The warning from the man at Banco de Sonora, along with Herman's presage about murder without provocation, bellowed louder than the barrage of bats. He expected the worst. Panic led to terror that his and Sheldon's lives were about to end. But disappointed, the desperado walked slowly backwards to his mule, spat into the dirt, slung himself up into his saddle and disappeared behind the rocks.

Karl collapsed. "Let's get back to the bunk house and start this day over," he jested. He sagged further and rested prone. It took several minutes for his heart to quit hurling itself out of his shirt.

That evening at the house, Sheldon and Karl were taking stock of a slice of mango moon shimmering in the river, when Paul appeared, leaning in the doorway, his arms crossed. "Heard you two had a run-in with a gunslinger today," he said. "Scared him off did you?"

"Nothing to give and nothing to take," Karl replied.

"How'd you know?" Sheldon asked.

"He came into town cursin' and bawlin' to a couple a compadres," Paul said. "Word got around fast to watch out for him. S'pose he's long gone by now."

"We weren't sure we'd see you again," Sheldon said.

"Me neither," Paul admitted.

"What's her name?" Sheldon asked.

"Tequila. She's a medicinal problem. Nothing I can't cure in time, I guess. Time I'm not takin'. Got word of another mine though. It's a long shot, but not too far from here." Paul scuffed across the terrace to survey the river.

Karl peered at Paul's back. Something about the way Paul held himself—a restlessness, lodged between his shoulder blades, buried deep under his shirt—was reminiscent of Jack Farnel. Karl thought, *Pay attention. This man is fragile.*

An eagle swooped upriver early the following morning. Paul's mood brightened. The pack-mules were readied to travel on the first of their forays west to Choix in Sinalo, just beyond the high mountains. They started out with a glint of hope.

Francisco decided to stop along the way to bathe at an unmarked spot in the El Fuerte where a hot spring—the only one in this part of the country—emptied into the river. As the day wore on, Paul's previous promise of "not too far," comical at first, became more and more so, until after a twelve-hour day on the trail, they had yet to reach camp and were still riding along a small stream in the dimming light.

Nearly rocked asleep, Karl was suddenly thunderstruck as the mule beneath him lunged forward and backward in a violent series of plunges.

Taking a second to gather his wits, Karl wondered, *was there a snake bite? An earthquake?* The mule dropped his head to the ground. *Oh, my God,* Karl thought—*we're going down.* He jumped off and immediately sank to his knees in what he recognized was the source of the problem: "Quicksand!" he yelled, and reached backward toward the bridle of Francisco's mule behind him. "Hold still!" he pleaded, pulling to hoist himself out. The mule's forelegs were submerged. Francisco rode around and threw a rope over its neck and one around its hindquarters with the help of a branch-pole, lashing them both to his pommel.

Although it seemed impossible, after strenuous effort, with Karl coaxing at the reins, they pulled out the mule.

"Could 'a gone either way." Paul said. "If I'd had to wager, I'd have guessed we'd lose the old guy."

"One fine beast," Karl said, patting the mule's neck and rubbing him down.

"We'll camp here." Francisco acknowledged there was adequate level terrain away from the quicksand.

Paul's mining prospect proved yet another disappointment. After returning empty-handed to their house by the Urique River, once again, Paul scuffed across the terrace on a morning after having stayed out all night. He chugged his coffee, wiped his long mustache with the back of his hand, and announced that he was leaving on a lengthy trip to inspect some gold placer properties in Sonora.

As soon as Paul stepped out, Sheldon and Karl concurred that he should not venture unaccompanied. Sheldon agreed to travel with him because Karl wanted to pursue a lead he had received from Mendez, a local Mexican who told him there was a promising old shaft about four hours down-river with a wide strong vein carrying copper pyrites—fool's gold, which Mendez asserted with persuasive emphasis, had often indicated silver values at depth.

Alone in the deserted house after Sheldon and Paul had departed, Karl promised himself he would only make one or two more forays at mining, then head back to Law School. If this wasn't going to pan out, he realized, he'd better get back, help his father, and earn a living. Months had passed. It was time for him to come to a personal reckoning as to where to draw the line between perseverance and profligacy.

Wind kicked up through the valley. Karl gathered his gear, threw it over his mule's back and headed out to meet Mendez. This time he had his gun.

25

The Vision

ON AN EVENING PRIOR TO Sheldon's and Paul's return, as Karl approached the new mine to measure the drill holes in order to account for payment to the miners, he was knocked over backwards by a terrific blast. Rocks shot high and out toward the river. At first he thought the men were trying to kill him, but as he got closer, he saw them on their knees murmuring, "Jesus, Maria. Santa Maria Madre!" Karl soon realized that, in his absence, they had been blasting to increase the number of feet they would receive compensation for.

After that, things began to look up. Mendez's prospective mine near the Urique River, which Karl had named "the Lincoln," was showing real enrichment. Drilling was being paid for by the foot, and Karl had added more miners to hand drill the shafts—three-hundred feet along one of the veins, with a tunnel one-hundred feet below the bottom of the old shaft. They had cut into three parallel veins.

On the twentieth day, workers rushed from the tunnels, jumping high and shouting: *"Plata! Plata! Oro! Plata!"* In the old shaft, they had discovered tetrahedrite, carrying high silver values.

Karl asked Mendez to go to Urique to send a telegraph summoning Sheldon and Paul:

COME QUICK. SILVER. NEED ASSAY.

It took almost a week before Paul and Sheldon arrived. By then, Karl was convinced the mine must be promising, since he noticed pockets and saddlebags bulging on many of the men. But he was also aware that a defining assay had not yet been performed to confirm values. Only Sheldon had the expertise to do this in the stone furnace he had constructed, where samples wrapped in lead foil were placed in a small container—a capel—for twenty minutes and exposed to extreme heat so that lead would draw out the base metals.

Before Sheldon had had a chance to assess the ore, however, Paul went berserk. He descended the old shaft, looked at some of the ore and became so excited that he fell to the ground, completely out of his mind. He ran up over the small waste dump, delirious and delusional, staggering and stumbling down the path into camp, shouting: "I want my Packard! Where's my chauffeur? Damn it all, don't keep me waiting!"

Sheldon called for Karl. "Hurry! Paul's gone loco." Together, they chased and caught up to Paul near the river. They wrestled him to the ground and held him there for a while before carrying him back to camp. He struggled in their arms the entire way until they laid him on a cot and bathed his head in cold water. He continued to moan and babble.

Paul was sick for several days. Sheldon offered to watch him until he realized he would need to leave to do the assay. So Karl stayed with Paul. *Success can exact a precipitous shift in personality. At least I still have Sheldon,* Karl thought. *A trusted friend is priceless.*

Sheldon came back with a positive report. The sampling indicated an average per ton of four-hundred-twenty ounces of silver to three-quarters of an ounce of gold and about sixteen percent copper.

Gradually, the miners' families arrived. A small village of bush huts sprang up along the river. Months of slow development of the veins at the Lincoln mine lay ahead before the final assessment.

Paul remained mercurial. He appeared and disappeared like a strange mood—never to be trusted. Sheldon, on the other hand, kept on with continuous enthusiasm.

One night as the campfire glowed and Karl and Sheldon listened to coyotes howl, Sheldon spotted something—peripherally—something moving high in the hills: Faint lights, barely visible, were moving on the mountainside above them.

"Look," Sheldon said, pointing up.

"What is it?" Karl asked Francisco.

"A funeral procession," Francisco said. "It's the Indians."

Thousands of feet above them, a graceful line of torches, held high by white-sheeted figures, glided along the cliff. The ancient ritual floated through space like a mystical chord.

"No one knows them, even though they sometimes come to Urique with nuggets of gold. They are secretive—never tell where their gold is found. They do not mingle with us," Francisco said, "Like eagles born in the sky."

The scene held Karl entranced. Unspoken beyond the string of hypnotic lights was something he knew he could never verbalize— akin to mysteries more sensed than seen, as if in a dream. But as he glimpsed the Indians' solemn ritual, he knew that unto itself it was sublime. And he wondered what power an evil, like greed, could wield over their camaraderie in a world where gold was plentiful and their gods within their reach.

When the haunting vision disappeared, Karl was struck by an epiphany—the time was drawing near for him to go home.

Max and Herman stood in Karl's room at the apartment in New York, watching him unpack while they inspected the fifty-pound bag of ore he had brought back from Mexico.

"I think our mine's a winner," Karl said. "But only time will tell. Hey, Herm, you were right about a few things."

"What's that?"

"Well, there was a man—an American—who rode up to our house in Urique one night. After we helped him unhitch his pack and water his two mules, he sat down to dinner with us at our porch table, candlelight glossing the rowel of a spur he wore as his belt buckle. He said he'd heard that we were interested in mining pro- spects and he claimed he had the richest gold prospect in Mexico. He brought samples for us to assay and proceeded to tell us that an old

Indian, for whom he had done some good turn, had taken him secretly to a vein that was almost completely covered by a landslide. He said he'd show it to us if we'd be interested in putting up some money to do a modest job of further sampling and prospecting. The ore was so rich he said he'd be satisfied with a half-interest—wanted no money for himself. He laid large chunks of ore (one weighing over thirty pounds) right out on the table. It dazzled like diamonds in the candlelight. Sheldon assayed them the next morning and found that they ran over one-hundred ounces of gold to the ton!

"It was Sheldon who suspected him. 'I bet these came from Illuvia de Oro,' he said—a famous gold mine not too far away. We wired over there with a description of our visitor and they sent us a message right back saying he was a recently discharged foreman. He was the big swindler you predicted. It was the first part of his story—the part about the Indian—that was the real giveaway."

"What did I tell you," Herm affirmed, "prospectors can't be trusted *no matter what* their affiliation or nationality!"

"And I, um, did get held-up at gunpoint."

"Oh! Just when were you planning on spilling those jumping beans?" Max asked.

"Tonight at the dinner table when I could build enough suspense to see if you cared about your little brother," Karl said, patting Max's head.

"So what happened?"

"You'll have to wait to hear the story," Karl teased. "Where's our old pup, Shirley-girl?"

Max's response was quick: "Up where bones are free," he said. "She's sniffing out the trail for us."

"Oh," Karl said, sadly, "what happened?"

"What a sweet old dog. Soon after you left, she couldn't walk; everything inside her shut down. I held her while she was released from earthly miseries."

Just then Sarah came in, looking radiant in a simple blouse and dark skirt with a wide sash. Her smile brightened the room and the mood. She hugged Karl, gathered his laundry, reminded him to telephone Charlie about the wedding plans, and strode out of the room as though this was the same as any other day. Then she turned around and asked, "What's in that bag?"

"A sampling of our future wealth, I'm hopin!" Karl said with a bi-coastal grin.

Fritz and Alice joined the family in New York for dinner that night, eager to hear some of Karl's stories—in particular, how much he expected to make from the mine, and when. More often than not, Fritz interrupted to add a "better" story of his own. Karl tried to explain the terror of being caught in quicksand, but before he had completed his third sentence, Fritz jumped in with a saga about a long-lost uncle of Alice's who died in a swamp decades before.

"Tell us about the hold up." Max said, returning to Karl.

"Hold-up? What's that, son?"

"Maybe I should tell you about that later, when we're not eating. But, well, let's see—two other frightening moments come to mind," Karl said. "One while riding; the other on foot."

He lifted a piece of bread and tore it in half, thinking about how to proceed with his description. "I was alone, riding the trail late on a Saturday afternoon on my way to spend Sunday in Urique. It was a four-hour trip and getting dark. I pressed my mule just to wake him, along a section of good wide trail cut out of the cliff. We were hundreds of feet above a barranca gouged out by the river below when my mule suddenly stumbled down on both forelegs and went into a complete somersault. I flew over his head, landed hard on the stony trail, and sprained my ankle. I got up and limped over to him. He was standing still but trembling all over, which made me realize that somehow he knew what a close call it had been. If he'd rolled over sideways instead of straight on, we would have careened headlong down the cliff to kiss that sweet river goodnight."

"Oo. Ow! That's a nasty one," Herm said.

"What's the other? I've got goose bumps," Alice said, squinting at Fritz.

"Oh, the other time was almost worse: when Sheldon and I thought we'd try a short-cut on foot down an arroyo to get to the Urique River by avoiding all the dense underbrush. As the slope increased, we started to slide faster and faster on the smooth rock. We were laughing and hootin' up a storm. But looking ahead, I got worried and yelled to Sheldon behind me to slow up. When we finally managed to slow down, after a great deal of difficulty, I warned him that it was looking too steep ahead. I said I was afraid we'd get hurt. He laughed at me, called me lily livered, said I ought to be more trusting—let loose a little more, have fun. Well, within not more than fifty feet, we saw what was looming right ahead: a sheer drop and I mean *SHEER*! The arroyo led to, I'd say, a five-hundred-foot vertical plunge straight to the river—way, *way* down, below."

Alice swooned.

"Well, at least I wasn't the only worried man after that! It took us well over two hours to get back up to where we'd started."

Fritz threw his arm up, draped it around Alice's shoulders, and said, "That reminds me of..."

"Pass the chicken, Fritz would you," Herm intervened.

"And the salt," Max added.

Soon it seemed to Karl as though he had never left home. He noticed his father was aging, which made him glad he'd come back to help out. He could look at the photograph of his mother, knowing he'd been able to carry on with his life, which was vastly different from the time when she had been his main source of certainty.

Only three weeks into Law School at Columbia, Karl received a wire from Sheldon:

LINCOLN VEIN GONE BORA, WRITING.

Karl knew this meant that the veins were superficial and had ceased to carry values. Their dreams of wealth were smashed. Both the promise of the mine and his relationships in Mexico would be over; Karl was stunned by incredulity. As though he was witnessing the demise of a treasured possession—helpless to prevent it from being smashed to smithereens. He wondered how Sheldon was coping with Paul's inevitable depression compounded by the disappointment of Mendez and all the families who had settled to work at the Lincoln. He wished he hadn't left Sheldon alone with all of that.

He wired back:

CRUSHED. HELP?

But he did not hear anything for many weeks, until a wire from Sheldon finally arrived, the tone of which was incidental, typically optimistic—about a few more new prospects he was pursuing.

26
Fairy Tales

*T*HERE IS A THICKENING IN THE AIR. Helen lies on her bed with her head in her hands. She is aware of every breath she takes. The stillness is dark as danger, intense as consciousness, a sky of stone. Her sense of the grand sweep of the world and its indifference elicits memory of a time when she was younger:

She is walking blithely, sure of the forest trail, until, without a clue as to how she has gone awry, she realizes she has no sense of where she is relative to where she is headed, or even where she wants to be. Darkness begins to augment illusions. The trees and thick understory close in around her. She rests on a rock. All she can think about is having been in these woods with Bud just recently— realizing that it was always he who knew the way. She pictures him digging through mud for salamanders after instructing her to follow his footsteps soundless as a squaw. And she remembers that, years before, she had been nestled inside a rocky cave next to him, reading a book of Grimm's fairy tales she had carried from home. She recalls, in particular, the one entitled "Brother and Sister" where the brother becomes a roebuck and the sister promises never to leave him.

She had ventured out to find that cave, and now scans the various branches and pieces of wood in her vicinity, as Bud always did, scrutinizing their potential for carvings. She pictures herself— the obsequious way she had shadowed him through fields, bramble patches, over rock ledges; examining fungus, lichen, wild flowers, insects; how they made spears or walking sticks; launched elf-boats made from shagbark hickory chips or wild violet leaves, tucked around and turned inside out, to watch them spin and sink.

She leaves her resting place and walks on, hoping that she will come full circle, or at least recognize something familiar. Miles of forest surround her. She enters a grove of pines where there is a clearing. She tries to avoid admitting to herself how completely disoriented she is.

A groundcover of pine straw, comforting underfoot, renders the space visually expansive, simplified. She rests on a log near a round depression in the forest floor—a deer-pit filled with rainwater. All around her she senses an invisible, whispering pulse. Then, feeling ridiculous, but out of sheer fatigue and frustration, she calls her brother's name.

From less than a hundred feet away, she hears him answer, "Why, here I am, m' lady!"

"What! Where?"

"In my castle—yonder!"

Helen sighs, incredulous. After looking into the cathedral canopy high above, scanning the tree-tops and noticing the way their branches almost touch like asterisks swaying against the sky, she closes her eyes and turns her head slowly, laughing and smiling in the direction from whence the voice had come. She spots a rudimentary shelter of tightly angled poles under camouflage of pine needles and walks over to it, bending down and giggling at the sight of her brother bunched up inside the hut with his arms wrapped around his knees. She crawls inside to join him.

"I was *lost*," she says. "*Desperate*," she admits.

"But now you are *found* my child," Bud drones with intonation.

"Do you believe my luck in finding you here?"

"Never doubt the power of luck, m' lady," Bud says, placing his arm over her shoulder. "Shall I escort us home, then?"

Remembering this true "fairy tale" as she lies across her bed, Helen thinks of her promise never to leave her brother. Time contracts upon itself. She relives the moment she learned that Bud had suffered a sudden and fatal heart attack while he was driving home from having completed a complex and arduous, but for him wonderful task of creating a survey map of a vast area of Canadian wilderness.

27

True Blue Scouts

*T*O COMPENSATE FOR THE MONTHS he had been away and acclimate to the rigors of Columbia Law School, Karl was trying to concentrate on his studies. Slumped over Contracts and Constitutional Law, he found that he was rereading the same sentence over and over while struggling to remember why he had returned to the confined canyons of New York, since he ached to be back riding the hills of Mexico.

Fortunately, action and fellowship of evening and weekend participation in the cavalry of Squadron A had eased his withdrawal from the wild. Composed of recent college graduates, Squadron A consisted of four troops with about seventy men in each with a high military ranking in the National Guard. Karl joined Troop A, the oldest of the four, because one quarter of its roster consisted of young lawyers. Along with serious training for military duties, the evening rides in New York City provided a release from his sedentary studying.

Despite his deficient eyesight, Charlie Engle had joined Karl's group, which was a welcome distraction for him because Emily's parents had decided that it was imperative to take their daughter to Europe for several weeks; their reasoning was transparent.

"They'll do anything short of murder," Charlie said, explaining to Karl that there would be yet another delay in his wedding plans. The two men stood together next to their horses on bareback drill night at the Armory. "It's brainwashing—two against one. They continue to poison the well, hoping Emily will shun me by the end of their sojourn."

"She won't," Karl said in a manner he hoped was adequately curt to be convincing. In fact, he worried that she might be swayed, and he regretted the small hesitation that preceded his assertion.

153

"I'll kill myself if she..."

"Don't say that!"

Guiding the reins over his horse's head, Karl turned away from Charlie and jumped on. Charlie did the same. He was a competent rider. But many in the Squadron were not—especially one man Karl referred to as "old friend Turner" who weighed upwards of two hundred pounds and had insufficient spring in his legs to mount a horse, barely even from the block.

Karl rode up next to Turner, dismounted, and with a huge grunt tried to boost Turner onto his horse. But Turner only got part of the way up, and was lying on his stomach when the horse took off at a gallop with "old friend" draped over its withers, bouncing like a sack of flour. Karl and Charlie chased after him trying to grab the runaway horse, but the sight of Turner, coincident with his desperate cries of "Whoa, whoa, *WHOA!*" was more than Karl and Charlie could bear. They slid off their horses onto the tanbark, landing in perfect synch, and sat rocking back and forth in gales of laughter.

Seeing Turner released from his horse, Captain Arthur Townsend cantered over to Karl and Charlie to deliver a tongue-lashing, which made their struggle not to laugh even harder. They stood up and dusted themselves off, but as soon as one or the other started to sputter, they both gave way to the pressure like a couple of busted spigots.

That night was intended to be the beginning of bareback jumping practice, but everyone had a saddle, and as Captain Townsend assessed the burgeoning failures around him, his disgust evolved into indignation. Anger began building under apprehension that he would become the leader of a miserably embarrassing bunch. So he called a halt and stood before them, mustering command and magniloquence. His lecture on how to jump waxed lengthy and strident. The horses grew more and more restless, snorting and pawing as the men yawned.

Finally, Townsend said, "Watch me now as I take that jump. See how I loosen the reins and urge my horse forward, just at the right moment."

Swinging into the stirrups, sword and buttons flashing, he spurred his horse and took off in a rocking, circular canter approach to the jump. He gave the horse his head, then reined him in before signaling him to go on. The horse took off at a gallop with his head shaking wildly; then pulled up short of the fence with all the braking power of a freight train. Captain Townsend sailed over the horse's head as if in slow motion. The entire ensemble—rider, sword, buttons, and pride—landed on the other side of the fence with an undignified THUMP.

Fresh from their previous laughing fit, and seeing that Townsend was not hurt, Karl and Charlie couldn't contain themselves. Once again, they kicked back and forth, beating the tanbark, knees to ears in fits and tears.

Captain Townsend, embarrassed and shaken by his fall, limped, strutted, then limped again over to Karl and Charlie, ordering them out of the riding arena.

Convinced that they could be in for strict discipline, Karl anticipated the worst, but Townsend, who turned out to be a fine fellow, never said another word and some time later actually promoted Karl to Corporal of his Squad.

Merriment at the Squadron continued at a summer maneuver in Pine Plains, New York, where each squad slept in a large conical tent. Karl's friend, Elton Parks, who had been the leader of the Yale Glee Club, led nightly singing. The melodic paeans so enticed two songster sergeants that they requested permission to join the same tent.

"Fine idea. Certainly you may," Elton replied. "All you'll have to do is abide by our rules and regulations: The loser of our nightly spelling game cleans and polices the tent in the morning."

The sergeants glanced at each other and readily nodded in agreement.

Subsequently, losing the spelling games, either one or the other was obliged to pick up cigarette butts and put the tent in order while

Karl, Charlie, and several other troopers stood happily amused, lording over them and mercilessly criticizing their work.

Maneuvers to educate the troops were inculcated in serious order. Amidst the sham battles staged at Pine Plains was a two-day event—one of the largest ever held. It consisted of twelve thousand Regulars (the Red Army) versus fifteen thousand or more National Guardsmen (the Blue Army).

On the day before the battle, the Red Army had marched some twenty miles from camp while Karl's Blue Army moved a few miles out and spent the night in shelter half tents. Karl gazed across the vista of hundreds of campfires, thinking the scene a replica of an army camp during the Civil War. This reminded him of a lecture at Lawrenceville when the impassioned General John B. Gordon, a tall man with a small white goatee, the former Governor of Georgia and Major General in the Army of Northern Virginia, had inspired everyone with his flowing oratory of the old South.

General Gordon's message stressed the imperative to be prepared to give one's life for the Stars and Stripes—even as Gordon's own immortal Army of Northern Virginia had fought and died for the Stars and Bars of the Confederacy: "No one could love the American flag more than we did," he explained. "But during the war, everyone was doing their duty as they saw it." General Gordon spoke about the dire circumstances—including the fact that, for sustenance, Confederates picked pieces of corn from the hooves of their horses. General Gordon broke down during his explanation of how he had prevented "the godlike soldier and gentleman, General Lee, from leading a forlorn, hopeless charge in the battle of Spotsylvania Court House."

At the campsite, Karl closed his eyes, recalling the sight of Reverend McPherson holding General Gordon's quaking shoulders and leading him to a chair to recuperate.

The plan for the next day's sham battle called for the Blue Army to find and engage the Red Army, which simulated an invading army from Canada. Karl was awakened at 3 a.m. by Lieutenant

Copperthwaite, who shook him out of a sound sleep. "Get your equipment and report mounted on the road in fifteen minutes," he said.

Six other specially selected scout troopers joined Karl. They took off and rode half a mile or so; then they stopped for bread and coffee at a place where Lieutenant Copperthwaite stood in shafts of lantern light—his shadow casting long beyond him like ink spilling into dark, unfamiliar space.

"Each of you will be assigned a trail or road on this map to travel in your effort to locate the enemy's main forces," he said. Backlight filtered through the burnt-umber, crenulated map as he pointed to various locations. Karl stared transfixed—as though the map was iconography for a treasure hunt. Copperthwaite continued: "As Army scouts, you are now free and independent Troopers. You have two hours before the battle that begins at six. Locate the enemy and return to the Commanding General with your information. Along the way you will undoubtedly meet the famous U.S. Tenth Cavalry, fresh from the Philippines. They are acting as part of a screen for the enemy. Get through this screen without detection or capture."

Karl was the last to slip into the dark. His assigned trail was little more than a path with grass growing down the middle, along which he trotted for about three-quarters of an hour, until dawn began to break and he slowed to a walk.

Half an hour later he heard scouts of the Red Army troop laughing in the distance and saw that they were riding in a long line across the country, with about a hundred feet separating each man.

He dismounted, led his horse into a thicket, removed the bridle and replaced it with a feed bag to keep him from neighing at any other horses.

The scouts passed by. Karl continued on, stopping before every open space and galloping from cover to cover until arriving at a small hillock where he waited in hiding again to watch the road below. There he got lucky. He spotted the Red Army approaching in the distance—first a small column of vanguard cavalry, then sometime later, the men who constituted the beginning of their full infantry.

With detection inevitable from the burgeoning light of day, Karl galloped back. He heard scattered shooting, hid in the bushes, and watched a few troopers pass by only thirty feet away. Relieved that he hadn't been seen, he remounted and raced on, meeting Major Bridgeman at the head of two troops of Squadron A as they approached him in a column up the road.

Saluting, Karl shouted, "Entire enemy infantry about two miles away, Sir!"

Major Bridgeman immediately wheeled around and ordered Mitchell, the Squadron bugler, "Blow dismount." Then he continued (with no word to Karl) to canter back along the short column of troops, saying: "Form a line of skirmishers on foot. Advance and engage the enemy!"

"With all due respect, Sir!" Karl said, riding to catch up to Major Bridgeman. "All the enemy is on your front. You'd best wait for the infantry to back you up!"

The Major muttered the equivalent of "mind your own business" and spurred forward into a fast trot.

Neck-reining his horse into a spin, Karl galloped back down the road. When he reached the Colonel of the Fourteenth New York Infantry, he reported the information to him; whereupon the Colonel turned to one of his lieutenants and coolly told him to ride back to the Commanding General with this new information.

After Karl followed the lieutenant and heard him report to the Commanding General, he felt relieved from further obligation and took the liberty to ride back to the front to see the show. There, he watched, incredulous, as an absurdly small coterie of dismounted Squadron A troops advanced on foot through the brush and high grass with their short front a mere three-hundred feet in length.

A long line of enemy infantry rose up out of the high grass and fired just one volley at a distance of about four-hundred feet.

In an instant, an umpire rode up and shouted to Major Bridge-man, "Your outfit's all killed! Mount up and get on the road. Pass through the Reds in your front. You're finished for the day!"

Karl took it upon himself to return to the Colonel of the Four-teenth Infantry where he warned: "Two Troops of Squadron A have just been wiped out. The entire enemy force is directly on your front!"

By this time, the Fourteenth was engaged in a long line of battle on both flanks. Karl followed the left side of their line. Shots died off for a while. Then a sudden, tremendous firing burst across the front and rear left flank. The whole regiment had been caught in a cul-de-sac.

"Cease fire! You're captured!" the umpires yelled.

Karl watched, bitterly disappointed as the rest of the infantry regiments, each going to battle alone, met the same disastrous fate. *A prime example of the old fault of the Union Army in the first years of the Civil War when they engaged in piecemeal attack, and an apt illustration of exactly how crucial effective leadership can be,* he thought.

In 1912, a two-day maneuver took place over Lincoln's birthday in Bardtown, New York, which consisted of an attack on foot by one troop of the Squadron and two companies of Infantry against trench-es with cardboard targets, firing live service ammunition by cannon and machine guns.

From his sprawled position, Karl heard shells whistle overhead. He watched them hit the trenches and ricochet off an old stone farmhouse. Keeping tight to the ground, his adrenaline rushed with apprehension. Next to him, Charlie raised a shoulder just half-an-inch too high. He was hit.

Karl hadn't heard Charlie's gasp, but in turning, saw him writhe, holding his shoulder. When the short firing-round paused, Karl stood up, waving frantically to capture the attention of the

Captain, who ambled over, shaking his head, prepared to preempt any claim that the firing practice had been misguided.

Charlie was helped off the site where he, Karl, and one other infantryman waited for his evacuation as he was wrapped, then whisked away for transport to a medic.

It was one of the coldest days on record. The thirty horses were hardly slowed to a walk during that afternoon's ride from the Armory to Bardstown until they were finally rested for the night— picketed off lines that ran from wall to wall in an old abandoned hay barn. The temperature plummeted below zero.

After dinner, Karl and a group of men went to check on the horses and found them so cold they could hardly stand still. Three were shivering violently.

On the way out the barn door, the Sergeant turned to Karl and said, "Behr, I'm going to ask you to stay with the horses tonight. I think you are stronger than most of us. If you want another man with you, I'll leave one, but the fewer out in the cold, the better." Handing Karl a pint of whiskey, he left for the farmhouse, a full quarter of a mile away.

With one small lantern and a bottle of spirits, Karl realized that there was little he could do to help the horses, aside from re-securing the few blankets they had and giving them more grain, supplemented with some bits of cracked corn he found in a bin. Trembling in the pitch-dark, coal-black barn, Karl arranged what he hoped might be a fairly insulated place to sleep under hay and extra blankets. Wind whistling through holes and slats between the barn's wall-boards, blasted an agonizing cold into his bones. Everything ached. He pulled his jacket tighter, but it might as well have been made of ice for the amount of warmth it provided. He couldn't stay still, so he draped burlap sacks and blankets around himself and jumped in place. He heard a rat scurry across the beam overhead and took a swig of whiskey. *Empfindlich.* He thought of the word his father had once called him—"*weak,*" he added.

"I should have warned him," he said aloud, berating himself for not having reminded Charlie to stay low in the trenches. Every chance Karl might have had to save someone, to avert a death, assailed his conscience. *Jack, Oscar, my mother and now possibly Charlie. ...I need to be more vigilant,* he thought.

His teeth chattered. He jogged in place. When he stopped he thought he heard someone whisper at a far corner of the barn. Darkness intensified. He considered running for the house. He stepped outside. The wind was murderous, so Karl turned back in, paced and talked to the horses, rubbing them for warmth. He practiced swearing in every language he knew: Spanish, French, English, and German. Then he tried to settle under the blankets, lying on his side, hugging his knees to his chest and crossing his arms close over his heart for warmth against the chill that overwhelmed him.

Just after dawn, when the sergeant arrived, he thought Karl must have left the barn, until he spotted the tip of a boot jutting out from under a pile of blankets and discovered him there, quivering and delirious. They stumbled outside, Karl barely able to walk. The sergeant helped him mount and ride to the house.

"We had open fires blazing all night," the Sergeant said. "The men were piled together here on the floor. No one slept a wink. The temperature fell to eighteen below zero. When the farmer from next door came to see if we were alive, he told us every single one of his chickens had frozen inside the coop!"

"Mmm," was the only sound Karl could murmur through his blue lips, wondering if anyone had considered him.

Although consequently ill, Karl improved immeasurably when he learned that Charlie's wound was just a deep grazing without impaction and that he would recover with only a scar.

28

Reflection

*H*ELEN GETS UP TO SHUT THE WINDOW and returns to sit at the edge of the bed. She can't decide which chore to tackle next in preparation for their departure from the summer house, so she reaches for the pen and ink in the drawer of her bedside table. Ruminations of her father, of Bud, of Karl soon to join them, inspire her to write:

Dash to Alchemy

Oh Death within whose forest we abide
Aspect of brittle leaf and wizened stream—
The questioned course we pause to stand beside,
Quell our yearning sleeplessness and dream
To resurrect the sun, reset the day
Where disappearance seeks no further measure,
Nor comprehension light to lead the way.
For love will shine removed from earthly pleasure,
Though loss decreed the end's necessity;
Eternal absence begs an empty question,
Yet limns through time all possibility
That thoughts transferred might bear a new dimension—
   We hear a river of souls inside our heads
   Declare beloved voices never dead!

Amused when she imagines Gertie ridiculing the sonnet's somber tone, Helen tucks the poem into the drawer of her writing table and goes down to gather towels that are hanging out on the line, remembering the day she and Gertie met:

On her first morning in the hall at Briarcliff College, Helen overheard a slender girl with a shrill voice, holding court with three other freshmen who had broken into gales of laughter. Later at lunch, when Helen spotted her sitting at a corner table, she approached, asking, "Are these seats already spoken for?"

"Only by my imaginary friends!" Gertie grinned, introducing herself.

"I heard the girls laugh at something you were saying this morning and wondered what I missed," Helen said, as she lowered her tray, noticing Gertie was wearing an identical skirt to one she also owned.

"Hi, I'm Helen. But I don't much like the name. You could call me anything else!" When Gertie smiled, Helen surmised that she had already picked out several odd and/or funny names to choose from.

"Well, let's see, how about Guzzy? We could be a circus act— two bears—Gertie and Guzzy! Or run away with gypsies—a couple of gymnasts! Something like that?"

Helen laughed. "Great idea! We'll skip college and have fun instead."

"The joke I was telling in the hall was on me, really," Gertie said. "When we first arrived here, my mother sang my praises, saying that I didn't have a mean bone in my body. You know, sentimental stuff like, 'She's my baby—neat, sweet, tidy and kind.' Ooh, and that was just the beginning! She went on and on and on and *on*, drenching me in syrup 'til I ossified!" As Gertie gestured, her beautiful hands caught Helen's attention—each finger like a dancer with long-straightened grace. She went on, "Of course, Mother's candy-coating became a big joke. I didn't know what to say when the girls started clucking at me saying, 'Come along, Chickabitty!' I must have been peeping and twitching to make fun of myself when you walked by."

"Oh," Helen said with a grin. "I thought you were saying something coherent! I can't imagine my mother ever praising me, let alone saying anything sappy. She's not easy to please."

"You're lucky!"

"Maybe," Helen said, but the doubt in her eyes gave sincerity away.

Gert looked up at her—Helen caught sight of a sparkle with a wry twist that jumped the space between them. Gertie continued, "My mother's name is Grace, and she's never done a single thing that didn't ooze with it. I'm her complete opposite; I don't let other peoples' opinions get under my skin. With five older siblings—four boys and my sister Margaret—I had to get used to being plunked into bed by six o'clock and forgotten. I was a redundant addition to an already over-active household and I've yet to figure out why my mother's so nice to me. Except that I am her baby—after Margaret, our beloved beauty queen. Maybe it's pity!" Gertie sank her teeth into her toasted cheese sandwich and munched while she waited for Helen's response.

Helen eyed a reflection caught in the curve of her spoon. "I have one brother, Bud—my best buddy in the world—good-for-nothing that he is, always hidden away somewhere in the woods."

After taking the towels off the line, once back in the kitchen, Helen empties the icebox to defrost it. She has returned to her chores, but recalls how concerned she'd been that she could think of little with which to impress or entertain Gertie on that day they met. Compared to Gert's life, hers had seemed so simple. And she knew she could not engage a new friendship by describing how affected she'd been by something so mundane as the way snow-cover enhanced the contours of rocks and ledges at the farm where she had grown up, after the acres became a wasteland without all the activities of apple-picking, hay-baling, feeding cows, sheering sheep, watching lamb tails shake a-mile-a-minute, dodging the ram, tending vegetables, harvesting, pruning, digging postholes, riding through

fields on the open-back platform of a green stake truck, holding on
for dear life.

"Well, I've got more brothers than I can handle, so I never try to
handle them at all," Gertie said when she saw that Helen's attention
had drifted. "They're so different from one another. They fight all
the time. It can make your head spin!"
"Must be fun, in a way?" Helen countered.
"It's a battle zone. Karl, the youngest, is the only one who really
understands me—we have a lot in common. For some reason we
agree on most things. He usually seems sure of himself, but underneath his big act is a sensitive boy waiting for manly self-assurance
to drop down from on high."

Helen rubs soap on her rag, pensive about Gertie's comment,
realizing how important a single utterance can be. She scrubs the
icebox shelves and wipes them dry. Without awareness of Karl's
humility, she doubts she would have fallen in love with him the way
she did. She dries her hands and stands transfixed by leaf-shadows
dancing on the wall; their frenzy grows impassioned. They weave,
shudder and clap silent applause.
She approaches the window. Feeling the sun's warmth penetrate
the glass, she notices light gleaming on blades of grass that bend and
shiver in a breeze at the edge of the field. Natural clarity of the scene
rekindles a memory of innocence—the dilemma she had faced at
midnight, standing at the rail of the *Titanic*.
Up to that point, she had been—like the grass outside with the
sunshine on its back—swept off her feet, quivering with giddiness,
wanting to make love to Karl, although she had taken her mother's
quip to heart: "Affairs expire like butterflies that have lost the dust
on their wings." At the ship's rail, she had wondered why the expression of love was so fraught with guilt and danger. But most of all she
worried that her fear of it would haunt her.

Looking back on this now, Helen realizes she had yet to learn that physical intimacy was not so much a Rubicon compared to the loss of it...compared to missing it when it was gone.

She writes a note to tell the milkman to stop delivery, then she moves inward—toward the rest of the chores that remain for her to close the house.

29

A Glimpse of Music

*A*FTER SPENDING AN ACCUSTOMED predawn hour working at the firm of McKeen, Brewster and Morgan at 40 Wall Street, Karl strode to rendezvous with Charlie for early breakfast. He spotted his friend down the block, reading the newspaper while leaning against a wall near the restaurant door.

They talked as they weaved around tables toward their accustomed nook by the window and, before sitting down and removing their hats and gloves, had already settled the affairs of the world. Karl reminisced about various parades for which Squadron A had provided primary escort. "Oh, remember how bloody cold it was that day we led Governor Hughes to the Capitol for his inauguration?" he said, not really anticipating a response.

"Boy, *do* I! Those full-collared coats and wooly hats we sported made us look like Russian Cossacks!" Charlie replied, grinning over the welcome arrival of unsolicited coffee.

"Fetching, weren't we, in the midst of spectators crammed along Fifth Avenue for a glimpse of Roosevelt. I was lucky to be nearby to watch him greet his cavalrymen from the Spanish War. I am forever amazed at his genius for recalling names. How do you suppose he does it? By mnemonics, or visual associations? I'll have to ask him. He shocked me when he cupped his hands together and shouted: 'Karl! How's that bullet serve?' "

"Oh, *now* I know why your head swelled!" Charlie said, twisting his earlobe. His eyes narrowed. "And think of our Naval Parade for Henry Hudson with the international fleet assembled on the river! That was quite a scene! I was wishing for an aerial picture of the spectacle: British Marines, West Point Cadets, and German Sailors marching one flank after another down Fifth Avenue. I came upon the exact image I wanted in the *Times*."

"Me too!" Karl exclaimed, "It's already pasted in my scrapbook. Hey, speaking of great events, are you coming to our hockey game next week?"

"Hell. Do I have to?"

"Friday night. If you're not there, I'll…"

"Cry?"

"Uh, well, no. Anyway, we'll probably lose. As you know, our Squadron A team is capable of beating the Seventh Regiment, but the Regiment's tough. They've been on the ice and we haven't!"

"Right, we've been out getting shot and frozen in the hinterland."

Karl shivered and returned to the subject of hockey. "Marshall Peabody, Captain of the Regiment's team, plays for the Saint Nicholas Hockey Club. He's a good friend of mine."

"Heck, then you don't need me! By the way, aren't you recovering from a broken collar bone after the first game?"

"Yes, but…it'll be fine. Actually, Charlie…"

"What?"

"There's a girl."

"A *girl*?"

"Helen."

"Of Troy?"

"Practically."

"Really?"

"Helen Newsom of New York; originally Ohio. I met her through Gertie."

"Gertie? Who's that?"

"Oh, you know, my baby sister!"

"Well, of course I remember Gertie, but you rarely talk about her, *or* Margaret. Sometimes it seems they don't exist!"

"I know. It's inexcusable. But the name Charlotte hasn't crossed your lips lately. How's *your* sister?" Karl asked.

Charlie shrugged his shoulders, so Karl continued: "I met Helen in Morristown. She's a friend of Gert's from Briarcliff. She has dark hair and dark eyes—portals to a magnetic personality."

Charlie wiggled his brows, tweaking an imaginary mustache while Karl continued, "She's planning to come with Margaret and Gertrude to watch the game, and I'd really appreciate it if you could meet her—be a gentleman escort, if possible, then let me know what you think. Know what I mean?" Karl took a sip of juice without budging his wide-eyes from Charlie's reaction. He considered asking about Emily, but put his glass down, deciding not to.

"Emily wants to take some time off," Charlie said as if he had read Karl's mind.

"Oh, guess I'm not completely surprised, given the pressure she's been under, but how do you feel about that?"

"Half alive. She tells me it's not 'good-bye' forever. Maybe it should be for *her* sake, but I refuse to believe that. Getting shot in the shoulder helped me rethink a few things—like how lucky I am to be around and how hard it is for me to be patient. But I'm holding out for Emily to see beyond her parents. If not, well, then I'll have to deal with it. Anyway, I know there's no one else for her. Not *yet* anyway."

"No other way to look at it," Karl said. "You're still my inspiration, you know!"

"Horse poop!" Charlie said picking up the check.

Karl walked back to McKeen, Brewster and Morgan where he had assumed the position of managing clerk after graduating from Columbia Law School in 1910, a job that had helped to hone his experience while affording him valuable time to remain involved at his father's abrasives company. He enjoyed getting to know the lawyers and matters they handled. He especially valued working alongside the Labor Litigation attorney, Walter Gordon Merritt. Karl was rapidly promoted from his position as the clerk.

One day, Mr. J. Newton, of Abro J. Newton & Co., a doors, sashes, and interior wood manufacturer in Brooklyn, called the law firm for help when his men had refused to join the United Carpenters' Union. Consequently, representatives of this powerful Union had arrived in Brooklyn, called on Mr. Newton, and advised him that they had come all the way from the Indianapolis headquarters to force his workers to join the Union, or they would mandate that all Union carpenters working on buildings in Brooklyn not use his products. And they said they planned to do the same thing to every other non-union shop in Brooklyn where workers had refused to join.

At the firm, Walter Merritt obtained a temporary injunction, forbidding the organizers of the Union from calling a strike on buildings under construction, and he appointed Karl the task of serving papers at Union headquarters on Atlantic Avenue in Brooklyn, which Karl performed in short order—confronting the men where they skulked at a table manacled in dust and smoke in a cavernous room near the wharf.

Not long afterward, although wishing to remain anonymous, a man who had quit the Union, apparently sought vindication against it. He stopped in at the law office and handed the Union's strike book over to Karl. Despite the injunction, the book indicated ongoing orders, instructions, and a schedule to strike, written in longhand by three or four individuals.

At the trial in the Supreme Court of Kings County, the Union men vehemently denied having issued any strike orders subsequent to the temporary injunction. However, when Karl brought in two handwriting experts to prove otherwise, they backed down, attempting to amend their testimony. They were jailed for perjury. The Court made the injunction permanent, and the borough of Brooklyn was freed from enforced closed shops for many years.

Charlie arrived with Charlotte, Helen, Margaret, and Gertie at the Squadron A hockey game just in time to watch Karl rush down-ice and shoot the puck past Washburn for the first goal during the opening period. Peabody answered it, scoring two in a row for the

Seventh Regiment. The players' interaction was exceedingly rough, with more than a few tripping penalties.

Between periods when the spectators were treated to a contest of speed skating, followed by a spectacular exhibition of pair skating, the hiatus provided a chance to chat.

Seventh Regiment vs. Squadron A
N. G. N. Y.

❊

ANNUAL HOCKEY MATCH
AND SKATING CARNIVAL

FRIDAY, FEBRUARY 24, 1911

❊

PROGRAM

The rival teams will take the ice at 8:20 P.M.
The probable line-up will be as follows.

Seventh Regiment		Squadron A
	GOAL	
FRANK WASHBURN		QUENTIN FEITNER
	POINT	
M. WASHBURN		B. ROLSTON
	COVER POINT	
F. RICHARDS		FORD JOHNSON
	LEFT WING	
VAN VECHTEN		HOWARD BOULTON
		W. B. BOULTON, Jr.
	CENTER	
WILLIAM STRUTHERS		ROBERT LEAKE
	ROVER	
MARSHALL PEABODY		KARL BEHR
Captain		Captain
	RIGHT WING	
A. MILLIGAN		A. CAMPBELL SMITH
		T. FARRELLY
		MACKENZIE

NOTICE

After the first half, and during the interval between the halves, there will be an exhibition of Pair Skating in the Continental style by **Irving Brokaw,** the Amateur Champion of America, and **Herr Held,** formerly of the Ice Club of Berlin. The program will be the same as that skated by Herr Bergler and Fraulein Hubler, Champion Pair Skaters of the World, together with some original single combinations by the skaters.

This will be followed by expert skating races, for which the managements of the two organizations have offered silver medals.

At the end of these exhibitions the last half of the hockey game will be played, and at the finish of the game general skating will take place, for which skates may be obtained at the rink.

Hot chocolote and refreshments are being served, a la carte.

"Quite the rivalry!" Charlie said, turning to Helen.

"It would be great fun to skate like that, but I'm not much for pain. Why, in the name of *sport*, do men have to *injure* one another?"

Charlie, taking this as a rhetorical question, smiled blankly, then said, "Actually, I wish I could answer that, but I have to admit nothing logical comes to mind."

"It's lunacy." Charlotte said with a small wave of her hand. "Wouldn't the game be better, minus the tripping and slashing going on behind the referee's back?"

"Sure, I guess," Charlie agreed. "More *civilized*, like golf or tennis."

A brass band revved the fans back up for the hockey game.

Charlotte turned toward Gertrude and started talking about her cat, so they missed seeing Karl avoid a defenseman as he advanced toward the goal. Fans were chanting: *"Squa-dron, Squa-dron, Squa-dron!"* echoed by *"Se-venth, Se-venth, Se-venth!"*

Karl's attention was on the puck as he passed by flashes of color—appendages, shapes, handkerchiefs—and voices cheering. Then, in a blink, there were two sticks crisscrossed in front of him. He attempted to jump, but instead of clearing the sticks he was catapulted into a full somersault. His head hit the ice with tremendous force. He bit straight through his bottom lip.

The crowd hushed. He was out cold.

"Oh, my God, he's not moving," Gertie said.

Helen stood with her hand over her mouth.

"Someone help him!" Margaret called out.

"They will, Margaret, don't worry; they know what to do," Charlie said, hoping he was right.

"Oh, move Karl, *move!*" Charlotte whispered.

It was a long time before he was taken off the ice to the hospital where a physician stitched up the gash on the back of his head and in his lip. Karl was kept awake; his concussion was severe.

When Helen arrived to visit him in the hospital, Karl's mood improved the minute he saw her. He extended his hand, melodramatically slanted his brows, and asked, "Do you take great pity on me?"

"You look like a war-hero all bandaged up."

"A Civil War soldier?"

"A mummy in the Cairo Museum."

"A vanquished prize fighter?"

"A sorry one who has bitten his lip with remorse!"

"You would make a nifty nurse, by the way."

"Do you need something?"

"To know if you came out of pity or affection."

"Affection when you scored that goal. Panic while you were unconscious for so long. Pity ever since."

"That's what I thought—pity outweighs everything else." Karl tried to fake a grimace, but settled for a weak squint.

Although she hadn't stayed long, Karl was elated by Helen's visit well beyond her departure. He stared at the wall, wishing to heal quickly.

Charlie arrived an hour later.

"Hey there, old chum, you're looking better. Or, should I say, *bitter?*"

"She held my hand."

"Whoa, slow down, big-shot. You must be seeing stars again. Which *she* is she, the brunette or the blonde?"

"Ha! So, what d'you think?"

"A-one. But I think she might like *you*, so I have to omit the plus."

"Hmm," Karl managed a thin grin.

"I guess it's my turn to worry about you," Charlie said.

"Now you know how sympathy feels!"

"Not too bad from this side of the bed."

"Well, you're a kindhearted fellow, and just when I thought you cared," Karl mumbled lightheartedly. "Bring me some water would ya, Nursey? Where's your cap? You need something to hide those horns of yours!"

Charlie folded a napkin and shoved it on his head.

"That's better! Now check me out of here!"

Karl suffered wicked headaches. Losing a battle to rise above the pain, his temperament swung low. Impatience overwhelmed him. Long days loomed with malaise after he had moved from the hospital to his father's new apartment at 777 Madison Avenue. But on the afternoon he listened to a recording of Mischa Elman's 1908 debut performance of Tchaikovsky's violin concerto with the Russian Symphony on the phonograph, the virtuoso inflections of emotion were transcendent, even cathartic, and his outlook improved.

Sarah waltzed in. "Been dancin' outside your door," she said. "What's it like to have to relax?"

"I haven't even made a difference in a dog's life. I'd change places with you any time, Sarah!"

Karl followed her into the kitchen to slice bread while Sarah pirouetted from ice-chest, to cabinet, to table, to the laundry, dishes, glasses, food, utensils, napkins, condiments—

"Feeling better?" She stopped to ask.

"The best so far! Maybe I'll be able to get back to work soon… and see more of Helen."

"Helen?"

"Gertie's friend—from Briarcliff."

"Why not ask her to join us for dinner soon!"

Karl was relieved when he was finally able to return to his desk at the law office. When a gentleman by the name of Mr. Griffin, of the Griffin Wallpaper Company, entered, expressing terrible angst over a breach of contract with the potential for a devastating loss to his business, Karl's compassion was aroused.

Mr. Griffin had closed a contract with an inventor of photographic wallpaper for exclusive use of it in New York. He had financed this because he thought it would revolutionize the industry. His mistake was in taking a trip to Europe under the impression that everything was secure. Upon his return, he discovered that, during his absence, one of his largest competitors had moved the inventor up to Worcester, Massachusetts, along with all the equipment.

Once the particulars of the situation had been explained to him, Karl stressed the need for truculence. He suggested obtaining an injunction to prevent Griffin's competitor from learning secrets of the process, which would have destroyed its value to Mr. Griffin. "If I were in your boots, Mr. Griffin, I'd fight these people without too much legal courtesy," he asserted.

Mr. Griffin persuaded Mr. Brewster to allow Karl, that "fighting fool" lawyer, to represent him. However, when Karl consulted Mr. Brewster as to strategy, Mr. Brewster dismissed Karl's plan, saying, "Well, I see little likelihood of your ever obtaining a mandatory injunction against the Worcester Corporation."

"Meanwhile, Mr. Griffin is in a state of agony," Karl said, not knowing what alternative course he might take.

No better plan surfaced. On the afternoon when he was retained, Karl told Mr. Griffin that he would call Judge Dugro to persuade him to issue a mandatory injunction, ordering the officers of the Worcester Corporation to cancel their arrangements with the inventor. When Judge Dugro hesitated, then refused, Karl persevered: "With all due respect, sir, there is something wrong with the law if no way can be found to protect Mr. Griffin from this clear case of theft!"

"Come to my apartment at the Savoy Hotel at 10:30 tonight with all the case authority you can find on mandatory injunctions and we'll discuss it," Judge Dugro said.

In his library of leather-bound books, Judge Dugro perused the Temporary Injunction Order and handed it back to Karl, shaking his head. "I'd be the laughing stock of the Bench if I signed something like this. It's completely unenforceable."

Karl interjected, "Sir, I remember at Columbia Law School, having a mandatory injunction order of yours pointed out as a borderline case. It was touted as a *daring* borderline case, if I recall correctly, and, although it was unenforceable, it achieved its purpose—the contractor was ordered to return and clear out a vacant lot. If you sign this, maybe the Worcester people will be embarrassed into surrendering Griffin's property."

Judge Dugro massaged his chin and reached for the papers. "All right, I suppose it might do some good. I'm really too old to be worrying about my reputation. I'll sign it and I wish you luck, although I very much doubt this will help."

Via wire to Worcester, Karl suggested that the officers of the Worcester Corporation come to New York for a conference. As soon as their representatives arrived on the night before the scheduled conference was to take place, Karl had the Injunction Order served to them in their hotel room.

Their elderly lawyer called Karl the next day rife with indignation that they'd been tricked into thinking they were to have a business meeting, only to be served an injunction. "We are going right back to Worcester," he said.

Karl requested a meeting, asserting: "It would be advisable for you to know certain facts that I've gathered."

The two representatives and their counsel agreed to meet after all. They convened in Mr. Brewster's own large office that afternoon with Mr. Griffin and Karl.

Previous to the meeting, Karl cautioned Mr. Griffin not to enter into the discussion until he had tapped him on the foot. "At which time you can go ahead and express your feelings as strongly as you want to. But don't be surprised if I act shocked. Then, when I tap your foot again, stop immediately. We have to frighten these people. It's our only chance."

The adversaries settled opposite one another.

"Your corporation was fully aware of Mr. Griffin's previous relations and his contract *before* negotiating with this inventor, was it not?" Karl said. "We have the injunction order in place and we will fight you in court until we win."

"Counsel in New England never prejudges the outcome of its litigation," the polished lawyer asserted.

"Well sir, I'm fresh out of law school. Perhaps I've had too little experience to be fearful of not obtaining justice in the courts," Karl said, tapping Griffin's foot.

Griffin let loose his fury, "Just what would you do if the shoe was on the other foot? This is the worst piece of thievery in the history of any corporation. Yours is a dirty, sly, no-good operation run by the rottenest concern the Wall Paper Industry has ever…"

Karl tapped Griffin's foot, but he wouldn't stop.

All three of the opposing men prepared to leave.

"Gentlemen! I apologize for my client's outburst. Nevertheless he has just cause for his disgust," Karl said attempting to stop them.

The men had gathered up their papers and were about to walk out the door when Karl quickly added: "Mr. Griffin, I recommend that you publicize your complaints and facts in the newspaper and by direct mail to the industry. If we can't get relief through the law, then at least we can pillory the corporation and its officers before the business world; in which case I doubt very much they'll increase their profits next year one whit!"

The Worcester men walked out.

Left alone with Karl in the office, Mr. Griffin heaved a sigh of frustration. "We've lost haven't we?" he said.

"We'll see. I doubt it. I found out that the president of this corporation is a church-going man. He's a respected citizen of the town. I don't think he would want bad publicity. I'll go ahead and just prepare a report for the papers," Karl said.

After a few days, along with a boy carrying a suitcase, the Secretary of the Worcester Corporation walked into Karl's office.

"Our directors have met, sir," he said. "On being informed by the President of all the facts, the Vice President who made the decision to bring in the inventor has been repudiated. Furthermore, we would like to make restitution."

The boy produced a pile of books from the suitcase that had been created to exploit the photographic wallpaper invention, along with all of its stock, as the Secretary added, "We would appreciate being able to pay for the expense of returning this inventor and his equipment to New York."

Despite awareness that his method of intimidation was unorthodox and that few lawyers would have used it, Karl took great pleasure in the ability to give Mr. Griffin back what had been stolen from him. He sat down immediately to write a letter to Judge Dugro, telling him about the positive impact of his borderline mandatory injunction. As soon as he was through, he walked home to conspire with Sarah and Gertie to invite Helen to the apartment for dinner.

Left to right: Max, Herman Jr.,
Herman Sr., Karl in Geneva,
Switzerland, 1896.

The abrasives company building
in Brooklyn, NY.

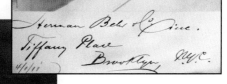

Herman Behr, Sr.

Karl leaping on the deck of the *Saxonia*.

Barrett and Gore (in foreground) vs. Wright and Behr in
All-England Championships, 1907.

Lawn Tennis
and Badminton

Vol. I. (New Series.) No. 3.   Wednesday, June 26, 1907.

THE U.S.A. DAVIS CUP TEAM.

Karl Behr and Beals Wright.
U.S. Davis Cup team, 1907.

Norman E. Brookes (foreground)
vs. Karl Behr, 1907.

American Lawn Tennis

Official Organ of United States National Lawn Tennis Association

Volume I   *AUGUST 1, 1907*   Number 6

The Battle for the Davis Cup

By George W. Pratt, AMERICAN LAWN TENNIS Special Representative

London, July 16.—The effort of Beals Wright and Karl Behr to bring the Davis cup back to America has proved to be a vain one, but let no one think that Australasia's victory was an easy matter or that Wright and Behr played tennis that was not a credit to themselves and their country.

Brookes' two victories were decisive and it must be acknowledged that to-day he stands at the very top of the lawn tennis ladder. He has mastered the art of service to a degree beyond that reached by anyone else; his volleying at the net is as good as Beals Wright's at its best, and in the matter of temperament, Brookes is well qualified to be a champion. He is always calm, determined and careful.

In Wilding, Wright and Behr found an opponent who was a tremendous fighter, a player who had as much

tennis in him as they themselves had, and who was their superior in endurance. Wilding cannot kill lobs and he is not the equal of Beals Wright as a tennis tactician, and perhaps this explains why Wright was able to defeat him. In both his matches, however, the New Zealander played very high grade tennis, and his victory over Behr was won by superior physical condition alone.

Behr lost both his matches, it is true, but it would be unjust to accuse him of playing anything but the very best of tennis. Indeed the London papers were so much impressed by his playing that they refer to him as the best of the younger men and a future champion. The English critics have much to say in praise of his game, and indeed they should, for Behr fought Brookes harder than anyone else has been able to do.

The first match of the series was the Wright-

Norman E. Brookes versus Karl H. Behr.

Mexico river valley, 1908.

Sheldon with Karl's horse.

Paul, Sheldon, and Karl in Urique, Mexico.

Assay furnace, used to heat ore and determine which metals are present.

Urique's entire male population, 1908.

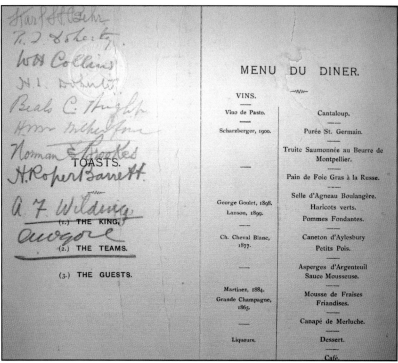

Davis cup dinner menu, 1907.

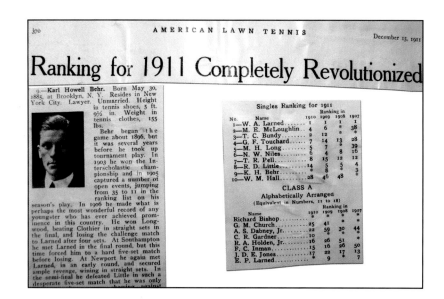

Ranking for 1911 Completely Revolutionized

9.—Karl Howell Behr. Born May 30, 1885, at Brooklyn, N. Y. Resides in New York City. Lawyer. Unmarried. Height in tennis shoes, 5 ft. 9½ in. Weight in tennis clothes, 155 lbs.

Behr began the game about 1896, but it was several years before he took up tournament play. In 1903 he won the Interscholastic championship and in 1905 captured a number of open events, jumping from 35 to 11 in the ranking list on his season's play. In 1906 he made what is perhaps the most wonderful record of any youngster who has ever achieved prominence in this country. He won Longwood, beating Clothier in straight sets in the final, and losing the challenge match to Larned after four sets. At Southampton he met Larned in the final round, but this time forced him to a hard five-set match before losing. At Newport he again met Larned, in an early round, and secured ample revenge, winning in straight sets. In the semi-final he defeated Little in such a desperate five-set match that he was only ...

Singles Ranking for 1911

No.	Name	1910	1909	1908	1907
1	W. A. Larned	1	1	1	1
2	M. E. McLoughlin	4	6	*	38
3	T. C. Bundy	2	12	*	*
4	G. F. Touchard	7	14	13	28
5	M. H. Long	5	7	*	39
6	N. W. Niles	6	4	8	16
7	T. R. Pell	8	15	12	12
8	R. D. Little	14	5	5	4
9	K. H. Behr	*	8	8	3
10	W. M. Hall	28	46	48	*

CLASS A

Alphabetically Arranged

(Equivalent in Numbers, 11 to 18)

Name	1910	1909	1908	1907
Richard Bishop	*	*	*	*
G. M. Church	25	41	*	*
A. S. Dabney, Jr.	22	59	30	44
C. R. Gardner	10	*	*	*
R. A. Holden, Jr.	16	26	51	*
F. C. Inman	15	16	26	50
J. D. E. Jones	17	22	17	13
E. P. Larned	*	9	*	7

Squadron A military parade, 1909.

Karl Behr (standing far right) with Squadron A, 1909.

Helen Newsom and Karl Behr,
March, 1912.

PART THREE

All across the far-flung globe, small lights…

Photo from postcard of RMS *Titanic*.

30

A Chance For Love

"**K**ARL, COULD YOU TELL ME MORE about this nameless inventor of scenic wallpaper? It seems to me that while the financier fared quite well, the inventor might have wanted to move to Worcester, but had no say in the matter a t'all. Did you speak to him? Was he upset to have been such a pawn?" Margaret asked her brother at dinner.

While he formulated an answer, Karl watched candlelight flicker on Helen's soft chin. She sat directly across from him, next to his brother Herman. He noticed how adept she was in the atmosphere, easily gliding in and out of conversation.

"No, Margaret, I never met the inventor or learned anything about him. He broke his promise, and I don't think he was coerced." Karl answered.

Behind his father, a fire affected a fleeting reminiscence of sun-glazed mountains in Mexico, but Karl's attention gladly returned to the table when Helen spoke:

"I'd like to go along with you, Karl, when you visit Griffin's some day. I'm intrigued by the idea of photographic wallpaper, wondering what it would be like to be surrounded by an ocean scene, a forest, or a lake like Squam." Helen's eyes circled to encompass everyone gathered at the table; her dark hair was contained, flattering. "You'll be coming up to visit us at Squam again this summer, won't you Gertie? Margaret, you should come too! And Karl, Mr. Behr, Sarah, Herman? Actually, Max and Evelyn, Fritz, Alice—our house is very accommodating! It has a wide porch overlooking the lake where we perform silly skits in the evenings with the loons calling us back to our senses!" Helen blinked once, a little hard, as she considered that she may have rambled too long and gone overboard by inviting everyone—even the absent family members!

"I look forward to coming so much!" Gertie said, soothing her.

"I'd love to see it," Margaret added.

"Count me in!" Karl said. "What about you, Dad?"

"I'll give it a dream or two," Karl's father replied. "It may be a bit more journey than I'm game for, much as I hate to admit it. Thank you for the invitation Helen." After he spoke he looked into Sarah's face. She adjusted the position of the utensils on the platter that she was serving, lifting her brows ever so slightly. They were both thrilled by the hint of romance in their midst.

"I've been too busy at the firm to ask what's been happening at the company," Karl said to his father.

"More of the same usual rush of production and inventory. But there is one thing that is pressing and needs to be addressed soon: The renewal of our contract with the Austrian Bank for importation of Adamant. The contract is about to expire and someone has to go to Vienna, but no one appears to be available."

"Adamant is an abrasive produced by an electric furnace, Helen." Karl said.

"Oh," Helen reacted, grateful that Karl considered it important to inform her. "Well then, Karl, maybe you could finagle the trip?" she said. "My stepfather is keen to go to Europe in February. We're sailing on the *Cedric* for the Mediterranean with Mother and their good friends, Mr. and Mrs. Kimball."

"I'll speak to Mr. Brewster and then inquire if I could get a cabin," Karl said, short of receiving a formal invitation.

Margaret smiled at Gertrude, who grinned as they dove back into their plates.

Herm had been more silent than usual during dinner; he didn't know what to think of this change in his little brother.

Karl spoke to Mr. Brewster and received permission for his trip to Europe with the promise that someone would cover for him while he was away. He was able to secure a cabin on the SS *Cedric*. Although Karl had recovered from his concussion, he continued to suffer occasional headaches and welcomed the chance to travel.

Once again while Karl was packing, Herm came to his room—this time to wish him well, but also to report that the Works Manager had been undermining their father's authority at the Company. "I can't put my finger on it, exactly. I just don't trust him anymore. He's fine one minute; then he finds something to complain about the next. Worst of all, he has spoken to some of the other men, insinuating incompetence in Father, casting aspersions and pointing out problems to other partners—Robert and Gustav. Of course, what he doesn't realize is that they relay his disaffections right back to me. So far, I've not spoken to Father about this; I'm keeping an eye on it, that's all."

"Do. I've had my suspicions. Father is dependent on him."

"And so loyal that he would never let him go," Herman said.

"It would be beneficial for you to learn as much as possible about whom and what the Works Manager controls. Watch the accounts, and record your reactions to everything he says—whatever you hear." Karl said as he lifted a pair of pants from his drawer.

"She's a sweet one," Herman blurted. "Mighty young though, don't you think?"

"Oh, Helen's wise beyond her years. The way she puts me in my place makes my head spin. There's nothing immature in her that I've seen. We have an awful lot of fun together. A cruise with her mother and stepfather—well, that should be quite the acid test. Wouldn't you say?"

"I envy you," Herman said.

"And I see you as more admirable than you'd ever recognize for yourself, Herman. I wonder if you have any sense of just how much your vigilance over everything here with Sarah is valued by the rest of us good-for-nothings. Max agrees. By the way, what have you heard from Fritz, lately?"

"Not a peep," Herman said, then gave it more thought: "He's married in every sense of the word, I suppose. Left us in the dust."

"Maybe we'll hear from him when he needs us."

"Well I need you, pal. So take care to stay safe."

"Hey, I survived the tussles in Mexico."

"I'll be waiting—as usual," Herman said.

At the rail of the *Cedric*, Helen and Karl caught a glimpse of Gibraltar against the dawn's pastel aurora. "Helen, I'm sorry I haven't made a favorable impression on your mother," Karl murmured sleepily.

"She likes you Karl," Helen countered.

"I botched everything in Madeira, at Funchal."

"Everyone seemed amused by our mistake."

"We were lucky they kept the boat waiting for us. I fully understand why your mother was furious, after all her warnings to be back at the dock by four. I had no excuse—other than having been swept away by…" Karl left his sentence open ended. He rocked back and forth against the rail like a school boy.

"We couldn't help losing track of time when every new garden was more glorious than the one before. I'd make that same "mistake" again right this minute if I could! Oh, just think of those trees, butterflies, flowers—the birds we'd never seen before, and imagine what we missed!"

"We were a long way from shore at four o'clock. I don't know how I could have been so oblivious; I was supposed to be the time-keeper. It's a lucky thing you didn't twist an ankle when we flew down those hills!" Karl steadied himself, reaching to take the blame. The sleeves of his white shirt ruffled in the wind. He rolled them up.

"But it was funny, Karl. Remember how passengers cheered at the rail!"

"Do I! I recognized your mother's embarrassment in having had to alert the Captain that we were missing. And now I can still hear her tongue-lashing: 'What would you have done, Karl, if the ship had left without you?' It sends shivers down my spine, and I've been cold before I can tell you that! Your mother sees me as an irresponsible fool and I can't say that I blame her," Karl said, looking sheepish.

"Oh, Karl, don't be upset. She's tough because she feels she should be, that's all."

"I wish I could agree with you," Karl replied, picking up her hand and bringing it to his lips.

The word *storybook* echoed in Karl's mind as he wandered the narrow Moorish streets of Algiers with Helen, admiring every sensual nuance—flowerpots placed under canopies of vines cascading in lantern-light. From there, they traveled up to Nice, then to Monte Carlo by train to spend their last day alone together. All too soon, it was time for Karl's solo trip to Vienna, via Rome and Venice, leaving Helen in Nice to continue on to Portugal with her parents.

On the train from Nice, Karl read an account in the *Paris Herald* about the elder J. P. Morgan's recent visit to Rome, describing Morgan's stay at the Grand Hotel where he had engaged the services of an astute professor as his courier.

The moment Karl arrived in Rome, he went straight to the Grand Hotel, checked himself in for two nights and requested the name of Mr. Morgan's guide from the manager who grinned politely and asked, "How much of Rome do you think you can see in forty-eight hours?"

"Far too little. That is why I wish to get the best courier available," Karl answered, puffing himself up a bit.

With help from the manager, Karl was able to contact the professor by telephone to verbalize his request.

The professor replied, "I am no guide, sir. You should employ one of those recommended by the city so that you can see its churches, the Vatican…"

"I am not interested in those. My interest lies solely in ancient Rome, particularly in the Forum. If it takes two full days to learn about it, I'm eager to do so," Karl said.

"Mr. Behr, you intrigue me," the professor responded. "I shall call on you at eight o'clock this evening and we will discuss the matter further."

"I have a chance," Karl reported to the manager, who had awaited the reply.

"He is a prominent archaeologist," said the manager. "If he likes you, he will devote his time to your service. If not, he will refuse. Money is of no interest to him."

The liaison was a success. Erudite explanations flowed in paragraphs as the professor spoke to Karl before a model of Rome at the time of Augustus. At the Capitol Museum, Karl was transfixed by the small marble statue of a young girl known as "Venus of the Capitol." When he gushed with praise and questions, the professor embraced him, exclaiming, "If I were given a choice between all of Rome or this statue, I'd toss Rome into the Tiber!"

History sprang to life in the professor's vivid recapitulation of events at the ancient Forum where they convened until late afternoon—leaving all too soon as far as Karl was concerned. After attending the Italian theater, Karl boarded a midnight train to Venice and was rocked to sleep.

Just outside the City of Canals, he was awakened by talk of the night's gala event—the presentation of a meeting between the King of Italy and the German Kaiser on the Kaiser's yacht, *Hohenzollern.*

That evening, Karl reclined in a gondola, marveling at buildings and bridges as he glided passed them, alongside various elaborate craft—even a few motorboats—in a stream of eager onlookers that rushed to reach the harbor. Oil torches blazed along the Grand Canal, glazing the water with undulant seduction toward the formidable, bright-white *Hohenzollern* highlighted from every angle in a theatrical display. A brass band on the forecastle blared the Italian National anthem, followed by an explosive version of *Deutschland über Alles.* There was a momentary flash of light, during which the Kaiser and the Italian king were visible—standing together on the afterdeck. Effusive calls of *VIVA!* resounded. Then light dimmed and the crowned heads disappeared from view. Fireworks and revelry ensued, but Karl decided to abandon this much too romantic setting, unable to shake his longing for the girl he had left behind in Nice.

After having traveled to Vienna, Karl soon discovered that renegotiation for the crucial "Adamant" contract with the Kaiserliche Königliche Landerbank was no easy task. Herman Behr & Company had competition from another strong American concern. Eight days of negotiating, however, were relieved by the comforts of accommodation at the Bristol Hotel, which Karl considered a *grand step up from that Bardtown barn.*

By 1912 the charm of this imperial city was derived, in part, from the survival of venerated customs that afforded stability. The vivacious people of Vienna lived in much the same manner as their great grandfathers. Karl found the continuity in protocol, reinforced by decorum in aspects of everyday life, both pleasing and curious. According to a hierarchy of nomenclature, a military title was acknowledged as having precedence over a professional title and the latter over any business title. Upon arrival at the hotel, Karl was referred to as *"Herr Direktor."*

"I am afraid you might have made some mistake, sir. I am only Mr. Behr, a young businessman from New York," Karl said, at first unaware of the custom.

"Yes, I know. You are *Herr Direktor*, Karl Behr. The Landerbank has advised me of your expected arrival. I shall inform them at once that you are here, but first I would like to show you to your room," was the firm reply.

During negotiations for Adamant, the Landerbank's Director Kaufmann advised Karl that he should procure a solicitor.

When Karl refused, saying he didn't need one, Director Kaufmann became incensed, so Karl admitted that he was a lawyer himself.

"Mein Gott! You—*Herr Direktor*, also a lawyer, at your age! It is too much!" said the Director, wiping his forehead. "In Austria one is not permitted to practice as a solicitor until after attaining a Doctor

of Laws degree. And only pursuant to many years of practice would he receive admission to the Bar!"

All work ceased at noon in Vienna and would not resume until mid-afternoon; so directly from his meeting with Mr. Kaufmann, Karl decided to walk back to the Bristol for lunch—a ten-minute stroll. Coffee shops were crowded with businessmen playing chess and smoking. Along the way Karl noticed that the men who apparently occupied junior business positions were lifting their hats high up off their heads as they passed by their seniors who merely tipped theirs in return.

Upon arrival at the hotel, Karl went to inquire about his mail at the reception desk. "There is no mail for you this afternoon, *Herr Doktor*, the concierge said, lifting his hat high.

"Excuse me, but why do you refer to me as *Herr Doktor*?" Karl asked.

"The bank has telephoned to inform us that you are a lawyer, *Herr Direktor*. Therefore, we must take pleasure in addressing you henceforth as *Herr Doktor*."

Karl smiled, thanked him, and walked from the desk to the dining room where the headwaiter bowed deeply and greeted him in a bellowing tone: *"Guten Tag, Herr Doktor!"*

Once negotiations to secure the Adamant contract appeared to have been successful, Karl ventured to catch a glimpse of the Emperor Franz Joseph, appearing for spectators at an overlook window. Afterward, Karl spent his most heartening evening in Vienna in the company of a young courier from the bank at a "folk" restaurant. In the middle of dinner, five hundred people rose from their seats and sang to the music of a large orchestra that performed Viennese waltzes and folk songs. Holding hands and swinging the arms of his new acquaintances, Karl belted out the words to Strauss's *The Blue Danube,* with pleasure and abandon.

Before leaving Austria, Karl had one more assignment, this time for McKean, Brewster & Morgan's client, The Franklin Trust Company. As Trustee under the will of an elderly American who had died in the Tyrol at Bad Gastein, Franklin Trust had received outrageous hotel and undertaker bills, which the Company had resisted paying due to concerns of increased liability. Despite months of rankling, they were unable to obtain the deceased's personal effects, which were being held as security for this payment.

Rendering the prospect of settling more discouraging, the owner of the hotel also owned the undertaker establishment, as well as being the Bügermeister of Bad Gastein. He held every card in the deck and even managed to convince the supposedly impartial Austrian Consul to recommend full payment of these bills.

Karl traveled via Salzburg to Bad Gastein to meet with the Königliche Notar, a young, Austrian sportsman who was sympathetic to their predicament.

Together over lunch, they sat at a table in a small inn overlooking the village—its scenic valley spread below, including a mountain river.

"Das ist schön" (This is beautiful), Karl said, hoping his German was accurate. The conversation languished. "Was amüsiert Ihnen während des langen Winters?" (What amuses you during the long winter?), Karl continued.

"I ski, skate, and hunt chamois," answered the Königliche Notar.

Silence intervened.

"And what occupies your summer months?" Karl asked.

"I play tennis. I am Champion of the Tyrol," he announced with pride.

Conversation lapsed again.

As if to break the awkwardness, the Austrian launched into a colorful condemnation of the Bürgermeister.

Greatly relieved, Karl presented a "ploy" to advertise a condemnation of the hotel. In synch, they laughed uproariously about the possibility of embarrassing the Bürgermeister. But their exchange ebbed back to prolonged silence.

"Do you ski or play tennis in America?" asked the Notar.

"I play tennis, but have never skied," Karl answered.

"Have you ever seen any of your great tennis players like Larned? I would give my left arm if I could, but once, go to Wimbledon," he said.

"Yes, Wimbledon is quite a different surface to play on," Karl said. "I have had the great privilege of playing Larned many times."

Silence resounded loud as a drum roll.

The sportsman stared at Karl. Then suddenly he pounded the table, jumped to his feet, and struck himself hard in the head, his face beaming. *"Dummkopf!"* he exclaimed. "You are the great tennis player, Karl Behr, are you not?" Karl was surprised by his excitement, but readily admitted his identity.

Standing and clicking his heels together, the Königliche Notar turned serious. He loomed and stared at Karl with enough intensity to spark fire. "Herr Behr," he said. "I, a little champion, beg you, a great champion, not to call on the vile Bürgermeister this afternoon. I shall not allow you to soil your hands in the company of such a swine! As an Austrian sportsman, I ask you to take the next train back to Vienna. I promise you, on my honor, the trunks you desire will be expressed to Vienna tomorrow morning, and I shall see that the hotel and undertaker's bills are reduced by half. They will be mailed to you forthwith. Herr Behr, you must trust me!" He stood at attention awaiting an answer.

Although not altogether sure he should, Karl extended his hand saying, "This is too good of you. Of course, I shall follow your advice, and I am deeply grateful for your kind interest."

Within a few days, two trunks and a large bag arrived by express at the Bristol Hotel, accompanied by two reduced bills and a flowery letter of apology from the infamous Bürgermeister himself.

31

Beyond Any Heaven

$\mathcal{K}$ARL DEPARTED VIENNA AND VISITED with the Herman Behr & Company sales agent in Berlin. About to return to New York on the Hamburg-Amerika line, he changed his plan when he received a wire from Helen:

SAILING HOME FROM ENGLAND ON *TITANIC*'S MAIDEN VOYAGE

On Wednesday, April 10th, after shipping the newly acquired trunks and bag to The Franklin Trust Company in New York, Karl traveled by train from Berlin to Paris and on to Cherbourg where RMS *Titanic* was to pick up more passengers, arriving there from Southampton, England, its port of embarkation.

Near the dock in Cherbourg when Karl's hat blew off in a gust of wind and was crushed by a carriage, he recalled his mother's chagrin over the loss of essential items when he was a boy and chuckled to realize how little the hat's demise had upset him—due to the fact that he was able to purchase ticket #111369 for First Class aft cabin C148 on the *Titanic*.

Briefly, he considered how he would reckon with his frugal brother Herman's inevitable ribbing for the extravagance, but he was bound to celebrate the success of his trip and could concentrate on only one idea: being with Helen again.

Luggage, brought to the quay from the station, was delivered to the tender, *Traffic*—the vessel to ferry Third Class passengers out to the *Titanic* when she arrived. The other tender, *Nomadic,* was to carry Karl and 273 First and Second Class passengers to the ship at around 4:30 in the afternoon.

While Karl was waiting on a rock, a young man struck up a conversation about weather-related speculations, saying that he hailed from New York. He mentioned having heard a rumor at the railroad station—something about a near collision with the *Titanic* outside of Southampton harbor in the River Test—a possible cause for the ship's delay. Concern was sidelined for a moment when Karl and his new acquaintance chortled over the fact that they were wearing the same make of shoe.

"8th Street?" the young man asked.

"Duane," Karl answered, adding, "Stood me straight as an arrow these past few weeks!" Bending forward to wipe dust off the toes of his shoes, Karl considered that his comment might have been misconstrued since the young man walked away.

Karl stood on the rock and surveyed the horizon. He thought he could see *a dot? Or was it a flash of light?* He could not be sure. But then, no doubt; there was a hint of inspiration pending—a small dark smudge, a shadow unsure of itself, although steady by immeasurable degrees, advancing unnoticed as a minute hand, the passing of a cloud, or a day. *She is emerging as though born from my expectation,* he thought.

The ship grew—a sown speck becoming recognizable, taking shape like a seedling sprouting from a dish of indigo. It approached in the waning light across the English Channel near the western passage of the French peninsula. Before her, the water reflected ampersands of pearlescence, streaks of green, tildes of amethyst. At a mile out, she gleamed—her windows a sudden blaze of copper and gold. She carried herself high above the water, welcoming, yet self-contained as a fortress. Formed from a mere notion at a dinner table in London, there she was, resplendent—casting a favored profile with the unfathomable heft of her sleek bulk—*tantalizing as Lady Luck incarnate,* Karl thought. She held his prize and he could hardly wait to take his chance with her.

As *Nomadic* approached, the *Titanic* grew gargantuan and the sea darker, more agitated. Compared to this tremendous ship, the tender ferry looked like a gnat at a giant's eyebrow. *La Marseillaise* wafted through the wind, uplifting Karl as he listened while attempting to take in as much of the scene as he could.

He climbed aboard—following, leading, watching patiently along with others in the crowd. He turned to look into the faces of people coming behind him through the gangway; their eyes, like his, were suspended in expectation.

Amidst effusive greetings from the stewards, Karl found the First Class reception room and the purser's office where he learned how to access C deck aft. Preferring exercise to elevators, he ascertained how to take the stairs to his cabin.

Once inside, he fell onto a chair and scanned the room, noting a space heater in the wall next to the bed, a white-marble sink, a small well-appointed desk, a colorfully patterned rug, embroidered trims. But dwelling on the fact that the room was lavish (the most he had ever seen on any ship) could not quell Karl's impatience for his trunk to arrive. He began to pace until he decided to abandon the vigil, assuming that his belongings would be delivered *if* and when he was no longer waiting for them. There was only one thing to do: leave a tip with a note for the porter and race to Helen's cabin to surprise her.

The ship's purser provided directions to Helen's room, D47, near the bow. Karl walked steadily toward it, taking in sights, sounds, and smells. Being in motion soothed him. But the longer he continued to search for Helen's cabin without being able to find it, the more the ship's four-city-block length, with her complex system of passageways—a maze of white walls, iron railings, and protruding nautical devices lodged beneath stairwells or around corners—confused him. More often than not, his forays returned him to the vicinity from where he had started rather than making headway toward his destination.

Finally relieved to be standing in front of Helen's cabin door, he knocked. There was no answer. So he ventured up and out onto B deck, into the gathering darkness, to take in some fresh air and scan the steamer chairs—searching, searching everywhere and every-one—for Helen. He saw a couple wrapped in blankets watching their child spin a top. He rested there. Slowing down was a mistake; it triggered concern that Helen's mother disapproved of him. Wondering how he might impress her, he was also worried about the possibility that he could be entering an unresolved purgatory akin to the one Charlie suffered in regard to Emily's parents.

"What if I don't find her until tomorrow? I'll never get to sleep!" he said aloud, not caring that someone might see him talking to himself. Exasperated, he made his way back to his cabin where, to his burgeoning chagrin, his trunk had still not arrived. To pass time, he sat at the desk and jotted a note to Charlie, venting his frustration about the ship's complexity on White Star Line stationery that he found in the drawer, and planned to send it via the ship's Transatlantic Post Office. Then, thinking he might have better luck this time, he ventured out to search for Helen again.

He decided to investigate the dining saloon after restudying a diagram of the ship. But as he stood in the dining-room doorway, he realized that surprising Helen there would be awkward and impersonal, so once again he opted for the chance of finding her near her room. This time, as he consulted the diagram, he spotted the words "Squash Court" and decided to take a detour, hoping to find it on his way.

A steward in the purser's office directed him forward toward the bow, with turns, descents, and ascents to keep in mind. As he went along, Karl became lost in the muddle of directions and returned to the office to get a new route from a second steward. This one he thought more promising and set off yet again. But oddly, this too proved inadequate. Realizing he was only temporarily "lost," he relied on simple intuition: *just keep walking*. Soon, in front of him, was a heavy white door marked SQUASH COURT.

Surprisingly, the door had been left unlocked. Karl was impressed to see that the court appeared to be regulation size and was pristine. There was not one mark on the floor or white-white walls and he was eager to christen them.

The court was not far forward below Helen's cabin, so he ventured up and aft from there. This time, lucky enough to have taken the requisite flight of stairs, he followed a corridor that led to the companionway where, serendipitously, he had entered the narrow but pleasant hallway to her room. And...

There she was!—standing alone, reaching her hand toward the doorknob, her broad shoulders turned above her thin waist; her delicate mouth; her chin at an angle to her graceful carriage. Karl wanted to freeze that moment forever.

"Helen!"

She turned to see who... *"Karl!* Is that really you?"

They rushed into an embrace, which might never have ended had Karl not noticed a reticent crewman attempting to inch his way past them by pressing flat against the chair-rail.

Karl pulled away from Helen, mumbling a pretense of embarrassment. Colors in the carpet blurred since he had squeezed his eyes tight for so long, overwhelmed as he was by the intensity of his feelings. When they were alone again, he looked into Helen's eyes, stroked her hair, and held her dear face in both of his hands. "I missed you," he said and kissed her.

"I missed you *more*," she said.

They stood transfixed, staring at each other, then burst into laughter at the image of their awkwardness.

"Helen, don't you think we're meant to be together—*forever?*" Karl blurted, grinning.

"Oh, Karl, yes; I mean, I hope so. But my mother bristles. She says I'm much too young to think of a permanent relationship."

"She doesn't approve of me! Does she? Does she know you sent me the wire?"

"No. I doubted you could join us. But, it's not you, Karl. She still sees me as her dependent child—an immature girl. What do I know, after all? She holds on to me for security, hoping I'll always need her as much as she needs me. You know, other than me, there's only Bud. And he escapes to the woods with his guns and his dreams. She doesn't have many close friends."

"She has Dick Beckwith."

"Yes, but after my father died at Middle Bass Island, Mother was terribly lonely. She needed me—when she was home, anyway." Helen drew a breath and added, "She still does, sometimes."

"But she'll have to accept that you're in love with me. That's all there is to it!"

"Am I?"

"Aren't you?"

"Mmm, maybe a touch, but..."

"BUT?"

"You're so *old*. Look at you—twenty-six! I am only three quarters your age," she teased.

"Well, let's see, that makes me one quarter wiser."

"Leave it at older, that's all I'll concede. Don't go getting a superiority complex over a few years now. ...Umm, have you seen the darkroom? I was thinking of searching for it. Somewhere in the bow, I think."

"A darkroom? Really? Amazing!"

"Oh, I'm so glad you're here. We're going to have such a grand time exploring. Have you seen the Café Parisien? It's a garden room—ivy climbs on trellises covering the walls and ceiling, with wicker tables and chairs—my favorite place so far, aside from the Reading Room, of course. Oh, and there's a most impressive wood-carving at the clock on the center landing of the Grand Staircase. A steward told me it is called, "Honor and Glory Crowning Time"—at least I think that's what he said. It was rendered by extremely labor-intensive efforts, with an ornate cut-glass dome overhead—allowing light to pour in from above! Personally, I prefer the newel-post carvings at the aft staircase because they're more delicate. *When* did you say you came aboard?"

"Hours ago, from Cherbourg, and late because of *Titanic*'s near collision when she left Southampton. Was it frightening?" Karl asked, taking hold of Helen's hand.

"At the time I didn't realize how dire it might have been, but I was told we came within only a few feet of the little *New York*. Considering the massive size of this ship, I'm sure that if the captain hadn't managed to divert us, something horrendous would have happened!" Helen said, letting go of Karl's hand.

"I arrived with passengers who were brought to the ship by ferry at least a mile from the Cherbourg dock. I found my cabin and waited for my trunk, which never arrived (probably still hasn't), and I've been searching for you ever since—from stem to stern as a matter of fact! I was misdirected over and over! Where were you hiding?"

"Nowhere really. Guess I was swallowed up by a cavernous Chesterfield with my book, next to the fireplace in the Reading Room."

"*Fireplace?*"

Nodding, Helen said, "Come with me, I'll show you! Let's find my mother and stepfather first. You could join us for dinner. We always seem to eat late. Where's your cabin?"

"Miles aft. By the way, I was just at the squash court, not far from here. It's miraculous!"

"Oh, so you weren't searching for me the *entire* time."

"Yes I was! The court was on a slight detour, along with all the other involuntary ones."

"This ship is too big," Helen said. "So easy to get lost in it. I want you to tell me about all your adventures in Europe."

"Happily," Karl answered, hugging Helen. "Everything went well. You're my good-luck charm."

"Oh, there's our stewardess." Helen gestured toward Violet Jessop who was passing by and asked if she had seen her mother, Mrs. Beckwith.

"We passed on the Promenade Deck about an hour ago," Violet said.

"Thank you, " Helen replied.

Helen and Karl ventured on to survey various rooms. At a glimpse of the molding around the ceiling of the Smoking Room, Karl recalled a wintry afternoon at Yale. He recounted the event to Helen as they stood together in the doorway:

"I wandered up to a second-floor apartment that had been rented by my pal Harris Hammond, and saw him there stark naked, suspended by his fingertips from the molding. He was 'in a swivet' as my mother liked to say, endeavoring to maneuver himself around the entire perimeter of his living room. After I walked in, he managed to gain an additional three feet before slipping off with a crash that shook the whole building. Immediately, a door downstairs opened, slammed shut, and the two old ladies who owned the house came thundering upstairs to find out what 'n Hell had caused the quake! At first they knocked politely, but when Harris shouted, 'You'd better stay outside!' he might as well have issued an embossed invitation to come right on in.

"In lieu of running for cover, Harris merely leaped up on a table, so that upon entry, the biddies saw him—posed and frozen into a statue S, with one arm arched up to the tip of its index finger and the opposing leg suspended, knee bent, foot drawn up daintily behind for dramatic effect. Through his lips squeaked a tremolo question: 'Grecian Mercury?' The two matronly voyeurs ran off squawking loud as hens from a fox-ridden coop. From some distance, we heard one yell: 'Hammond! You're evicted!' at which point I crumpled in a ball of hysterics."

Helen laughed, adding a small anecdote about skinny-dipping with a hungry snapping turtle.

Karl was consumed by his desire to sit alone with her forever—to tell her everything that had happened to him in his entire life. *All in good time,* he reminded himself. First, he would have to put his best foot forward. He wondered: *Which would that be?*

Karl planned to join Helen and her parents for dinner. He was elated to find that his trunk had arrived when he returned to his cabin to freshen up.

"So Karl, how did you manage to secure a ticket at the last minute?" Helen's mother asked, dabbing at her mouth with a napkin.

"By an incredible stroke of luck, Mrs. Beckwith," Karl said, shifting in his seat to stave off the awkwardness he was feeling. "There were places available at embarkation from Cherbourg, which was convenient for me because I was leaving from Germany and I had heard that the ship was not fully booked due to the coal strike. Even still, she's carrying quite a fair number of passengers, don't you think?" Karl said, shifting a tad stiffly to assess the crowd in the dining hall. "I assume that leaving from Cherbourg was logistically more difficult than the departure from Southampton. At least from the standpoint of having to be ferried to the ship if one was encumbered with mounds of luggage. I travel light. And my cabin cost only twenty-eight pounds, which I consider a decent price, really, don't you?"

Immediately, Karl tried to recall what he had just said, wondering what inaccuracies might have escaped—thinking that normally he would only be this nervous if a four-legged carnivore happened by.

"A bargain," Sallie said, grinning, then grimacing at Dick behind her napkin.

"I should think you're right about transferring the luggage Karl," Helen said to support him. "I watched a lady come aboard at Southampton with so many trunks that I couldn't resist counting them—plus suitcases, crates, and a monstrous chest marked Medicine, in red letters. Good Lord, I wondered why on earth would anybody need, or want to carry so much."

"She's probably moving to New York permanently, dear," Dick Beckwith said, slanting his brows back at Sallie.

"Pass the mustard, would you Karl?" Sallie said to change the subject. "Such a sweet little pot with all those handles! What's this gorgeous music?"

"Puccini," Karl answered, aiming a covert wink at Helen.

"Tell us about your business venture, Karl. We want to hear everything," Helen's mother said.

With no strict attention to chronology, Karl regaled and surprised them with his tales of success in renewing the Adamant contract as "Herr Direktor," then "Herr Doktor." He pontificated about cajoling the intriguing Professor of Rome into spending precious time with him, and embellished the grand finale—his out-of-the-blue surprise from the Austrian sportsman—after quickly ruling out mention of his lonesome night in Venice. *At least Sallie seems to be listening,* Karl thought. *Is there any chance that she is impressed? Or is she just pretending for her daughter's sake?* He took a deep breath, held it, and let it out slowly.

"Oh look! There's Dorothy Gibson! Isn't she stunning!" Dick elbowed Karl.

"Mmm," Karl mumbled.

"She's an actress, you know," Dick said.

"Not nearly as pretty as our Helen!" Karl said, nudging Dick back.

"Of course not! Impossible!"

"Oh, cut it out you two," Helen said. "This crowd is way too plucked-eyebrowish for the likes of us! I know you agree. Entitled extravagance is a source of false pride. Mr. and Mrs. Kimball are our friends, and of course Mr. and Mrs. Harder, but overall, I feel like an imposter in this crowd—not that it isn't inspiring! Over there are Mr. and Mrs. Astor, and then, let's see, Ben Guggenheim…"

"Turn back around and don't point, dear," Sallie said, sternly.

Karl laughed, "Well, Helen, let's just pretend we belong. We are sitting here after all, aren't we! Right behind you is a fascinating scholar I'd enjoy *communicating* with," Karl said. "I recognized him right away. Have you heard of William Stead the spiritualist author? His work intrigues my father, which is how I became acquainted with his writing. I found his books in Father's collection—one about a steamer that sank with a horrible loss of life because there weren't enough lifeboats. The other, I think, involved a ship that hit an iceberg—oh, yes, I remember it was a White Star Liner named *Majestic*. Survivors climbed onto an iceberg—struck me as highly unlikely! Margaret knows all about him. Take a gander at the intensity in his eyes when you have a chance."

"Not *now*, dear," Sallie said to prevent Helen from twisting around.

Suddenly, a young woman rushed up to Karl, stopping just short of throwing her arms around him. "Karl! Hello! That's you, is it not? *Karl Behr?*" He blushed with embarrassment. He had no memory of her. She was astoundingly stunning in a natural way and she seemed to know him somehow, intimately. Recognizing his bafflement, she quickly introduced herself: "Kate, Kate Buss. Oh, I'm terribly sorry, I really have no idea what's come over me. I must have thrown decorum to the wind. I've been entirely seduced by the spell of this luscious ship. There you are, the handsome young American—looking so marvelous—and here I am, ecstatically engaged and giddy. I'm on a journey to California to marry a heavenly man and I recognized you from having watched every match you played at Wimbledon and for the Davis Cup. I'm a tennis enthusiast, you see. Of course there is no reason for you to have the foggiest notion of me. Please forgive my intrusion!"

"Not at all, Miss Kate…?" Sallie said.

"Buss, Kate Buss," she repeated, extending her hand.

"I'm Sallie Beckwith," Helen's mother said, reaching to shake Kate's hand. "Won't you join us for coffee? We'd be more than pleased to have you stay. What a long way for a lady to journey alone."

"No, no. Thank you. I'm actually traveling in Second Class," Kate replied, blushing and pointing aft. "I was sneaking through to verify a game of bridge tonight with the ladies at the table over there.

Thank you again, though, and good night. I hope we'll meet some-where, someday, again." Kate turned and continued to weave her way around the chairs.

"Phew," Karl whispered.

"Such a lively lady," Helen said.

Sallie settled back, sipping at her demitasse.

"Mr. Beckwith, *Dick*," Karl corrected, remembering having been urged to call him by his first name, "what would you think about a game of squash in the morning? We could exercise before we dock at Queenstown."

"A fate worse than death, I'm afraid, Karl—for you that is. I doubt if I could give you much of a match."

"I'll take my chances. All we need to do is find two squash racquets and a ball, which I assume the ship could supply. Helen and I were planning a small explore, weren't we, Helen? Afterwards—let's say at ten o'clock—I'll meet you at your cabin, racquets in hand; then Helen and her Mum could go for tea or take a stroll."

"Might you be on time?" Helen's mother said with a smile.

"Yes," Karl answered in earnest.

The next morning Helen and Karl walked the length of the ship, ogling a wealth of aesthetic accoutrements. "Phenomenal, amazing," Helen said over and over. "I don't see how it is possible to create a ship so lavish."

"I heard a steward claim that this is the largest moveable object ever built and she's even got a double bottom," Karl said. "But the crew is unfamiliar with her. I've been misdirected four times so far. Soon, though, like most crews, they'll be able to navigate her with their eyes closed—by instinct—even in the pitch dark, which is expected, you know."

Karl and Helen stood on deck wrapped in each other's arms, staring over the vast expanse of ocean, reveling in their euphoric sense of comfort, security, and peace. Karl closed his eyes, over-whelmed by his connection to a benevolent universe.

"Have you seen Captain Smith?" he asked Helen. "EJ? You know, white beard, heavy scrambled eggs on his hat brim, medals on his lapel, four stripes on his sleeves?"

"Yes—in the dining hall."

"Let's find him and have a chat," Karl said.

"He wouldn't have time to talk to us, would he? What would we ask him about?"

"The weather, time, his family, the course—how he steers this behemoth—you know, winkle a wee bit outta 'im. I hear this may be his last crossin'," Karl said, struggling with his pseudo accent.

Helen perished the thought of intruding on Captain Smith, but she was spared because Karl realized the time was getting late and gasped. They sped to the inquiry office to find squash racquets, which were located by the racquet professional, Fred Wright.

Karl arrived with Helen, one dollar in his pocket for the hour of squash, and his right hand poised to knock on the Beckwith's door—smack on the dot of ten o'clock.

32
Heaven's Amphitheater

ON SUNDAY MORNING, APRIL 14TH, 1912, Karl awoke in his cabin, supremely content, if a touch lonesome. He threw off the covers, eased out of bed, and went to the sink where he prepared to shave, working up a lather from the much-touted Vinolia soap. Since Sunday was considered family-day in his household while growing up, he did not want to appear intrusive, so he hadn't planned a rendezvous with Helen. He also suspected that she might be overwhelmed by his advances, for which he couldn't blame her. But the thought of not being with her depressed him, and his inclination toward restraint lasted not quite half a minute before he recollected Sallie having mentioned her plan to attend Captain Smith's service in the First Class dining saloon at ten-thirty.

Invigorated by the thought of finding Helen, Karl quickly stooped at the mirror and muttered, "Oh, Lady Luck, keep shining down on me!" Then trying not to jumble the items in his trunk too much, he lifted out a clean white shirt, a starched collar, his vest and tie, and pulled on his undershirt and socks in a sudden irrational rush. He finished dressing, hastily reached for the hat and jacket he had worn when he was in Germany, and turned back toward the mirror to check and smooth his hair. He thought of Fritz as he surveyed the "unruly mop with a mind of its own." *Not such a detriment any more,* he thought.

Karl left his cabin, passing by the barbershop, to recline on deck with a glass of juice that was offered on a silver tray at the door. As soon as he caught sight of the expansive horizon, his spirit soared. Sheering through the vast ocean plane, with its multiple stabilizing guy lines extended from the funnels, and perimeter flags flapping cheerfully, the massive ship seemed a quintessential inspiration—*the epitome of all that might be possible when great minds converge,*

Karl thought, *a floating palace for one's wildest dreams of escape, of relocating to a better life, or for venturing to visit a treasured place or person.* Unencumbered in vast expanses of air and water, the ship seemed a home for the soul, and at that moment Karl saw himself in glorious context as a small but integral piece of the design. *Grand by association with the privileged entourage—like life amongst the Alps,* he mused.

As he observed a young man who was standing apparently comfortable in shirtsleeves at the rail, Karl wished he had been endowed with a similar constitution so as not to be perturbed by the cold. He hastily retreated inside to relax in the lounge, and watched the languid parade of First Class passengers, noting that some seemed to exhibit haughtiness.

Karl realized that humility was one of the qualities he most admired in Helen—her ability to see through and beyond presumption and pretense. She had pointed out that, although many of these people possessed fortunes that could stagger the earth, they had commensurate weaknesses and flaws and were often immensely generous. He remembered her saying, "I find it so terribly unfortunate that, in this world, either abundance or the lack of it wedges a barrier between people."

Karl waited for the morning service to end before bidding an exuberant "good-morning" to Helen and her mother, thus initiating another jubilant rendezvous.

At the end of the day, however, he bid "good-night" to Helen reluctantly. The flat-calm ocean had rendered dining and dancing fluid as a dream. For dinner, Karl had chosen consommé Olga and filet mignons Lili, with Parmentier potatoes and peas, and peaches in chartreuse jelly for dessert. Having curiously anticipated the hue and flavor of that jelly, he was not disappointed. He amused Helen by snitching a taste of her éclair the moment she swiveled around when he announced Lady Duff Gordon's late arrival in the dining hall as a decoy for his theft. The meal was so superb that he slipped the menu into his coat pocket for a keepsake.

Helen and Karl left the dining saloon when the musicians stopped playing. He invited her to accompany him to his cabin to "fetch a warmer coat for stargazing," pulling her along as they giggled about the prospect of being alone there together. "I want the whole beautiful world to know how much I *love* you!" Karl said, grasping Helen's hand and leading her into his room.

Helen sat on the edge of his bed, smiling but locked in thought.

Karl reclined next to her. Their hands explored one another, soft as air, until Karl stood up, walked over to his trunk, crouched alongside it, and searched for something—finally lifting out a small box clamped tightly in his palm, which he brought shyly over to Helen. Without a word, he raised the lid so that she could see the diamond ring he had brought along with him.

"It belonged to my mother. Dad slipped it into my hand just before I left. 'Take this along with you, Karl,' he said. 'I know how much you adored your mother and I sense a similar intensity of affection brewing in you. I want you to have this in case you should be overcome with desire to give it to some beautiful young woman.' …That's what he told me."

There was an awkward pause. Karl continued, "Do you like it? Shall we see if it fits?" Then seeing Helen's hesitance, he added, "Just check? For the *future*, that is?"

"Karl, it's beautiful. Gorgeous! I adore the ring, but I can't put it on. It's just not the right time. Will you keep it for me a little longer? I need to wrestle with things my mother has said, and when I'm done, I'll ask you if you still want me to try it on—if you can wait." Helen held Karl's hand, kissed him gently, stood up, and left his cabin.

He followed her. He wanted to say he would wait forever, but all he could muster was, "I'm sorry, I didn't mean to…"

Helen turned and smiled, but walked away.

Once inside her cabin, Helen found her warmest coat and went out on deck. It was bitter cold but she welcomed the invigorating chill. The sky was a teeming dome of stars that glistened as though still wet from having been lifted out of the sea. She leaned forward against the rail, wondering how to convince her mother that she was sure of herself and her feelings for Karl. She felt the wind river through her hair and across her face. She shivered, then tilted her head back to listen to the night, as though a voice might speak through the space of it. At once, the darkness seemed an unfathomable abyss, then close and protective, wrapping a flinted cloak around her, making her invisible. The stars presented myriad possibilities gold-flecked and scattered. Damp air, enhanced by the smell of the sea and mystery, overwhelmed her with a sense of how small she was within the vastness of it. She grasped the rail and leaned forward, breathing in deeply. Apprehension entwined around her—her mother's warnings: "Darling you have no idea what this boy is really like! You've only known him for six months! When a relationship changes, one can not go back." Was love drawing her to happiness, or to the myth of it? She pulled herself tight to the rail, exhaled and continued to stare into the night—into the back of her future.

Although he respected Helen's rejection, Karl sat still on his bed—stunned, utterly flummoxed, and uncomfortably equivocal about having acted rashly. He had scared her away. *How could I have been so unprepared, such a bumbling, unromantic fool, after that dinner and dancing! After our day together! Why didn't I gather words before presenting the ring as if it could speak for itself? That wasn't even close to a proper proposal,* he realized. *What did I expect she would do?* He hadn't wanted her to feel pressure. Instead of being seen as earnest, his approach was a half-baked catastrophe. The more he replayed it, the more he considered how Fritz would have had a field day ridiculing his flat-footed maneuver—a brush with disaster. Patience was the only resource he could call upon—a chance to win, next time. But after this false start, how could he convince her to marry him before someone else came along?

Humility from having hung his heart on his sleeve caused confusion to swirl; Karl couldn't rest. He sat upright on the edge of his bed, perplexed, until he was unable to tolerate self-doubt one minute more and strode out to the Smoking Room in search of male camaraderie.

When he spotted Dick Beckwith and Alexander Compton playing cards he was relieved. "Ah, there you are, you scoundrels! Seizing a chance to pilfer from the innocent are you?" Karl joked as he approached them.

Earlier, during dinner, Karl and Dick had chuckled over a notice that had been circulated to the passengers, warning them to be on the lookout for unscrupulous professional gamblers in disguise. Discouraging games of chance had been advised in order to prevent such individuals from taking unfair advantage of the unsuspecting.

"Sit yourself down, you scalawag. Seven-card stud's the game. Twos and one-eyed jacks are wild," Mr. Compton announced.

"Deal me in," Karl said, dropping like a rock into the chair and leaning back to peruse the ornate rosettes in the ceiling.

"Watch out, Karl. That card-shark smells blood tonight," Dick said, squinting over the top of his glasses with a glare directed toward Alexander.

Close to eleven-thirty, Karl and Dick were alternating between yawns and accusations that Alexander must be one of the dreaded gamblers because his luck had burned their money like coal fire. He beat them, drawing aces and other cards he needed, repeatedly— even a royal flush. So the two losers slapped their cards down on the table, claiming they couldn't take Alexander's thrashing one minute more. They bid adieu and wandered off to retire to their cabins for the night.

33

Tears of Ice

$\mathcal{K}$ARL BEGAN TO UNDRESS IN HIS ROOM. He took off his collar, vest, and cutaway coat, anticipating the comfort of his pillow and a soothing slide between the sheets. Suddenly, he felt the ship tremble, but heard nothing other than a muted rumble. Having experienced a ship's violent shaking on previous passages, he thought that maybe *Titanic* had broken a shaft. He stood still for over a minute. Since the engine continued running, he surmised that it couldn't have been a shaft—*I doubt if there was anything to worry about,* he thought, continuing to undress. But then the ship's engines stopped and he began to feel uneasy. So he put his collar, vest, and cutaway back on, opened the door and peered down the hallway. There was no one in sight. *It must be nothing,* he thought, and closed the door to undress again. As his hand was reaching back up to his collar, however, he said aloud, "I'll just go to Helen's cabin and make sure everything is all right."

He walked half the length of the ship along the gangway for-ward, never seeing a single soul, until he arrived at Helen's cabin where he was taken aback—*elated,* in fact—to see her in the hallway fully dressed. Dick Beckwith was standing next to her, along with Sallie, Mr. and Mrs. Kimball, and a few other passengers.

"A great deal of ice has gathered on the portholes of our cabin," Sallie commented. "Did you hear that pebbly, scraping sound?"

"Like tide receding from stones." Helen added.

"Hmm," Dick said with a small smirk aimed at Karl, "Like the sound our cards made being thrown on the table in disgust!" He and Karl grimaced together.

"Actually, I felt a shuddering when I was back in my cabin," Karl said. "I think we should do some reconnaissance to see what, if

209

anything, we can find out. I'll go up to the Boat Deck and look out from there."

"I'm coming with you, Karl. Wait for me," Helen said, walking toward her cabin to get her coat.

"Perhaps someone should have a look around the bow, maybe at the squash court," Karl suggested to Dick.

"I'll go down there. Afterward, let's meet back here," Dick rejoined.

Helen and Karl passed through the main lobby where they saw one or two officers and a few sailors, but no passengers. Once up and outside, they walked the length of the Boat Deck, which was completely deserted, damp, and bone-achingly cold. Stars flickered in the night's black cave. Nothing appeared amiss. Karl and Helen hugged, exchanging shy endearments. He apologized profusely for his bumbling as they returned to the gangway by Helen's cabin.

"There's water in the squash court," Dick reported, arriving in the hallway just after Helen and Karl.

Sallie reemerged from her cabin fully dressed, a coat draped over her shoulders.

"We'd best go back up to the Boat Deck again." Karl said, aware that the squash court was mid-bow on G deck, just above the water line.

A crewman passed by, saying, "As a precaution, sir, I've been advised to issue an order for lifejackets." He walked on.

Karl and Dick went to find the requisite jackets and figure out how to fasten them.

"I must say, this all seems unnecessary," Sallie quibbled.

"I certainly hope so, my dear," Dick agreed.

On their way up the main stairs to the starboard Boat Deck, they passed Captain Smith who appeared self-immersed as he hurried down alone. Karl observed him intently, unable to detect concern.

Once outside again, there were a few small groups of passengers on the Boat Deck, but this time, a torturously loud noise—steam, venting from a pipe on the side of the forward funnel—emitted such a deafening high-pitched whistle that shouting was the only (although still nearly impossible) means to communicate.

A forward lifeboat was being unlashed, but there was no motion to load it. Using hand signals, Karl indicated to Helen that he was going to wander toward the bow. He saw lights there, apparently from a ship not far off the port bow—*only several miles away,* he surmised. He returned and reported this to Helen through cupped hands over her ear.

The effluent steam ceased screeching and there were audible sighs of relief. Karl told Dick and Sallie about the ship nearby. In place of what might have become a state of limbo accompanied by projected apprehension, Wallace Hartley's band music wafted up, brightening the wait with tempered ragtime. More passengers had gathered on the Boat Deck. Karl recognized Bruce Ismay, the tall Chairman of the White Star Line, as he shuffled by in a dressing gown and slippers, then overheard Ismay clear his throat and instruct a group of forward passengers to enter the lifeboat that was being prepared for them.

Gradually that first boat (No. 7) filled up with some passengers; Karl counted ten men and ten women. Helen was amused by First Officer Murdoch's timid handling of a feisty, thick-furred little dog she thought was a Pomeranian, realizing it must belong to one of the prospective passengers in that boat. After scrambling to catch it, Officer Murdoch managed to toss the dog into a lady's arms. Located directly across from the entrance to the gymnasium where a few people were occupying themselves and keeping warm on the exercise machines, No. 7 was held even with the gunwale for a while until a few of the people in it started to climb back out. Karl wondered if there had been any practice of the lowering procedure, along with questioning its necessity.

Helen looked ahead at the lifeboat. "Oh, those people are brave; don't you think, Karl? The thought of being lowered down to the ocean from way up here terrifies me!" She said, shivering, her breath exhaled in a vaporous cloud.

"It does seem that the boats would be better surface-loaded at the waterline on a calm night like this."

As soon as he said it, Karl heard an officer order lifeboat No. 7, which had proceeded downward, to be held near the forward gangway door to await more passengers once it reached the ocean.

"If need be, more can be brought aboard down below," said another man, echoing the sentiment. This made sense to Karl. It seemed an undue risk to lower the boats more than eighty feet, bearing the weight of as many people as they might conceivably hold. *The boats might buckle. The davits look small 'though they appear brand new,* Karl thought to himself.

As Karl was assessing the lifeboats, he spotted George Harder, a fellow Brooklyn manufacturer, standing by his wife, Dorothy. Karl had joined George after breakfast on Saturday when they had conversed at length—comparing George's work to Karl's at his father's abrasives business. Karl walked over to speak to him.

"I caught a glimpse of the iceberg we must have scraped," George said. "It passed by my porthole—partly blue, immense!"

"Oh," Karl said, distracted because he was keeping a watchful eye on Helen over George's shoulder. He saw Ismay approach her mother, so he returned to Helen's side. She told him that Mr. Ismay had told her mother to board lifeboat "number five" as he referred to it, which had been swung over the side and was being held flush with the deck in the process of being filled, this time with many more passengers. The lifeboat looked diminutive against the black abyss, *like a fishing boat used for off-shore haul-seine forays,* Karl thought.

Sallie didn't answer Ismay. Instead she shrugged and waited, disinclined to do his bidding. "Isn't this just precautionary?" she asked. "It is preposterous that the ship will sink, is it not? I have no desire to be dropped into frigid darkness." Her coat, although well cut, was sleek and thin. She was trembling, stifling yawns, obviously inclined to return to bed. None of the passengers or crew appeared anxious, which augmented her lack of concern. The prospect of trusting one's life to being cast off and away in a flimsy-looking boat was undoubtedly foolhardy whereas staying on deck seemed a preferable option.

Rockets were launched. Their small explosions, followed by trails of cascading white stars overhead, seemed to Karl *like sparks from a welder's torch,* but he felt sure the signal was adequate to lure the ship he'd seen off the port-bow. However, the urging from Ismay and First Officer Murdoch, assisted by Third Officer Pitman and Fifth Officer Lowe, grew more forceful. The Boat Deck passengers and crew were mercifully unaware that, below them, two engineers—Shepherd, who had broken his leg, and Harvey, who had gone to rescue Shepherd—were being swept under by a wall of water at that moment, as the band played on till lifeboat No. 5 was filled with thirty-some passengers. It hung suspended, awaiting more. Ismay approached Sallie again, this time he spoke emphatically, saying that she must board the lifeboat and added there was "no time to waste."

"I think you should do as he says," Dick encouraged.

Sallie turned to Ismay and inquired: "May *all* of my party enter this boat?"

"Why certainly, Madam, every one of you," Ismay answered.

Sallie sighed and looked askance to Dick for his opinion. He answered by taking her hand and stepping in with her. They entered with Edwin and Gertrude Kimball. Along with them, Helen climbed over the sloping boat-side into the stern.

"Come help row!" Dick said to Karl, pointing at the oarlock next to him. "We need your strong arms!" he said.

Sallie bid Karl "Come along!" in a forceful tone.

Helen held out her hand for him to join her; her eyes were pleading.

Karl swung his leg over the edge of the boat. He squeezed Helen's hand saying, "Don't worry. We'll be fine—most likely hoisted back up right after we touch down and row around awhile."

Passengers in the lifeboat waited while Ismay, Fifth Officer Lowe, and First Officer William Murdoch looked around for more women in the vicinity. There were only a few men.

"Who is in charge of this second boat?" Murdoch shouted over a crescendo in the music.

"I am Sir!" Pitman said, approaching from a few feet away.

"In you go then, along with Quartermaster Olliver," Murdoch said.

Third Officer Pitman resisted: "All due respect, Sir, I'd be better off up here."

"You go in charge of this boat. Hang around the aft gangway," Murdoch insisted. He waited for Pitman to settle in, before stretching out his hand with noticeable solemnity and bidding him "Good-bye and good luck."

"Are there any more women before this boat goes?" Ismay called out.

A lady appeared from the shadows.

"Come along madam; jump in!"

"I am only a stewardess," she said.

"Never mind—you are a woman! Take your place," Ismay said.

"Lower away!" Pitman said.

Bruce Ismay bellowed: "Lower away! Lower away!"

Commencing their descent, Ismay's orders grew more strident and Karl heard someone snarl at him—the equivalent of "get the hell out of the way!" Then a heavy set man suddenly jumped into the lifeboat without warning (ostensibly to join his wife), severely injuring one of the ladies toward the bow. There was great commotion. The lady had apparently been knocked unconscious. Thereafter, the crewmen who were maneuvering the hoisting tackle ropes (the falls) from the davits, fell out of synch with one another. The bow dropped drastically, then the stern, then the bow again.

Holding her hat with one hand, Helen reached out to Karl with the other. They both grasped the edge of the boat for dear life, anticipating a drastic plunge. Officer Pitman called up to the crew to steady and level off. Once leveling was accomplished, the lowering proceeded without mishap. The boat was near the water when, abruptly, one of the officers on the lifeboat blew a whistle and shouted to the crew above, "Stop lowering! Is the plug in the boat?"

"That's your own bloomin' business!" came the retort from above. Karl looked up, attempting to identify the source of the voice, but could not detect any silhouette. In passing by the outer edge of the *Titanic*'s hull on the way down, he had tried to discern damage, which he assumed must be below the water line.

Once the inquiry about the plug was voiced, Karl saw Quartermaster Alfred Olliver lunge past several passengers and plunge headfirst directly underneath Helen. Either he replaced the plug, the "stopcock" as he called it, or had seen that it was already there and secured it—Karl was not quite sure which, but was relieved when Olliver come back up from his mission, apparently satisfied. Olliver crawled back over the tangle of passengers—this time to reach the trigger, a new gadget intended to release the falls. Chatter broke out, insinuating that the trigger wasn't working—there was speculation about needing a key. At the same time, Karl learned that the woman who had been knocked unconscious was all right. He was relieved to hear her moan when her name, "Annie Stengel," was mentioned.

"Cut the trigger to release the falls," Officer Pitman ordered.

A knife was found. Within a short interval the ropes were severed. Concerned about how they would get back aboard, Karl realized that this could easily be accomplished at the aft gangway; the sea was flat calm.

Instead of staying near the ship, however, Pitman issued orders from the forward helm to pull away and follow lifeboat No. 7 that had departed from starboard before them. They saw more rockets being launched—sparks merged with stars in the Milky Way. The sweet lilt of music counterbalanced the brutality of icy air.

Helen scanned the sky for familiar constellations while others around her searched for lights, food, water, or any supplies—finding none. At the stern oar, Karl rowed out, pulling hard, intuiting wisdom in Pitman's desire to put some distance between their small boat and the giant ship. The exercise felt good, warming, and it grew inscrutably advantageous to view the *Titanic* from some remove. Details aboard the ship were diminished, but her light was cast valiantly into the surround, coating the already glassy sea with a tinsel-sheen, which buoyed belief that she would remain afloat.

Officer Pitman assessed that there were fewer passengers in lifeboat No. 7 than in his boat, so he began the cautious transfer of two men, one woman and her boy, from No. 5 to No. 7. He lashed the two boats together with a heavy rope painter so that they would hold steady as a more cohesive unit. The undertaking was a welcome distraction that occupied time in order to be executed safely. A few of the passengers exchanged names and information between the two boats, mutually enjoying the proximity of each other's group. The waiting, drifting, and watching continued. A signal for them to return to *Titanic* seemed not to be forthcoming.

Although he fully realized that his riveted gaze could not accurately detect a small change in the ship's tilt, Karl continued trying to gauge the perimeters of her silhouette relative to the coordinate pinpoints of the slowly rising stars behind her. Briefly, he was reminded of his futile childhood efforts to detect the movement of a minute-hand. At the horizon, stars erased the parameters of sea and sky.

Expectation was superseded by calm. The longer the ship remained afloat, the more reassuring it became that her watertight compartments were performing as expected. People spoke in hushed tones, broken intermittently—sometimes abruptly—by small coughs, augmenting bits of unease as well as optimism. Although the ship's tilt had increased, the faith that she would stay upright held fast. Faint music oscillated like water-rings, dispersing a soothing emollient.

"The water is up to my ankles. This boat is leaking badly," Helen said, regretfully aware that she had spoken the obvious and immediately sorry to have brought attention to it. She whispered to Karl, "I can't feel my toes. Can you feel yours?"

Karl handed the large sweep-oar to Dick so he could reach beneath Helen to feel the perimeter of the plug under water. He prodded and pressed downward, trying to turn it to the right, but was unable to budge it at all, so he stuffed a blanket on top of it, which Helen then stomped and stood on in an effort to add the pressure of her weight to stave off further leakage.

"This little boat is brand new. I doubt if the seams were properly swollen. Must be why so much water is seeping in," Karl said, still searching for something else to do. *We'll need to bail out the boat, eventually?—with hats and shoes? But it's too cold to lose their protection,* he realized.

He heard gasps. The *Titanic* had lurched forward.

"Is she going down?" Helen whispered.

Her lights are still on, Karl observed; *the band continues to play.*

But the music stopped. Noise from the ship turned into shouts. Then blood-curdling screams severed all delusion of hope.

"Oh! Oh my God! There she goes. Oh God, *no!*" Helen's soft voice countered the unforgiving sounds—the shrieks of terror. Her eyes turned inward.

Karl stared at the *Titanic*—stunned by the grating, tearing screeches; the heart-wrenching sequence of rumblings; the stream of sparks as the ship's lights were extinguished. Her bow slid under water. She became tormented as a creature in the throes of death. There seemed a furious battle between air and water; then an explosion came from somewhere beneath. Her stern rose up high above the water—held in suspension, along with time—somewhere between eternity and a single second.

Karl and Helen watched in disbelief as the *Titanic* slid down and away with inexorable resignation like a tear, a scalpel, or a spade into the garden of stars that surrounded her.

Helen held her hands up to her face with her fingers pressed tight to her lips. Her eyes looked down in disbelief as she whispered, "She's *gone*."

From the bow of the lifeboat, Pitman announced the time: "It's 2:20," he said.

As preeminently unbelievable as the possibility that *Titanic* could or would ever sink, was the new reality: The magnificent, impermeable masterpiece, emblematic of the human spirit—*their refuge*—had been obliterated. But worse, and far more shocking, were the subsequent whistles and savage, heart-slicing screams, then moans from people in the scourge of death as they flailed in freezing water laced with the pain of a million machetes. A seething frenzy riled to smash the black-rock night.

Pitman released the rope that tied their boat to the bow of lifeboat No. 7. He ordered, "Oarsmen, pull back to the wreck."

Karl obliged as Dick handed him the sweep-oar. He pulled the lifeboat around, heading toward the vicinity from where the *Titanic* had disappeared. But after only a short time, two women near the bow pleaded forcefully and they were soon joined by other passengers, "We appeal not to go back, Sir. We will be swamped, and then we will *all* die."

Instead of disagreeing, Officer Pitman saw reason in their pleas. He slowed his rowing. Then he stopped completely. His inaction was verification that he concurred with them. Karl thought about this; he wrestled with it, assessing the level of water that was flooding their boat along with the number of passengers it already carried (almost forty after the transfer) and he didn't protest. As unconscionable as it was to stay away, he imagined the alternative scenario—*losing everyone to the sea—including Helen.*

Helen tried not to lose control, but could not contain herself. She shivered and cried, as quietly as possible, through clenched and chattering teeth. Karl hugged her and attempted to rub the circulation back into her feet. After a while, as the calls began to abate, she asked, between jagged sobs, "How long can people live in this water? Shouldn't we go search for someone who might still be alive? Boats near to them must have saved many by now. Don't you think?"

But shock, fear, and apprehension superseded any lingering conjecture to row into the human sea. *The lifeboat has no supplies, light, food or water,* Karl thought. *It might be better to die quickly.* Along with the group, he remained set against his desultory desire— sure that a rescue effort would be futile. The oars were raised.

A man nudged Karl while he was hunched over, rubbing Helen's feet. When Karl straightened up, he saw that this man was secretly revealing a nickel-plated revolver in his cupped hands. Leaning toward Karl, he offered no introduction before whispering, "Should worse come to worst, you can use this for you and your wife after I have finished with it."

"Thank you," Karl whispered back, taking his courtesy as a natural kindness and feeling no compunction about the fact that he had not corrected the man's inaccurate assumption that he and Helen were married.

Commiserating with her mother at the time, Helen had not been privy to their neighbor's offer. She turned, then squeezed Karl's hand, saying, "You saved our lives by urging us to the Boat Deck."

"Or at least prolonged them," Karl responded. "I wonder if any ship was reached during attempts to call for help." He remembered the ship he had seen off the port bow before their lifeboat was lowered.

Dick broadcasted Karl's query. "Does anyone know if a ship was contacted before we left?"

There was no answer. Few in their group had believed that the *Titanic* was doomed when they entered the lifeboat. *Not even Herbert Pitman,* Karl thought. But he recalled the somber tone in Murdoch's words of farewell to Pitman. *Murdoch must have known,* he thought ...*Bruce Ismay too. And the man who jumped into the lifeboat when it was already on its descent?*

Weak whistles and a few small flashes of match-light emerged though the darkness from widely scattered boats around them. One lantern swung out, spreading light in a seemingly furtive search to identify a source for its own paranoia. From time to time, muted prayers could be detected. Names were called out until the futility became too much to bear. There were intermittent "sightings"— lights of imagined ships approaching, each scrutinized at length before being roundly dismissed with somber mumbling. Then invariably relegated to the absurdity of wishful thinking, another would soon spring on its heels. Inherent silence, expanding like a universe, was flung like a fisherman's net—at first cast high into the air, then spread out wide to contain apprehension that the night could grow darker or the cold more intolerable. Occasional shooting stars, at first spectacular, were stunning ominous shards to accent obscurity and disorientation. Each one reflected an unanswered question. Collectively they clamored over the horizon, keeping their secrets locked in an invisible vault of unknowing.

As he watched Pitman wrap the boat's sail around a violently shivering woman, Karl blew into his hands, which refused to be warmed. He looked up into the firmament, its beauty was heartbreaking in contrast to his awareness of desolation—as limitless as the infinite stars. He riled against the indifference, every part of him stunned by pity and fury. In Helen's eyes he recognized an enigmatic stare that mirrored his own. It was the same as his mother's when he saw her watch Brooklyn burn.

34

Phantom Limbs

SCANNING A SPECTRAL ICE FLOE, Karl began to see mountainous bergs adumbrate with sinister foreboding around the lifeboat, and to assess the difficulty of navigating around them. Some other lifeboats could be dimly discerned. He looked for bodies in the water but was unable to see any—unaware that many had been carried away on a current. Time lengthened. Torpor turned desolation into vacuity.

People in the lifeboats called out names, scouring for evidence of their loved ones. Sallie stayed quiet with her eyes closed, resolute to meditation. From time to time she stroked the back of Helen's neck with long, downward sweeps of her hand. Simultaneously, they noted a cradle-moon just above the horizon, and also, at the same moment, Karl sighted...*something*. He blinked—convinced he had conjured a mirage; but the approach of a ship was no illusion this time. With rockets fired upward, and a green side-light, a vessel was steaming along rapidly—more lights strung along her sides could be seen.

Nearby, a flare signaled to the ship. Farther away, a small green light glimmered and another tiny light was being waved with a raging, twisting motion that formed figure-eights in the air. Sallie whispered to Helen, "*Tinkerbells.*"

A whistle sounded from the approaching ship, confirming that she had spotted the lifeboats. In a short while, although to Karl it was interminable, the ship came closer, turned around an iceberg, and dropped her sea anchor to avail her starboard side toward the lifeboat evacuees.

Night receded with reluctance; daylight was still a dream. But against the iceberg, Karl could see the ship's sweet silhouette with its single central funnel spewing smoke, and four tall mastheads, with flags at each, spaced evenly from stem to stern.

One-by-one, lifeboats approached the ship in a slow procession and the process of bringing survivors aboard as sensitively as possible was set in motion. They climbed a rope ladder, or in case they were unable to hold on to the ladder, they were lifted in a mail carrier, a sling, or a makeshift boatswain's chair. Occasionally, children were hoisted in ash bags. The course of this was arduous, fraught with relief and abject fear.

Morning's dawn-cast light laid bare a rising epitome of emotions—soaring spirits wrangling with shock and despair as the surrounding ice floes became gradually awash in soft pastels that illuminated them with a kind of glory, while at the same time highlighting the danger they posed and rendering them surreal above the shadows they cast across the channels.

When their lifeboat was unloaded, Karl climbed the rope ladder last, just after Helen, carrying her shoes in his hand. Once on deck, they were met by tempered greetings of "Welcome aboard *Carpathia*." They savored the comfort of blankets that were wrapped around him before being escorted below to food and coffee where they were informed that three doctors had been assigned to specific stations according to class. They were urged to report to their corresponding station in order to ensure proper position and care. There was a Dr. McGhee for First Class passengers, an Italian doctor for Second, and a Hungarian physician for Third. These various stations, organized in different dining saloons, had been set up so that survivors could receive adequate first aid or medicines if required. Directives to the locations were issued frequently in multiple languages. Much of the furniture had been removed from the small Smoking Room, the Lounge, and the Library, in order to prepare the areas for sleeping. The steerage passengers were told that they would be grouped together.

Listening intently to *Carpathia*'s Chief Steward Hughes's directives, Karl sipped and nibbled rapidly, then told Helen he was going back up to the rail to monitor the arrival of other lifeboat passengers.

From the deck, he watched with intensity, keeping count, noticing that some of the boats were collapsible types though they carried a great number of passengers: *Maybe thirty-some, or forty,* he thought. One corpse was brought aboard with great solemnity. Then a second collapsible was unloaded with someone he recognized: *Bruce Ismay.*

Finally, the last boat, still out at sea, was struggling to get closer. It was so overloaded that its side-rim barely cleared the waterline. From the deck of *Carpathia,* several onlookers pointed at it. Consternation was building. A williwaw stirred, and agitated waves swelled in the chop. Karl leaned over the rail, noting that the oarsmen were unable to make headway in their effort to reach the ship. To his relief, *Carpathia*'s captain ordered the crew to hoist anchor and maneuver toward the boat.

With her blanket still wound around her, Helen came up to join Karl. She stood tall beside him as they watched this last lifeboat being held at *Carpathia*'s side and unloaded. Like fire leaping beyond control, perception burned in Karl's consciousness and consumed him. He heaved a sigh and said, "The sight of so many in this last boat makes me sick. Oh our not attempting to rescue more people was sorely mistaken. It was pitiful, *shameful.*"

Helen immediately comprehended the unlikelihood of reckoning with the agony in Karl's expression. Sharing it, she responded, "If we had known *then* what we know *now*—that we'd be rescued..."

"We might have saved several people if we'd timed it right," Karl added, peering inward and gnawing on his lip.

"But Karl, we didn't know. Oh, but you're *right*; if this is the last group—the end—it is unbearable. Do you really think that everyone who survived is here now? Is that possible? Might some have been rescued elsewhere? How many passengers were aboard the *Titanic?* Weren't there more than two thousand? How many do you think are here?"

"Somewhere near seven hundred, if my estimate is right. I might have missed a few in my count when I went below."

"Oh, God, these poor people—missing their companions. But if the others weren't rescued, where did they go? Why can't we see them?"

"I've no idea. The lifejackets can't have failed."

As staggering as the loss seemed to them at that moment, the real impact of the misery had only just begun. It was not quite nine in the morning when the last person to board *Carpathia* set foot on deck.

There were some jubilant moments: Both Annie Stengel, who had been injured during the lowering, and Mrs. Dodge, who was transferred with her son to lifeboat No. 7, found their husbands. Other than these two joyful reunions, or seeing a single traveler who fully appreciated his or her luck, however, Helen and Karl witnessed meager relief. Confusion and sorrow seized those who had lost their friends and loved ones. The staggering vacuum—a complete lack of solace or sense—gave pause for grief to rush in, at first swirling, then growing to gale force. Hours passed. Desolation worsened exponentially amongst several hundred people whose multifaceted trauma was immeasurable. Many sat despondent, examining remnants of a hat or a shoe, unable to speak. Others chattered at length amongst themselves in raw states of shock, talking and analyzing in an attempt to uncover any shred of reason or blame; to reckon with the reality of their deprivation; or to communicate for the vague catharsis that sharing a story can elicit. They kept distracted by trying to formulate some course of action, but language barriers worsened the pervasive disorientation, and ramifications of the losses were further complicated by every new or obscure conjecture.

Walking by a woman who was rocking back and forth in silence, holding her child, Helen knew that she could only begin to fathom the woman's disbelief, and she was overwrought with sympathy and helplessness. Tender gestures unfolded all around them.

Dick Beckwith searched for Alexander Compton but never found him.

It was apparent that William Stead was gone.

So many, so many lost repeated over and over in Karl's mind. He spent time staring out at the vast ocean.

Before leaving the area where she had picked up survivors, the *Carpathia* circled slowly in search of bodies. Karl kept a lookout along with many others, but they did not see any more lifeboats, rafts or bodies. Only one corpse had been brought aboard. *Carpathia*'s crew hoisted thirteen of the *Titanic's* lifeboats aboard—as many as the ship could stow, leaving seven adrift to be recovered later by other ships.

Midmorning on that endless day of April 15th, Karl saw Helen where she had settled on deck, her coat spread over her, next to Kate Buss who was helping her attempt to console a grieving woman. He watched them for a moment and then went to find the Captain to offer help.

From the doorway of the Captain's office, Karl listened to him communicate with an officer of a ship in the area—the *Mount Temple*—saying that he could not find any more survivors in the vicinity and was requesting help to continue the search. He announced that the *Carpathia* would be heading west with the seven hundred and five *Titanic* passengers he had just brought aboard. Karl introduced himself, saying he wished to be of service.

The Captain, responding in kind, said his name was Arthur Rostron; he shook Karl's hand respectfully, replying that a plan was being formulated. With neither adequate supplies, nor the least inclination to continue on his way east to Europe, he told Karl he was ordering the *Carpathia* to reverse course—to proceed at full speed, first traveling south to circumvent the ice fields (adding several extra hours, he surmised) before heading west for what would be a four-day trip back to New York harbor.

Karl thanked him and continued to wander the ship, stopping to assess the dire condition of three men who barely clung to life after their prolonged exposure to the water, which he learned was 28 degrees. One man lay wrapped in blankets while his clothes were being dried in one of the ship's ovens. Recalling the pain he suffered after his freezing night in the Bardstown barn, Karl felt a cold ache spread into his hands as he looked at the three men who never regained consciousness.

Captain Rostron issued a request for the *Titanic* passengers to meet after lunch. A select group was assigned to oversee and assist in caring for and identifying the rescued. Karl became one of this seven-person Survivor Committee. The other members were his acquaintance, George Harder; Frederick Seward, the leader of the committee; Lieutenant Mauritz Björnström Steffansson of the Swedish Army; Frederick Oakley Spedden; Isaac G. Frauenthal; and Margaret "Molly" Brown, an optimistic, high-spirited millionaire from Denver who was returning home from a trip to Egypt.

Karl's responsibility was to procure sleeping locations for the steerage passengers while recording their names, addresses, and the identities of relatives they had lost. Working conscientiously through language barriers by soliciting help with translations, he managed to get information from as many as he could, preparing his list and rechecking it for the time when the names would be radioed to New York.

Later, in the Smoking Room, discussion raised speculation about the *Titanic*'s failure. No one knew enough to lace threads for cause or blame. A rumor circulated about Chief Officer Wilde, claiming that he killed himself with one of the revolvers he was handing out. Meanwhile, Officer Lowe was roundly praised for shuffling passengers and picking up more than a dozen people out of the water, some from floating objects. One moment Karl heard someone say that Captain Smith had shot himself. A second man mentioned that the Captain jumped off the Bridge. But a woman swore she saw him swimming with an infant in his arms. So, from the outset Karl learned that even *firsthand* stories crisscrossed, protestations notwithstanding, and variations of each rendered truth indistinguishable from rumor while all around them the gray sky blended with the gray sea.

Prior to his departure from Cherbourg, Karl had wired his father to inform him that he would be coming home via the RMS *Titanic*. Herm received the wire because Karl's father had fallen ill. Two doctors concurred that Herman Behr was suffering the onset of pneumonia. Sarah and young Herman were taking care of him with the help of a nurse. Max had visited, and Sarah became concerned enough to call Fritz. "Your father is very frail," she said. "You'd best come home and see him."

"Tell him I'll visit soon, will you, Sarah?"

"Yes, all right," she said.

The first words about the *Titanic* to reach Karl's family were laced with positive conjecture that most of the passengers were saved—including a report that the *Virginian* was towing the *Titanic* to Halifax. But by four-thirty on Monday afternoon, the truth emerged: There had been a horrendous loss of life. Reports claimed fewer than seven hundred people were returning on the *Carpathia* to New York.

Since many of the survivors' names had been interpreted over the wire, against loud static, there were errors in recording. A *Mrs. K. H. Behr* was included on the survivor list that was printed on the front page of the *New York Times*. Karl's brothers considered this a hopeful sign. In another paper, however, Max read an article asserting that Karl Behr, the well-known tennis player, was feared to have been lost. Max rang Fritz, and together they decided not to say anything to their father. But Herm had also heard this devastating report and he took it upon himself to prepare his father for the possibility that Karl was gone.

Two of Karl's Yale classmates spent the entire night at the White Star Line pier, waiting for news.

By four o'clock on the afternoon of Monday April 15th, an opaque undersea light spread like a layer of tulle over the ocean and a katabatic wind spun high-pitched whistles through *Carpathia*. Most of the *Titanic* survivors gathered in the main lounge.

Captain Rostron stopped the engines for a service led by Father Anderson to honor and precede a burial at sea of Edvard Lindell and the three other men who had died on board. Later, during the evening of this endless day, there was another gathering to pay tribute to all of the lost in an extended attempt to console the bereft. Despair intensified under a pall of senselessness.

The following morning, on his way see what could be done for the steerage survivors, Karl stopped to check on Dick (R. Norris) Williams, a young man he had met the previous day who was receiving care among the most critically afflicted because his legs had been frozen during hours of cold-water exposure.

Dick described to Karl how, at his father's insistence, he had jumped from the *Titanic* at the last minute, then turned to watch in agony as his beloved father was crushed by the ship's funnel when it fell. Dick had been able to swim to a half-submerged lifeboat. Because he had been advised that his legs might have to be amputated, he kept walking and in constant motion to bring the circulation back, fighting exhaustion and pain, as he was telling his to story to Karl. Awed by Dick's courage, Karl commiserated about nearly freezing to death in the windy barn in upstate New York. Dick had been born in Geneva, so Karl recounted his various escapades at La Châtelaine to amuse his new friend. The two men kept up a running discourse, sharing ardor for the game of tennis by mentioning their mutual acquaintances and recounting rivalries, although Dick was six years Karl's junior.

In *Carpathia*'s wireless room on the second day, Karl was scrutinizing the list of names for transmittal to New York when Harold Bride, the *Titanic*'s wireless operator, entered the room in a wheel chair. Bride had been urged to help *Carpathia*'s wireless operator, Harold Cottam, who was overstressed by the demands. Bride's feet were bound in wrappings—they had been wrenched during the night "Hell froze over," as he expressed it—in an awkward position underneath a heavy man on an overturned collapsible. He explained to Karl what had happened to him: how he was finally lifted into the overturned boat, beneath which he had first been caught.

Once names were relayed to New York on the wireless, Harold Bride relaxed, sighing and confiding to Karl and Cottam that the worst thing that had happened to him was not his injury, but the shock he received when one of the men who had succumbed to freezing was rolled over—revealing that it was his beloved friend and colleague, Jack Phillips, who had stayed at work in the wireless office long after Captain Smith said it was time to quit. Harold recounted their efforts to get help, praising Jack's sense of humor and confessed that he had walloped a bloke who tried to steal Jack's life vest from the back of Jack's seat. "I hit him so hard I believe I might have killed him just before the ship went down," he said. "But I have to tell you something amazing. We're a whole heap luckier than you might think! The wireless broke on Sunday. All messages and warnings backed up. We spent seven hours tryin' to figure out what was wrong with it. And we'd only finished repairing—just before the debacle. Shivers to think we'd never have been able to send for help. Not at *all!*"

That night, fully clothed and lying on top of a table in the Smoking Room, Karl had fallen into a deep sleep. There was a tremendous crash. He catapulted off the table and staggered out on deck, expecting to see another iceberg. Immediately, he was drenched by rain. He stood still, watching lightning rip through the sky, illuminating the ship's deck and the sea all around her. Thunder boomed like a blast at the mine in Mexico. Darkness leaped back. Karl turned to go inside, thinking that *never before had a violent thunderstorm been more welcome.*

When *Carpathia* approached Sandy Hook, Captain Rostron was perplexed about what to do in response to the deluge of requests— demands were fired from the press and even from President Taft for permission to board the rescue ship. "I'm opposed to having the survivors interviewed, but journalists are a mighty persistent bunch. What do you think, Karl?" he asked.

"You're correct to stand against it!" Karl said, supporting him unequivocally. "This is no place or time for interviews. These poor people are not in any condition to have to speak to strangers or to answer questions. They could be misinterpreted and their stories misconstrued. They should see their friends and loved ones first, as soon as...or *if* they are able."

Passengers were encouraged not to respond to the megaphones. The wireless operators couldn't keep up with inquiries. Cottam was given permission by Captain Rostron to ignore President Taft's demands. Taft had dispatched the naval warship *Chester* to meet the *Carpathia* because he was seeking information about his advisor and friend, Archie Butt, who had been lost; but this fact was still unconfirmed. Captain Rostron avoided a rendezvous with the *Chester* so he could continue directly to port.

Thursday evening, April 18th, the *Carpathia* entered New York harbor. Camera lights flashed around her. Karl and Helen looked out over boats of all sizes, overflowing with onlookers. Questions, wailing chaotic, were shouted over macabre mist and rain.

Captain Rostron first docked *Carpathia* at the White Star Line pier to unload the lifeboats. Once this was accomplished, he turned her to the Cunard pier to unload passengers. By nine-thirty the anguished crowd, later estimated to be approximately thirty thousand, seemed as likely to smother one another as the passengers they were eager to find.

Right after docking there was a great commotion near Karl, and he was told that Senator William Alden Smith had burst aboard *Carpathia* to speak to Bruce Ismay, Chairman of the White Star Line. Karl had not seen Ismay since the first day aboard *Carpathia*. Smith had come to garner Ismay's promise that he would participate in a hearing set to take place almost immediately at the Waldorf Astoria, although few persons could have been cognizant of the reason: A cryptic wire sent by Ismay with his name spelled backward, as Yamsi, had been intercepted, exposing the Chairman's plan to turn around and return to England on the *Cedric* without setting foot on American soil.

In spite of Captain Rostron's policy to disallow interviews, Guglielmo Marconi demanded to come aboard to interview Harold Bride. Since wireless operators aboard ship were employed by the Marconi Company rather than by the ship's operator, Captain Rostron acquiesced. Bride was a man of integrity, able and eager to answer questions, so Karl thought favorably of Captain Rostron's decision.

Amid cries, questions, exclamations, and lights flashing, Karl, Helen, Sallie, and Dick Beckwith exited behind Dick Williams, who was assisted down *Carpathia*'s ramp. Karl spotted Margaret and Gertrude at the edge of the crowd. His Yale friends, who had spent the night on the pier, ran forward, along with Herm who called out to Karl, waving.

Once together, Gertie embraced Helen, then Helen quietly turned and said "good-bye" to Karl, who looked at her with an intensity she welcomed just before she walked away with her parents when he said, "I'll call you very soon."

Once Karl's friends disbanded, Herm led Karl to the spot where their father was waiting, wrapped against the chill and separated from the crush of the crowd. Karl was shocked to see his father's demeanor severely diminished—his ashen face seemed half its normal size and indelible emotion in his eyes imparted suffering as words could not. Too weak to get up to greet his son, Herman raised trembling arms. Karl saw tears glisten on his father's cheeks. He bent down to hug him and all of their ineffable affection converged.

PART FOUR

A missive teemed with sparks of ecstasy;
A linnet's wing against the paper night;
Eurythmy ink, lightglide and gravitas.

Icefield, April 15th, 1912, near the site of the sinking of *Titanic*.

35

The Paper Sky

"*G*ETTING MIGHTY LATE, Claude, isn't it?" Karl questioned the office boy he recognized from Herman Behr & Company who was sitting at the desk in the hall when Karl entered his father's apartment the night he arrived back in New York.

Margaret explained, "There were so many inquiries about you, Karl, it was impossible to function without help to answer them."

From the kitchen doorway, Sarah emerged to help Karl's father when she saw him quietly struggle to remove his coat. Looking Karl up and down, she teased, "Travelin' a bit light, aren't ya?" Karl smiled and hugged her. "We thought we'd lost you," she sighed. "After we read a claim in the papers that you were probably gone. But here you are, fit as you were when you left. Thank the Almighty!"

"Yes, guess I am!" Karl said as lightheartedly as he could.

Finally surrounded by the comfort of his family, exhaustion and pathos overwhelmed him. "I'm here because Helen's mother asked the Chairman of White Star for permission for me, as one of her party, to enter the lifeboat; so I did—*just followed like a lamb*. We didn't think the ship was going to sink at the time. But now with so many lost, aside from being one of the luckiest men alive, I'm not sure I deserve to be! But I'll have to explain that to you—to *myself*— later, I guess."

"Oh, Karl, where's your faith," Gertrude inserted with clipped certainty. "Of course you deserve to be lucky, and alive!"

"Let's let Karl get some rest," Margaret interjected. "In the morning, things will seem better." She turned to help Claude prepare to go home.

Karl was grateful not to be further scrutinized. Alone in his room, he sat on his bed with the pounding rush of his experience inundating every part of him. On *Carpathia* he was distracted, attending to his committee duties and spending time with Helen and her parents. Sleep there had evolved from exhaustion. After returning to his familiar surroundings, the effect of having witnessed a living Hell plunged him into a morass, and he began to sense that he was caught between the devil and the deep sea. He wished he had saved someone from the water so that at least an act of heroism could have resulted from his survival, which was fraught with speculation. In his mind the words "*yes* and *no*" beat against the tick of the clock on the bedside table, which conjured a strange association with a metronome waiting for music. He imagined his alibi—*innocence*—flying out somewhere near the banks of Newfoundland where the *Titanic* sank. He blinked and tried to stave off his emotions. Opinions, convictions, conjectures—any capacity for certainty—drifted away. He was crushed by a wreck of inarticulate sadness beyond anyone's understanding, beyond reach.

Karl stood up and stripped off the clothes that by this time had molded to his body. He walked into the bathroom and turned the faucets on in the shower, adjusting the water temperature. He stepped into the rainy stream and rose up to meet it. Liquid heat penetrated his skin, soothing him beyond measure. He held his face and hands to the cascade with his eyes shut tight, turned around, felt the water run through his scalp, down his neck, his spine, opened his eyes, and reached out for the luxury of soap.

The next morning hard news arrived. Crewmen of a ship called the *Bremen* spotted more than a hundred corpses that had drifted on a current. Reports of wrenching sights poured forth: A woman with her baby at her breast; bodies clinging to one another in desperation.

Trying to counter his misery when his father and sisters had gathered around him in the living room, Karl recounted as much as he could about his successes in Europe, describing his initial days aboard *Titanic* as amongst the most euphoric he had ever spent in his life. He told them about the presence of William Stead and the consummate glory of the ship. But skirting his torment could last only so long—he finally touched on his proposal, Helen's postpone-ment, her sensitivity to her mother, how sorry he was to have lost the precious ring.

While he awaited his father's reaction, Karl lapsed into silence, pondering the way in which, after a few days on the *Carpathia*, Helen had suddenly said, '*Oh, Karl—your mother's ring? You left it in the cabin, didn't you!*' And when he had nodded, how she said: '*Oh, I'm so sorry; I wish I was wearing it!*' He was heartened by his thoughts of her tremulous candor, the genuine regret in her eyes.

Herman intuited that Karl was mired in equivocal ruminations. "My dear son, there is nothing so precious in a ring that cannot be replaced by another. In essence they are mere talismans. The bond that links true love will never be diminished by the loss of a material thing. As you well know, your mother was noble in her efforts to teach me to relinquish my attachments. We'll file a claim for the loss, that's all."

"But it was sentimental and beautiful. Helen thought so too. She said she…wished she had…"

"Well, I think she's all the more admirable for considering her mother first." Herman said, knowing how his son wanted to have finished that sentence. He preempted Karl's concern. "That's one hell of a fine lady. Now I'm convinced you ought to marry her! *Someday*…when she's ready," he added.

Consternation over the *Titanic* tragedy sprouted suppositions that were undaunted as weeds taking root between stones. Karl met each false assumption with frustration. He was aware that stories built on false premises had already rendered an accurate evaluation of the catastrophe impossible. Senator Smith's investigation attempt-ed to lay bare causes or blame for the calamity, but uncovered no clear scapegoat or villain other than a rumor that the *Titanic* ignored warnings because she was engaged in a competition with her sister ship for a speed record, which implicated Bruce Ismay as having ordered an increase in her speed. Knowing there was a shortage of coal aboard *Titanic*, Karl thought it unlikely that Captain Smith would have burned more than required for safe passage.

There were heroes—the musicians who kept on playing. And men who stood away from the lifeboats, preparing to die, were heroes in the making, praised by reporters as gallant and brave. In contrast to them, Karl plummeted to implied guilt by association with the male survivors who couldn't rationalize their means of escape. He recognized his situation as an uncanny replica of Jim's, in Joseph Conrad's *Lord Jim*—the consummate tale of a personal confrontation between perceived guilt and compromised integrity:

The moment Jim entered a lifeboat from the vessel *Patna*, his invincibility was irrevocably condemned along with his quest to secure any modicum of honor. The story was based upon a true event that occurred in 1880 when Muslims from the Malay states were traveling to Mecca for the Hajj on board a ship called the SS *Jeddah* that had set sail from Singapore under a British flag. The ship had sprung a leak, and an official inquiry was later conducted because the captain and officers abandoned the pilgrims on board.

Karl had read the book in depth when it was first printed and he had learned that Conrad, himself, suffered from a lack of self-confidence, which supported the empathetic way he portrayed Jim's facing the court inquiry alone after having been stripped of his navigation command certificate, furious to have lost his chance to be a hero. One line in the book haunted Karl: *"There was not the thickness of a sheet of paper between the right and wrong of this affair."*

At night, when darkness spawned cryptic shadows of regret, Karl reconsidered Conrad's interpretations of blind judgment from a precarious new vantage point—within himself.

In the light of day, he followed Senator Smith's Senate Investigation Hearing. Sensationalized in the newspapers, the Inquiry had begun at the Waldorf-Astoria Hotel in Manhattan and was moved the following week to christen the caucus room of the new Russell

Senate Office Building in Washington, D.C. where *Titanic*'s Third Officer, Herbert John Pitman, was interrogated extensively on the fourth day, Tuesday, April 23rd.

Karl read Pitman's testimony, sympathizing with the terrible humiliation Pitman suffered because he was unable to justify his decision not to have jeopardized the lives of his passengers in an attempt to rescue more. Hindsight could only vilify an attempt to rationalize the lack of action. It was morally impossible— *reprehensible* even to try. Karl noticed, however, that Officer Pitman was never given a chance to explain that, at the time, there was only agony in the circumstance of his decision to "raise the oars." *Of course, now he will have to live out the rest of his life, knowing he might have saved someone. That was the cross he would have to bear—the cross that I will have to bear,* Karl thought, alone at his desk where he had been holed up with the weight of the world's opinion pressing in on him.

Due to the accusatory tone of the Senate Hearing, along with a tacit imperative to assess blame, criticisms grew more harsh. Karl perceived himself affiliated with censure and backchat—judgmental, black-and-white gossip: If the men who died were honorable, then the men who lived were scoundrels or frauds by proxy or default.

When Karl entered Herman Behr & Company, he sensed the veiled question: *How did you save yourself when so many perished?* But he always avoided preemptive explanations. Instead, he adopted a profile of inner strength and outward humility, calling upon Sarah's advice when he was a boy: "Hold on tight to your pride no matter what happens." However, the longer inquiries continued in New York, Washington, then in England, the more Karl felt derision swamp him. He stopped being able to sideline his obsession to second-guess the speculation under which he imagined he might be viewed. Solipsism provided asylum, but not comfort. From time to time he received support from his brothers, but they were far too engrossed in their married, working, or private lives to communicate at any great length or depth about ramifications from the tragic event.

With others on the Committee of Seven, Karl worked to raise fifteen thousand dollars as a gift of gratitude to *Carpathia*'s crew, and to procure a silver loving cup to honor the heroism of Captain Rostron. At the time, Karl was unaware that this gift would be a precursor to others—Art Rostrun was recognized most prominently when Senator Smith concluded the Hearings with an emotional summation requesting a joint resolution calling for the coining of a one-thousand-dollar medal to be presented to the Captain of *Carpathia* by the President of the United States.

Karl attended the memorial service for William Stead. It was rumored that Stead dreamed he would die a violent death after being kicked by a crowd. As a writer he was praised for his psychic acumen during a lengthy service for him in New York, where Karl, along with his father and Margaret, absorbed eulogies for a man whose books and prophesies were heralded as marvels and whose work for the poor was praised, along with his pacifism.

On Sunday, April 28th, Karl read this headline in the *New York Times*:

BRAVE MEN MEET DEATH THAT
'WOMEN AND CHILDREN FIRST'
THE CHIVALROUS RULE OF THE SEA MAY BE ENFORCED
ONLY ONE OF ELEVEN HONEYMOON COUPLES WAS SAVED.

Still pondering this fact on the following rainy Monday morning, Karl watched pedestrians stream past the restaurant window where he and Charlie were ensconced, eating lunch. Also preoccupied by his thoughts about the afternoon's work that lay ahead, Karl was taken aback when Charlie said, "Emily and I are finally going to announce our engagement."

"Congratulations! Emily's my favorite of *all* your girlfriends!" Karl kidded. "How did you propose?"

"On one knee in the moonlight, after she'd been most expansively, or I should say, expensively, primed with wine, roses and confessions of my undying affection! I knew she wanted a formal proposal, although we made promises years ago!"

"Even before I went to Mexico. This is great! Wonderful news. Reward for your patience."

"I want you to be my best man, Karl. Are you available?"

"Of course...that is, I'd like to, but you'd be better off without me."

"I need you! Why are you hesitating, or shouldn't I ask."

Karl tried to answer quickly, but was distracted in thought. He reached for the reasons he hadn't lost his integrity—*Helen's hand stretched out to me for help; she was afraid; her mother beckoned for me to come; I needed to please her.* But another voice inside him said: *So many men stood back. What spurious rationale allowed me to climb into that boat to hold my beloved's hand? Will I ever retrieve my lost honor in the calculus of the world?* With his best friend sitting across from him, he blurted out his innermost feelings:

"Charlie, because a shadow of cowardice is going to precede and follow me for the rest of my life no matter how dedicated I am to creating a significant existence. I fall into spells of wracked contemplation and depression, which I struggle to hide even as I grow more grateful that chance favored my preparedness. The *Titanic* catastrophe is the sting of a scorpion. I can hardly function without thinking that I'm a pariah and I feel like that is written all over me. I can't tell you how much I wish I could reclaim that moment, and instead of climbing into a lifeboat, have thrown myself into the water along with the rest of the innocent survivors, as the world sees them."

"But Karl, if you had, more than likely you would not be sitting here telling me about it! Hiding behind a curtain of shame will make everything seem as if you were guilty—especially if you see it that way. You did nothing disgraceful or perfidious compared to men who jumped into boats *knowing* the ship was going down when there were women available to be in their places! You know that. All you have to do is face spurious judgment to the contrary. Blind prejudice abounds. You're learning this for the first time in your life. So far, you've had it easy—always a seat in the loge, right? Or, as our fathers would say, "Glücksfall" (good fortune), almost an embarrassment of riches has followed you all your life. Now you've joined those of us who have a few scars, imperfections, and history. So stop judging yourself the way you fear other people might. Remember how you couldn't willingly disappoint Helen's mother under the circumstance of needing to stay in her good graces! When she told you to come along, it was Hobson's choice. Knowing how afraid Helen was, you were considering her first."

"Was I?"

"Think back. You told me that you considered sending the lifeboats down was only precautionary. What was the last thing you looked at before you stepped over the edge into that boat?"

"Helen's eyes."

"There. You see…it was timing. The timing of *new* love."

"But of all *eleven* honeymoon couples, only *one*…"

"You've read Officer Lightoller's testimony at the hearings, so you know that, on the port side, men were simply not allowed into the lifeboats at all, unless they were sent to row. Lightoller said he thought passenger loading would continue down below. He was unaware that the *Titanic* would sink. The crewmen he sent to meet the lifeboats and continue filling them at the water level never showed up as far as he knew. Something happened to them, but he was too busy loading boats with women and children to find out. He saw lights of another ship nearby (probably the *Californian*) and thought that it must be on the way. He told them to head out to it. You read that too, didn't you?"

"Yes. I saw that ship. It faded away just as Lightoller and Lowe said it did. Charlie, it's a hell of a lot better having your help to hold me up and make sense of this. I realize there's little to be gained from self-recrimination. At least I'll try, but…"

"You do that. No 'buts' needed. Your despondency is helping no one. Maybe you ought to take a look at living for the reason you were saved. Rise to the challenge of whatever that is instead of wishing everything had happened differently. I'm sure as hell glad it didn't!"

As they waited for their lunch check, Karl said, "Charlie, I'd be honored to attend you at your wedding. Hey, did you catch the article on philately in yesterday's *Times*?"

"Missed it," Charlie responded, welcoming the new subject.

"I've just been pondering what to buy you and Emily for a wedding present. How 'bout a little missionary Hawaiian stamp?"

"A rare beauty!"

"According to what I read, a man named George Worthington owns the top collection in America—worth a *million* dollars and attended by a round-the-clock staff."

"Can you imagine owning something so valuable? You'd have to sleep with it in a bank vault. Not cozy! Your turn to pick up the check," Charlie said, grinning and sliding it across the table where it landed close to Karl's hand.

"I'll tell you what's really upsetting me," he continued—"the comments coming out of Germany, lately! The Germans are increasing their armed forces. General Frederich von Bernhardi, one of their most admired writers, says he considers war to be the best expression of civilization. He claims that the United States vies for peace under the guise of moneymaking. I read that Germany is accusing Americans of being globetrotting snobs after their 'questionable' *Titanic* hearings. As a German-American, this concerns me!"

"Quite a number of *Titanic*'s passengers were of Teutonic origin: Astor, Strauss, Guggenheim, and Roebling," Karl said.

"The French are alarmed about the German build-up."

"With good reason. Unprovoked, aggression can rarely be justified," Karl said.

Charlie and Karl bid goodbye to one another and strode out from the restaurant, each atilt against the slapping rain. Despite the cold downpour, Karl was eager to drive his father's Model T. He hopped in, heading for his father's company at Tiffany Place in Brooklyn—back to a familiar stomping ground over Roebling's monumental bridge.

At the company, unrest had whirled up like snow in a windy field since Karl's father had been taken ill. The four elderly directors were avidly vying for power. Karl had been named the fifth director, with voting control for his father. He had recently returned from a trip to Beloit, Wisconsin, where he had established Gardner Machine Company as their exclusive disk sales agent—an achievement that brought him much respect. Now the responsibility fell upon him to quell a rising controversy.

When Karl's father founded the company in 1872, his brother Robert had been his sole original partner. But after their sister Jennie married, Herman's mother Julie (as matriarch of the family) negotiated with Herman for the gift of a small-share partnership to Jennie's husband, Gustav Heubach, who became Secretary and Treasurer. Later, the Works Manager demanded a share. He had done such a fine job in developing and overseeing the factories at Tiffany Place that the partners were beholden to him and acquiesced to his wishes. Meanwhile, Robert, a wealthy confirmed bachelor with lavish tastes, steadily increased his share over time and had become the partner with the largest percentage. As Heubach's treasury assistant, young Herman noted that these aggregate inequities posed a threat to his father's rightful power. So he and Karl, the attorney, masterminded the plan that was about to be set in motion:

Karl parked the Ford, stepped out, and toweled off the seats. Above him, the schizophrenic sky, smudged to a menace earlier, was streaked with dramatic waves of light, *like an inverted watercolor seascape,* he thought. Before him, Herman Behr & Company, a rectangular, flat-roofed, brick and mortar building, filled out the block-front and exuded prominence with its name displayed in bold-black lettering. The Brooklyn branch made Pouncing Paper used to cut felt hats with precision, and Carborundum, an electrical, artificial abrasive composed of silicon and carbon for the shoe and leather trades. The business, comprised of a multifaceted interactive exchange, had gradually expanded across the country to Boston, Chicago, St. Louis, Grand Rapids, San Francisco, and into more than a dozen locations around the world, including eight European countries, New Zealand, and the East Coast of South America. Materials such as emery ore, used for polishing, were imported from Turkey and the Greek Island of Naxos. Pumice arrived from Vesuvius. Chalk flints came from putty manufacturers in England. Quartz was excavated and delivered from various quarries of finest quality. Garnet was garnered in the Adirondacks. The many kinds of abrasives manufactured from these materials were utilized in a nexus of entrepreneurial concerns: piano building, woodworking and furniture making, as well as leather, shoe, and hat businesses.

During the time Karl had become an expert "Maker" at the company, he mastered the essentials of the manufacturing process and compiled his own black book of secret formulas detailing the viscosity of glues and weights of paper for each grade and type of product.

Making his way up the staircase, Karl was hoping to affect a sea-change to insure his father's control. He greeted people kindly as he passed them, but headed on without stopping, sticking to his mission of the moment, which was to locate his cousin Edward Behr, who had been recently hired to create a testing laboratory for products and purchases. Karl needed to ask him one pertinent question.

Karl knew that Ed had previous experience at the Semet-Solvay Company and had been superintendent at American Cyanamid in Niagara Falls, Ontario. Ed was leaning over a table in the corner of the large workroom when Karl spotted him, walked over to him, greeted him, and inquired as to how he was getting along. They chatted until Karl was convinced that his cousin was thoroughly content to be employed at the company.

Without further ado, Karl jumped straight to the point: "Ed, you could run this factory couldn't you?"

"Yes, sure I could. Why?"

"All right, then from this moment on, you're our new Works Manager. Don't worry about Jebediah. He'll be promoted to Vice President with a whole new set of responsibilities, and I'm sure he will assist you if you need advice."

Ed soon caught on. The plan worked. The former Works Manager was pleased to be "promoted." Within the hour, Karl had jumped back into the Ford and was on his way back across the river to the law firm at 40 Wall Street. Mr. Brewster had offered him a partnership in the firm, which he was tempted to take, but while crossing the Brooklyn Bridge, glancing at sunlight gleaming off the river, he decided that he would have to leave McKeen, Brewster and Morgan. Time spent on affairs at Herman Behr & Company was slated to increase, and already his absences from the Brewster firm had compromised his effectiveness as a lawyer.

Titanic dinner menu
April 14, 1912.
(Cover)

R.M.S. "TITANIC."

APRIL 14, 1912.

HORS D'ŒUVRE VARIÉS
OYSTERS

CONSOMMÉ OLGA   CREAM OF BARLEY

SALMON, MOUSSELINE SAUCE, CUCUMBER

FILET MIGNONS LILI
SAUTÉ OF CHICKEN, LYONNAISE
VEGETABLE MARROW FARCIE

LAMB, MINT SAUCE
ROAST DUCKLING, APPLE SAUCE
SIRLOIN OF BEEF, CHATEAU POTATOES

GREEN PEAS   CREAMED CARROTS
BOILED RICE
PARMENTIER & BOILED NEW POTATOES

PUNCH ROMAINE

ROAST SQUAB & CRESS
COLD ASPARAGUS, VINAIGRETTE
PÂTÉ DE FOIE GRAS
CELERY

WALDORF PUDDING
PEACHES IN CHARTREUSE JELLY
CHOCOLATE & VANILLA ECLAIRS
FRENCH ICE CREAM

Titanic dinner menu
April 14, 1912.
(Inside)

THE GOOD SAMARITAN OF THE SEAS.
the Cunard Liner Carpathia, Who Brought
the Survivors Here.

Cruise ship *Carpathia* came to the rescue of *Titanic* survivors.

Titanic lifeboat and survivors
being brought aboard *Carpathia*.

k Times.

Showers and warmer to-day; showers to-morrow, cooler at night; moderate winds.
☞For full weather report see Page 17.

ITEEN PAGES.   ONE CENT   In Greater New York, | Elsewhere, Jersey City, and Newark. | TWO CENTS.

NEW LINER TITANIC HITS AN ICEBERG;
SINKING BY THE BOW AT MIDNIGHT;
WOMEN PUT OFF IN LIFE BOATS;
LAST WIRELESS AT 12:27 A. M. BLURRED

LATEST NEWS FROM THE SINKING SHIP.

CAPE RACE, N. F., Sunday night, April 14.—At 10:25 o'clock to-night the White Star line steamship Titanic called " C. Q. D." to the Marconi wireless station here, and reported having struck an iceberg. The steamer said that immediate assistance was required.

Half an hour afterward another message came reporting that they 're sinking by the head and that women were being put off in the oats.

he weather was calm and clear, the Titanic's wireless operator orted, and gave the position of the vessel as 41.46 north latitude and 50.14 west longitude.

The Marconi station at Cape Race notified the Allan liner Virginian, the captain of which immediately advised that he was proceeding for the scene of the disaster.

The Virginian at midnight was about 170 miles distant from the Titanic and expected to reach that vessel about 10 A. M. Monday.

2 A. M., Monday.—The Olympic at an early hour this, Monday, morning, in latitude 40.32 north and longitude 61.18 west. She was in dir communication with the Titanic, and is now making all haste tow a her.

The steamship Baltic also reported herself as about 200 miles east of the Titanic, and was making all possible sped toward her.

The last signals from the Titanic were heard by the Virginian at 12:27 A. M.

The wireless operator on the Virginian says these signals were blurred and ended abruptly.

Allan Liner Virginian Now Speeding Toward the Big Ship.

BALTIC TO THE RESCUE, TOO

The Olympic Also Rushing To Give Aid—Other Ships Within Call.

CARMANIA DODGED BERGS

Reports French Liner Niagara Injured and Several Ships Caught.

BIG TITANIC'S FIRST TRIP

Bringing Many Prominent Americans, and Was Due in New York To-morrow.

MISHAP AT VERY START

Narrowly Escaped Collision with the American Liner New York When Leaving Port.

Special in The New York Times.

HALIFAX, N. S., April 14.—A wireless dispatch received to-night by the Allan line officials here from Capt. Gambell of the steamer Virginian, states that the White Star liner Titanic stru an iceberg off the Newfoundland Coast t flashed out wireless calls for immedia. as ance.

The Virginian put on full spee headed for the Titanic.

No particulars have been receiv to the extent of the damage sustained

WHITE STAR LINER TITANIC.
Steamship in the World, Which Has Hit an Iceberg on Her First Voyage Here.

Titanic survivors in "collapsible" type lifeboat.

Helen Newsom, kneeling, aboard *Carpathia*.

Sallie Beckwith talking to Mr. and Mrs. George Harder
aboard *Carpathia*.

Titanic survivors aboard *Carpathia*.

Captain Arthur Rostron of the *Carpathia* and a letter from him to Karl Behr.

36

Owl-speak

"**W**HERE ARE YOU NOW?" Helen asks.

"In New York," Karl answers, trying to sit taller in his bed.

"Yes. No. I mean, where in the writing of your memoir?"

"Rewriting the day I opted to quit the firm. I needed to get to the point faster then, just as I do now."

"Oh, that was a tough decision. I remember when you told me that Mr. Brewster was disappointed, and so were you, after all your commitment to learning Law. You anticipated needing to help Ed run the company, as I recall, but he was masterful. You told me he memorized names and discharged duties, numbers, and details as fast as Roosevelt. And he never came to you with a *single* problem. Did he?"

"No. Not until much later. His efficiency allowed me time to pursue all my other interests, right up until the office cabal of 1918. But I'll never write about that. It's far too complicated."

"Having Ed as Manager gave you time to keep playing tennis. Best of all, time for us to be at Squam Lake, heavenly Squam."

Helen sees that Karl's vulnerability is returning. It reminds her of the ways he tried to hide his despondency after the *Titanic* tragedy when she and Charlie had been his mainstays. She knew how the sentiment BETTER DEATH THAN DISHONOR—printed boldly, assertively, ubiquitously—had affected him. So many prominent men died in a shocking, pitiful confluence of misjudgment. Writers had pained to compose eulogies. Since Karl lived in the shadow of his decision to accompany Helen in the lifeboat, she assumed her mission to bolster his self-esteem, rarely missing a chance to remind him that he had not compromised his integrity.

She knows now that she had been unaware of the gradual ebbing of his attention from her. Yearning for his company had taken hold, even as she encouraged his zealous pursuits. She ignored his abandonment of her until, bewildered, she realized how many nights she had lain alone under the drone of wind whirring invisible forces.

By the window Helen settles under a blanket with her feet tucked underneath her in her favorite calico rose-covered chair. She is sustained by the comfort of remaining daylight. She stares entranced, thinking of the night Karl proposed to her:

Flush as a harvest moon, a sense of ease had buoyed that summer evening of 1912 on the banks of Squam Lake at the house directly uphill from Sandwich Beach. Bud's banter had been so relentlessly amusing throughout the evening's dinner with their parents that Karl nearly slid off his chair seat more than once and had matched Bud's wit with his own.

Afterward, Helen and Karl leaned on the balustrade of the verandah, listening to the cicadas and bullfrogs. They decided to stroll down to the lake. As if polished and placed under klieg light on black velvet, crystalline stars complemented the night-music as Karl and Helen descended the veranda steps and meandered past a round reflecting pool at the far edge of the topiary garden. Gliding, as though on wings rather than feet, they slipped through shadows, striations, dark silhouettes.

In synch with rhythms of the unseen, Karl thought as he imagined indefinite shapes and eyes peering from somewhere inside them. He felt propelled by the soul of nature, until he stood still at the edge of the lake. In the water a half-moon was reflected. Then an owl's plangent *hoo–hoo* elicited the echo of another's distant response, as though the mystical ululation had emerged through hollow reeds from the darkest reaches of the lake to be limned in the throats of two sentinel birds.

Karl took hold of Helen's hand, leading her to sit with him on their favorite curved stone bench. Flecks of quartz glistened around her. He lifted her hand to his lips. The words coalesced: "Helen, I don't think we could be a better match for each other." He lowered himself onto one knee, still holding her hand, "As a matter of fact, there will never be anyone else for me. I love you with constancy and with all the passion of my heart. I want you to be my wife. Will you...will you marry me?" His voice trembled then, but he was smiling.

Moonlight reflected on the small seas in his eyes, over the receptive tilt of his head and the soul that surrounded him. Helen lowered her chin, peered at him, and quietly asked, "Would I have to watch you play in more hockey games?"

Karl laughed. The slope of his brows exaggerated. Pebbles sharpened under his knee. "No," he said emphatically.

"In that case, I think...I'll say...*Yes!*"

"Where did you go just then?" Karl asks.

"To Squam, with two loons and a squinting moon."

"You finally accepted my proposal there!"

"I remember how happy your father was. Can't think of another time I ever saw him so exuberant!" Helen said, surprised that Karl had guessed what she'd been thinking about and pleased that he seemed to be feeling better.

"I can't either. Not even later when he married Hedda, long after mother died. Hedda was a wonderful support, great fun. But he lit up brightest when you were in his company, it seemed to me."

"It was mutual affection," Helen admits.

"Did I ever mention that my father admired you for refusing me that night on the *Titanic*?"

"No."

"He did. He wasn't nearly as upset when I told him about losing the ring as I thought he would be. He was most impressed by the fact that you put your mother's feelings first."

That night of their engagement, Helen and Karl had raced back up to the house. They found Bud and Helen's parents in the living room. Karl took Dick and Sallie aside to ask them for permission for Helen's hand in marriage. Permission was granted. The engagement became tacitly official, along with Bud's smattering of sarcasm to amuse them.

Helen was relieved and elated when her mother said, "We're thrilled. You two are…what can I say…made for each other? Oh that sounds too simple. Well, maybe so! Simple and right."

Later, as Helen and Karl started to plan, they heeded Sallie's advice that "it would be best to delay before announcing this in any formal sense. Let's not print it in the paper until a month or so before your wedding. And let that be well into the future. *Titanic* news is still raw and this will rekindle it."

Helen uncurls her legs. "We waited ten months after the tragedy before announcing our engagement—with all the ongoing inquiries and sadness."

"Yes. I still cringe when I think of those articles about us even though we'd been patient—how embarrassing it was: *"Love Blooms from Disaster"*; *"They Found Their Love in a* Titanic *Lifeboat"*— illustrations of two oblivious lovers, kissing while the ship sinks in the background—calling me *hero…*"

"You were a hero, Karl."

"I never saw myself that way."

"Nevertheless, you did provide the crucial impetus for our survival. I hope you give yourself credit for it in your memoir!"

"I will; for you—for *us*. People enjoyed the image of our romance didn't they! But, for me, it was worse than embarrassing to be splattered in the papers that way—it made me out to be oblivious; crass, brash, insensitive as an egotistical kook."

"Reporters had been scrounging for a bright light to shine against the misery. If they'd known what it was really like out there—powerless to stop the Armageddon…"

"Well, they certainly pinned us under their melodramatic and mortifying spotlight. I recall the quote they invented: *"'He asked if he might row through life with her, and she replied, I'd go through all eternity with you!'"*

"You might have said that, mightn't you, dear?"

"Well, here we are, my darling. I'm still rowing am I not?"

"With a *little* help."

Charlie and Emily were married first. Their intimate ceremony took place on an early December evening, steeped in candlelight and music. They traveled south for their honeymoon and returned to live in New York City.

Following their lead, Karl and Helen were married at three o'clock in the afternoon of March 1st, 1913, at the Church of the Transfiguration in New York City, which was transformed into a tropical garden filled with potted palms and redolence of Easter lilies. Karl was attended by a self-described "modest" group of eleven ushers, inclusive of his brothers, while Helen had just two bridesmaids, her friend Bee Cook and Karl's sister Gertrude.

After a reception at the Beckwith's Riverside Drive apartment, Karl and Helen headed to see as much of the Wild West as they could. Upon their return, Karl unpacked a keepsake pile of postcards that he had gathered from every hotel they stayed in, pasting each into his scrapbook, complete with arrows drawn to every room they had christened.

On Karl's twenty-eighth birthday, the night of May 30th, he jumped into bed, yanked the covers up under his chin, aiming a ridiculous grin at Helen to gloat that he'd won their undeclared race into bed. She calmly joined him and reached over to turn out the light. Karl felt a lump under his pillow.

"There's something…" he mumbled, flipping the pillow up and switching on the light to find a small wrapped object.

"What's this?" he asked.

"One last little present," Helen said.

Karl opened the package.

"Baby powder?"

"Happy Birthday!" Helen grinned. "We're going to need it!"

Karl junior was born at the stroke of midnight, Christmas eve. Given her choice of birthdays, Helen registered his as December 24th, 1913.

Raising himself in his bed and lifting the papers in his lap to transfer them to the table next to him, Karl says, "Right, back to my quitting the law. There was one surprise windfall from my brief practice. Do you recall an incident having to do with wallpaper?"

"Oh, I do!" Helen says, "On the day I was about to purchase paper at Griffin's. I was giving the grinning salesman my name, when Mr. Griffin walked by and asked, "Did you say you are Mrs. Karl Behr?" As soon as I admitted the crime, he introduced himself, praising you in a barrage of aphorisms and declared to the salesman: "From now on there will be no charge on any goods ordered by Mrs. Behr in this store!" Although I should have been thrilled, I suddenly realized that I might have to stop shopping there if my "purchases" would no longer benefit the business."

"I remember that paper. Scenic, wasn't it?"

"Shepherds in a meadow with trees and sheep."

"Perfect for counting before sleep."

"I bet you don't remember it a t'all!"

"Well, what I remember most about our bedroom—is you. You know, darling, what I regret now is any and all of the time I missed being with you. I was always off on my latest, greatest, or worst new tangent, trying to prove myself to the world, wasn't I?"

"There was never a dull moment."

"But the wonder is how you raised our children without me. I was hardly ever home to lend a hand."

"You had things to do. I knew that. I saw you as vital and I was proud of you for setting an example for our boys to be independent and ambitious; to find and listen to a calling. Compared to my father's family (he was the ninth of Junius Newsom's eleven children) having four didn't seem so many to me. It was all my dogs that tipped the scale with their constant craving for excitement, and food!

"It was lucky."

"What was?"

"*I* was lucky, because you were there to catch me when I fell," Karl said, pressing his lips together.

Helen listens. Outside, she hears the rush of the imperative world. A horn honks down on the street. Someone cries out. Karl's words have brought him back to her. Now she realizes that what he always needed to help him understand the reason he had entered the lifeboat with her was something she could never revive—the intensity of his love for her at that particular moment in time:

She sees herself as she was—standing in the stern of the lifeboat, watching questions rise into Karl's face as he stays on deck— his expression changes while he weighs his decision whether or not to join her—she sees conscience give pause to action. She remembers how she had reached out, looking at him from her place there, willing him to be with her. She pictures the way he returned her look of desire with a craving of his own—at the zenith of passion, with superlative longing—as if he had scaled a mountain peak and was about to drink in the view.

37

Tennis

*O*N THE RUN TO PRACTICE FOR up-coming matches, Karl shuffled by, side-stepping and pointing to the patch of shade where his baby son was ensconced in a pram, fast asleep. "Sonny will be fine there!" he said. Everything was 'Sonny this; Sonny that.' Helen lived for this—having both her baby boy and her husband around her.

Karl's tennis game had been semi-dormant for some time. It was 1914 and he was eager for the challenge again. He worked with vigor—honing his skills, to measure up to the high standards that marriage and fatherhood rekindled in him. He was able to lose himself in concentration during his practices, increasing pace and stamina. The vision in his once-injured eye had deteriorated; however by wearing glasses, he had managed to raise the level of his game—to climb out of slumps—even sometimes exceeding his greatest expectations.

During the Middle States Championship against the champion, Gustave F. Touchard, Karl took the first two sets and lost the third. Then there was a fifteen-minute break. From the stands, Helen watched Karl guzzle oatmeal water while Touchard smoked a cigarette. The first game of the fourth set went to deuce. Karl won that game and charged through the next four without losing a single point. Touchard took the next two games brilliantly and seemed poised for a comeback. But to everyone's surprise, Karl secured the final set and match with a sizzling service ace.

At another match at the Orange Lawn Tennis Club in Mountain Station, New Jersey, fifteen hundred spectators gathered to watch a singles exhibition between Karl and his doubles partner Theodore Roosevelt Pell, holder of the Achelis Challenge Cup. The turf was soft and the sky's belly hung low as a waterlogged tent. But during the first set, sunshine broke from the clouds to spotlight Karl and Teddy as they teetered on a seesaw of wins and losses. After securing the first set, 8–6, Karl prevailed to take the next lengthy second set, 10–8. Pell then won the third, 8–6, and the fourth, 6–3. Karl seemed exhausted.

In the stands, Helen, Gertrude, and Charlie Engle's sister Charlotte had successfully set aside their quotidian obligations to come and support Karl. The women were also anticipating a late afternoon doubles match with Karl and Ted teamed together as doubles partners. Referred to as the Teddy-Behr team, the pair had been enjoying a long winning streak. Seeing them play against one another in the morning was an unexpected bonus.

Head in hand, elbow to knee, Helen leaned forward, attempting to detect Karl's state of mind over a sea of straw hats. Although he seemed ready to toss in the towel, she hoped not. Her thoughts strayed back to their previous night together when Karl had made love to her in the shadows of their bedroom, but afterward confessed that his self-doubt was unrelenting. Lying content, her head on his shoulder, her leg draped up over his, Helen had drawn the tip of her index finger through her favorite small dip in the center of his chest and whispered, "I love you the way you are."

Helen's attention turned to Charlotte. Posed like a butterfly at the edge of a leaf, Charlotte's delicate hand had emerged from a limp lace-rimmed sleeve to brush across her forehead. Never overly conversant, Charlotte was content to defer the chatter to anyone in her company who enjoyed it more than she did. "I'll be surprised if he can pull this out, won't you, Helen?"

Thinking Charlotte's diffidence endearing, Helen agreed: "He does appear depleted," she said, lifting her hat for air.

Gertie, who never missed a peep because she was endowed with invisible antennae, spoke abruptly, "Nonsense you two pessimists! Karl's a Gemini with a duck-soup chance of winning! He's hiding the evidence to fool his opponent and conserve energy. That's all!"

Everyone's best friend and harshest critic, Gert was always good at excavating layers for the gem-stars underneath. Occasionally, however, she spoke duplicitously without being aware of it—possibly to hide her insecurities.

"I have seen him come back from huge deficits before," Helen said in support of Gertie's prediction. But pressure on the thumbnail she was gnawing belied this assertion. She waggled her foot and pulled her shoulders back, perusing the crowd.

To the great surprise of many who shared a hunch that the match was all but over, Karl came out blazing: His glasses reflected sunlight like two merit badges. His racquet swung in graceful arcs from mid-court to baseline, to net, to sideline, and back to net again as he lunged and leaped in his black sneakers, white trousers, long-sleeved white shirt and bright white headband. Spectators who thought that Ted Pell was saving himself for a spectacular whirlwind finish were stunned. After Pell won the opening game on his serve, it was Karl who provided the whirlwind—he finished off the set, 6–1.

Once the victory presentation was over, Karl walked over to the stands, cupped his hands, and called up to Helen: "All for you, my darling!"

Helen said to Gertie, "You were right! How did you know? That was similar to his match against Fred Inman when it seemed like he was going to lose, but he won the first set, lost the second, changed racquets and scooped up the third—six games in a row!"

There was another notable match—in a semifinal round at Seabright on August 1st, 1914, between Karl and his friend Dick Williams. They had seen one another several times since the *Titanic* tragedy. Neither performed particularly skillfully during the first set. Karl's game was weak; he lost, 2–6. But he strode out on the court with a new strategy and swept the second set a dustless 6–0.

Thunder rumbled. Both players rushed their shots during the third set. Williams raised his level of play and took five out of six games. He cleverly concealed his shots by hitting cross-court winners after aiming down the line, which effectively fooled Karl over and over. At 5–1, the green-angry sky burst. Play was suspended, with everyone soaked.

The following morning, Karl started serving from this nearly impossible deficit. Few in the gallery thought he had a whisker of a chance, but he played as if possessed and brought the score to 5-all. Then Williams rose up scorching like the miraculous phoenix that he was, and took the next two games to win.

In the locker room after the match, Dick said, "Well, y'old coot. That's what you get for beating me at our other battle!" He was referring to an important decision that had just been reached about the national championships: With help from Julian S. Myrick, president of the West Side Tennis Club, Karl had spearheaded an effort to move the national championships (known as the All-Comers tournament then, and later as the US Open) from Newport, where it had taken place for thirty-four years, to Forest Hills, in 1915.

Dick, the rising star, had entered the key meeting dripping in garlands of applause. He was a Harvard man, and he bitterly opposed moving the championships away from Newport, primarily on the basis of sentiment. The argument he put forth, during what became the longest and liveliest meeting the United States National Lawn Tennis Association had ever seen (ending at one a.m. the morning of February 6th), included the detail that "it was terribly windy at the courts in New York" when he had played there.

Conversely, Karl stressed the point that tennis would benefit if a greater number of people could share in it where excitement for the game would be fueled in a more easily accessible place with better facilities and accommodations in the surrounding area. The fact that Davis Cup matches had previously been successfully staged at the West Side courts helped to support his argument.

Karl's advocacy for change won by a few slim votes: 129 for New York to 119 for Newport. He was hailed by New York as "Man of the Hour."

Later, at the annual Longwood singles championship, the two *Titanic* survivors played each other again in the finals. At the time, Dick Williams ranked second in the country and was well on the road to a superior career record to Karl's. Dick had come to Boston from Philadelphia heralded as the season's sensation, having completed an impressive unbroken string of victories.

From the stands, Helen and Gertie watched, not expecting to see Karl win a single game. Helen's heart sank—into a proverbial mass of mixed metaphors as she watched Williams streak through the first set like a hound on the scent of a fox. Karl stood marveling at his opponent's speed and agility while the shots flew by. Every attempt Karl made to win a return or to place a drive went long, slapped the tape, or flopped into the net like a helpless fluke. In one fell swoop, Williams had caught the fox and fished out the sea with a first set haul—a bountiful 6–0. Then, after 16 games of sensational rallies, Karl lost the second set, 7–9.

In the middle of a short break he squinted up into the stands to find Helen. When he spotted her, he thought he saw her move her hand subtly forward—a message he interpreted as *rush the net*. When play resumed, he tried this and it began to work in his favor. Regaining his bearings, he was able to revive the net game that had been his strength seven years prior. He ran through the third set, 6–2, then rolled on to take the fourth, 6–1.

Dick was winning, 4–3, in the fifth and coming up to serve. This time, Karl looked at Helen and saw her simply smile. He strode out onto the grass, gazed at the morning-glory sky, and broke William's serve on his way to winning the last set, 6-4. Helen was overjoyed when she heard a spectator say, "That was the greatest lawn tennis battle I've seen here in twenty-two years!"

Karl's roller-coaster tennis dipped into a depression of controversy when he was named a member of the 1914 Davis Cup team, but did not participate.

In Chicago, where he had gone to play a doubles match with Ted Pell, he awaited a telegram calling him back to New York for the matches. He was aching to play his old rivals—the familiar Australasian team of Brookes and Wilding. But no telegram arrived because the Cup Committee ultimately decided that the number one ranked player, Maurice "The Comet" McLoughlin, from California, would play with his usual doubles partner and great friend, Tom Bundy. McLoughlin and Williams (ranked #2) were slated to play the challenge singles matches.

Writers of New York tennis news regaled their audience with wild exaggerations of a great struggle that was going on for third place on the team. They said the Cup Committee was being pressed at the throat by McLoughlin's preference to play with Bundy, although the Committee had favored Karl, the third ranked player. Behind the printed lines, however, there had been no rancor. The players did not verbalize dissatisfaction with the committee's decision.

Australasia won the Davis Cup.

38

Taylor's Parade

CHARLIE'S CONCERN ABOUT THE MILITARY buildup in Germany proved prophetic. Every day during August of 1914 Karl could read multiple examples of German aggression on a single page of the *New York Times*. Then, on August 21st, the Imperial German Army marched through Brussels, leaving in its wake an inconceivable nightmare of violence. Belgians were starving to death. It was reported that some were forced to eat their dogs.

On the Saturday following May 7th, 1915, when the *Lusitania*, secretly carrying ammunition and explosives, was sunk by German submarine torpedoes, killing 1,198, including 128 American men, women, and children, Karl and Helen were walking in Central Park with Sonny to take in the early Spring. Their second son, Peter, remained at the apartment with the new nurse. As prearranged, they met Charlie, Emily, and their three-month-old daughter Isabel near the Reservoir. Within a short time, discourse between Charlie and Karl had grown inextricable.

"I know Karl," Charlie said. "We should be ready to defend ourselves. But that doesn't mean we're obligated to scuttle off to Europe to be killed or blown to hell by the leviathan juggernaut. You know, Karl, those tools of the Reichstag have embraced a military life since infancy. We have not."

"But if we don't adopt the state of mind that we might have to fight, it is conceivable that we could lose this country! Charlie, when Helen and I were in Pasadena visiting Senator Booth and I read Homer Lea's book, *The Valor of Ignorance*, I realized that his warnings concerning military inertia, published way back in 1909, were chilling! The danger posed by Germany, now, is potentially disastrous. If we turn a blind eye to this, we could be destroyed faster than we would ever anticipate. I'll give you the book. It backs up how I've felt since Yale days. I agree with Roosevelt so strongly I can taste the metal in it!" Karl looked into space, thinking, then added, "But you and I are of the same mind. We're Squadron A! No tin soldiers in *our* National Guard—especially not you, Charlie; you've already been shot!"

"Precisely my point. I'm done. Being prepared is one thing; but don't suppose I'd jump into a blood bath. I've taken my lickin' as you pointed out, and that's enough. I'm a family man now. I know who really needs me." Charlie smiled over in the direction of Emily where she was chatting with Helen.

Looking at Helen standing in the tranquil setting of Olmsted's magnificent park, Karl felt his need to protect her. A siren sounded a series of alarms on Fifth Avenue. A cardinal flashed through Karl's peripheral vision. He blinked, threw his head back, took off his glasses and rubbed his eyes. What he wished for—to be a pacifist in simpatico with his father, his brothers, and now Charlie—was no more possible than quitting a tennis match if he simply didn't feel like playing any longer. Underneath the instinct to enjoy his life, a seed of desperation was swelling to crack open despite his inability to comprehend it. What he knew, without a doubt, was that he would rather fight an enemy on soil overseas than face a threat to his loved ones at home.

Like Charlie, other close friends were disinclined toward involvement in Europe. They seemed glad to have Wilson in the White House. "It's Europe's war and we should keep the hell out of the mess," they argued. Coming from his once confrontational brother, this sentiment might have surprised Karl, but it didn't. Fritz was a dedicated father, enjoying the comforts of a fine life.

Max too, sounded skeptical. "Karl, are you advocating sending troops to Europe?" he asked.

"It looks to me like we're going to have to go," Karl said with forced resonance.

The family member in closest simpatico with Karl was Gertrude. "You're right, Karl. *Absolutely* right," she said. "There's no question in my mind that we'll have to sacrifice to keep our freedom. We're going to have to go to Europe and fight. There's no other way. I'm planning to be as active as I can—I just don't know how yet."

Gertrude found her means on the day Elihu Root sounded his slogan of preparedness at the New York Chapter of the Red Cross at Helen (Whitelaw) Reid's home at 451 Madison Avenue. She was encouraged by his words, which were printed in the *New York Times*: *"The American has been too prone to inquire not what can I do for my country, but what can I get out of it? It is time to consider what service we can perform in return for the liberty, the peace we enjoy."* Gertie signed up to become an active member of the Red Cross.

Dissension over allegiance caused a rift between Karl and his father, who continued to believe in Germany. Avoidance to confront their differences was a chasm unto itself. During their occasional games of chess, pieces removed from the board were no longer set aside with defiant clicks that might spark a discussion concerning conflict abroad. While America's relationship with Herman's beloved country had grown more and more adversarial, Karl's father made every effort to keep a calm vigil, but Karl knew his father's heart was breaking. Even though Germans corroborated stories of inhumanity and wanton destruction, Herman thought that the reports were scurrilous fabrications set to intimidate and therefore deter rebellion against the takeover. Although Karl's father had sent him off to the Davis Cup matches proud of his "American" boy, Karl was aware that the tables had turned on this magnanimity in regard to patriotic affiliations. Herman harbored a deep sentimental affection for the fatherland and he believed the hostilities would pass.

On the other hand, Karl's activities during that year of 1915, began to boil. He signed up to become an active member of the National Security League.

After a few months, Karl was elected the youngest member of the League's Executive Committee, and by year's end he was Chairman of the Campaign Committee.

On Wednesdays he lunched in a private room at the Bankers Club with several members, including former Secretary of State Robert Bacon, Henry Stimson, who would become Secretary of War, Frederick Coudert, Lawrence Abbott, Franklin Q. Brown, E. H. Clark, S. Stanwood Menken, Henry Wise Wood, former President Roosevelt, and George W. Pepper. Representatives of the British and French Armies, and members of the Military Affairs Committees of the House and Senate also attended from time to time.

The League advocated universal training as well as preparedness. Promoted through publicity, it had a substantially funded office force with branches and committees spread across the country, which attempted to arouse public opinion and awareness of the need for ready defense and the increased likelihood of being drawn into the war.

Karl considered the ability to appeal to a wider audience a necessity to raise money and support the League, so he spoke at numerous mass meetings that were staged in New York and in many other cities. During January of 1916 he received permission from the League Executive Committee to rent Carnegie Hall and the Century Opera House for a single night of meetings.

Promising to fill each meeting simultaneously with speakers who would draw interest, he secured Theodore Roosevelt, General Leonard Wood, and Senator Borah among others, for the task of engendering enthusiasm for preparedness. By sending a letter to each speaker, stressing the necessity of adhering to a time limit (a soft buzzer was set to sound a one-minute warning at each rostrum), Karl coordinated the timing of the meetings. He took control of the Century Opera House where "Colonel" Roosevelt (as Karl still preferred to call him), the last speaker of the evening, received an ovation so exuberant it bordered on hysteria. Meanwhile, Karl's friend, Guy

Emerson, monitored the meeting at Carnegie Hall where General Wood spoke last, capped by a commensurate burst of enthusiasm.

The intense campaign inspired such well-attended events that crowds of people were left on the street unable to get inside the doors.

While organizing a tennis exhibition match to raise money for the Red Cross, Karl received a phone call from Roosevelt's secretary, asking him to come to his office at four o'clock. When Karl entered Roosevelt's office at the Metropolitan Magazine, he immediately noticed the writer, Julian Street, sitting at a desk correcting a long printer's proof sheet with blue pencil. Then he spotted Robert Bacon hunched over what appeared to be the same document. When the Colonel bounded through the door, he handed Karl a third copy of this lengthy article that he had written to dissuade German-Americans from their passivity, assuming Karl had plenty of time to read it.

"Make any suggestions you think would be helpful, Karl," he noted and then left the room.

Without a word, Karl took it in hand and settled into a corner of the office to study along with the others.

Roosevelt's essay began with effusive praise for the fine service many Germans had performed for America—from Von Steuben in the Revolution to Carl Schurz in the Civil War. Then it condemned pacifist German-American attitudes against involvement in the current conflict in Europe, including an organization with many influential members called The Society of Friends of Peace that had spread pro-German propaganda across America. It also criticized the National German-American Alliance, which was promoting neutrality.

Karl read through Colonel Roosevelt's article, but did not make any notes on the proof.

Roosevelt returned, took Julian Street's marked copy in hand, and received verbal compliments from Mr. Bacon. Then he turned to Karl.

"It's much too long to begin with," Karl said, tapping his fingers and toes, searching for the right words. He considered how his father would have wanted him to hold his tongue, but said, "This will never gain front page coverage. If you want to deliver such a message I think you should do it in person—tell the German-Americans what you think in their own bailiwick. Your friends, Colonel, would expect you to go to these people and confront them face-to-face to convince them that their fidelity to the principle of freedom is central to the issue of honor and probity at hand. A speech in Cincinnati or Milwaukee would be first-page material all over the country."

Roosevelt hesitated for a moment. Then he shouted to his secretary, "Find out what Saturdays I have free. I'm going west to tell these people what I think, as Mr. Behr suggests!"

Roosevelt's subsequent speeches reverberated throughout the country. Afterward, from time to time, he continued to consult Karl, lunching with him at the Harvard Club when he apparently wanted a younger viewpoint on something.

During the first week of March 1916, Karl had received a visit from a gentleman named Lloyd Taylor, a retired New York Stock Exchange broker eager for the National Security League to organize a non-partisan parade in New York to stimulate interest in preparedness and arouse Congress. The executive Secretary of the League had told Mr. Taylor that the League itself was unable to organize any such affair, but to call on Karl Behr for assistance. Karl answered his pleading with a quick rebuff: "I'm sorry, Mr. Taylor, but I have no knowledge of how to run a parade and I'm much too involved in my outside business activities to take on anything more."

Lloyd Taylor rose up. His face twisted into a ganglion of fury and he bellowed, "I have seen at least a dozen men now, *prominent* men. And they are all too *busy!* Where, in heaven's name, are the *patriots?*" He stormed out of the office.

Two days later he was back, pleading: "Can you just imagine the effect on the country of a large non-partisan demonstration?"

Karl began to think about the strength of this—the vision of its power and persuasive energy—so he discussed it with some of his friends.

A few days passed. Mr. Taylor called on Karl a third time. "I'm coming in here and I'm going to stay until you agree to organize this parade!" he said, dropping into the chair with the everlasting heft of a pharaoh's tomb.

By this time, a grand picture of Taylor's parade had been playing over and over in Karl's mind. Just the night prior, Karl dreamed of the pageantry of thousands of men marching for this vital cause. As if the words were being channeled through another being's throat, he heard himself say, with uncharacteristic softness, "Mr. Taylor, I have changed my mind. We will have a parade!"

Lloyd Taylor leapt to his feet. His eyes filled with tears. He had finally succeeded in instigating the preparedness parade through his dogged devotion to the idea of it. "What can I do to help?" he asked, wiping his face with his sleeves.

"Bring all the friends you can muster to the Meeting Room of the Merchants Association in the Woolworth Building at four o'clock on the afternoon of March 13th. I'll bring mine. And we'll take it from there," Karl said.

At the first meeting, Lloyd brought three friends: George S. Brown, S. W. Fairchild, and Roger W. Allen. Karl gathered more than a dozen, among them James Barnes. At this first meeting they passed various resolutions, which a lawyer friend of Karl's had prepared. Among these was the specific declaration: *This parade is proposed for the purpose of calling attention to the wishes of the people of the United States that this country be adequately prepared for defense against attack from any quarter, and to urge upon Congress more adequate defense legislation.*

Karl hired the Large Room on the 18th floor of the Yale Club where the committee that convened each week grew from two dozen to two hundred men. New businesses were enlisted and numbers of marchers tallied. Karl handled the meetings, spoke at trade lunches, enlisted twenty trades, and secured the promise of Charles Sherrill to act as Grand Marshal, which he agreed to do if Karl could guarantee sixty-thousand participants.

This done, on the day before the parade, forty thousand more had to be refused due to a lack of available time to march everyone.

Aside from his efforts to insure the grandeur of the event, nothing seemed more imperative to Karl than to break the impasse between him and his father. At their customary breakfast meeting, Karl spoke passionately about this effort to influence Americans—its primary emphasis being on defense. Herman appreciated how crucial success of the parade would be for his son, but he could not subdue his angst and his pacifism. He refused to participate, explaining that to do so would be unconscionable. It would be "untreu" (unfaithful) he said, for him to appear as though he were taking a stand against his beloved Germany.

Consequently, although Karl had been invited to accompany Sherrill at the head of the parade and sit on the reviewing stand, he declined. Instead, he arranged for Squadron A to furnish more than a hundred mounted aides—one or more to serve as escorts for each trade. With this in place, he planned to ride as the Squadron A escort for his father's business.

To date, the Germans had torpedoed and sunk fifty-nine ships without warning between May 1915 and May 1916. On the morning of May 13th, 1916, less than a week after the first anniversary of the sinking of the *Lusitania*, the Preparedness Parade was set to begin. More than one hundred and forty thousand people from all walks of life converged to march. Representatives of cotton, rubber, lighting, fur, candy, oil, leather, lumber, and automobile industries. Teachers, doctors, lawyers, architects, and clergy were included. There were two hundred bands and fifty drum corps.

A sixty-four page official program could be procured for 15 cents. (More than a dozen counterfeit programs appeared.) The Independent Patriotic Women's Division formed the rear guard, with Mrs. Theodore Roosevelt as one of the Captains. Along with Grand

Marshal Colonel Charles H. Sherrill, other reviewing officers on the grandstand included Mayor Mitchel, General Leonard Wood, and Rear Admiral Nathaniel R. Usher.

Helen participated in an effort to decorate nearly every building with American flags. She stood waiting at a wagon that distributed flags to school children at Madison and 57th Street. Between the St. Regis and the Gotham Hotel on 5th Avenue, the largest American flag in the country had been unfurled and hoisted into place. Over the roof of the Ritz Carlton, hundreds of red, white, and blue electric lights were strung. A spotlight featured another giant flag displayed from the 46th street side of the hotel.

Early in the morning, Karl arrived at the Hall of Records where horses, gathered for the Squadron A aids, were lined up from City Hall to the Battery. He was astonished to discover that the horse set aside for him was a prize Arabian stallion—Champion of the Charger Class in the previous New York and London horse shows. A Mr. Borden, who had recently imported grand Arabian horses for stud purposes, had requested that Major Bridgeman have a Squadron A member ride this beautiful white specimen so that people could have the opportunity to see him. Major Bridgeman requested Karl for that honor.

Apprehensive to ride a high-strung horse amidst blaring instruments and wild excitement, Karl reached up to stroke the stallion's neck, getting a sense of his temperament. The groom, seeing Karl's reticence, said, "Don't worry. He's a nervous one, but you'll never have trouble controlling him, and he's been shod with rubber pads so he won't slip."

Karl secured his foot in the stirrup, swung himself onto the saddle, and rode directly toward a practicing band, happy to find that Mr. Borden's groom was right—the magnificent horse was fully responsive.

All the way from Fulton Street to Central Park the regal equine pranced from one side of the street to the other as people ran up to photograph him and Karl, posing proud by association.

Twelve thousand marchers passed the reviewing stand every hour. Lloyd Taylor's vision was executed to full effect. By the time the parade ended, at around ten in the evening, beams of light had crisscrossed salutations to the defense of freedom, and a river of impassioned people had roared through the chiseled gray banks of New York.

Once the last line of the final column passed the reviewing stand, a field gun, which had trailed the entire procession since daybreak, was wheeled up and fired. When asked to state his opinion of the parade, Admiral Usher shook his head solemnly, repeating, "The best ever, the best ever—that's all there is to say about it."

En route to his father's apartment that night, tired and satisfied, Karl thought of his father's apt saying, "Die Tat is alles, Nichts der Ruhm" (The deed is everything; fame is nothing).

At breakfast the next morning, Karl and his father sat in complacent if fragile silence, munching bacon, sipping coffee, and reading newspapers. Headlines in the Sunday, May 14th edition of the *New York Times* referred to the parade as the "greatest civilian marching demonstration in the history of the world." Karl was pleased when he read that the parade was described as having "exceeded the most romantic expectations—the number of marchers; the manner of their marching; their appearance as a multitude of individuals united in one mighty body to emphasize a single thought."

Karl's father buried himself behind the paper in rapt concentration, only occasionally stopping to stare out the window.

During the hour, Max called with kudos for Karl, noting how inclusive the list of parade participants had been. Fritz rang to tout his own synopsis: "But look at the reaction out of Washington," he pointed out. "Nobody's home. President Wilson is away on a yachting trip. Secretary Baker and Secretary Tumulty are snoozin' somewhere in Atlantic City. And Secretary Redfield is entertaining a 'party' down the Potomac, which includes both Secretary Lansing and Secretary Daniels."

"Yes, they're all elsewhere, effectively thumbing their noses," Karl said. "But I bet they've heard a rumbling!"

After absorbing his brothers' reactions, Karl continued to flip through the rest of the paper. An advertisement caught his eye:

PREPAREDNESS MEANS LIBERTY
Knox Hat Company
A Fragile Torch

Karl's father, still looking over his paper, whacked it with the back of his hand and, scowling, suddenly tossed an incendiary question: "Have you seen this report?" His glasses slipped to the tip of his nose as he read aloud: "Company C of the Seventh Regiment was effectively relieved from participation in the parade." Herman turned the newspaper toward Karl and pointed at the paragraph, adding with emphasis: "The *entire* Company was excused because it has so many members of German birth and ancestry. Did you see this?" he repeated.

"Many of them probably marched with civilian divisions," Karl answered, wondering.

"And look what it says here! Two troops of Squadron A with Teutonic surnames were 'ordered to duty elsewhere.'" Herman continued, "Did anyone mention them?"

"Not to me," Karl admitted.

"This is discrimination! What logic could explain eliminating men who are already serving in the United States National Guard?"

Karl could think of none. He wondered why he, with his German surname, had never been questioned. How and why had the decision been reached to disallow so many comrades from marching? He quickly answered his father: "I don't know. I'll try to find out. But it's doubtful I'll discover a reason other than fear or apprehension that men of German descent might become targets for reprisal."

Another British ship, the *Eretria*, was sunk overnight. Karl was unaware that his parade would spearhead others across America in an expansive and energetic movement for defense.

One Saturday, during the summer of 1916, Roosevelt invited Karl to lunch with him at Oyster Bay to discuss the renewal of their work on the heels of the parade's success. Since Karl and Helen were spending the summer in Greenwich, Connecticut, they traveled to Long Island by ferry in the Ford. Helen dropped Karl off at Sagamore Hill and drove off to have lunch with her friend, Bee Cook, at Glen Cove.

After juggling ideas about how best to fan the spark of the preparedness effort, Karl had a feeling that Colonel Roosevelt might have been instrumental in preempting inclusion of Karl's name from the list of scrutinized Squadron members. Roosevelt did not verify this; he expressed consternation in regard to excluding German-Americans from the march when Karl asked his opinion about it.

"I can't envision any Squadron A member without patriotism to America," Karl said. "Am I naive? Has there been speculation about infiltration of insurgents or spies? The exclusions are a violation of the liberty these men are willing to die for. How can this be justifiable?"

The Colonel began to explain the difficulty—the near impossibility of reckoning with the quandary of how to execute fairness and preemptive protectiveness simultaneously.

Helen's arrival with Bee to pick up Karl interrupted the remainder of Roosevelt's explanation, which was left to steep in conundrum. Seeing two attractive ladies in white dresses, waiting in a Ford in the driveway, Roosevelt charged outside to greet them. *"Mrs. Behr, get right out of that car! I insist,"* he said, bending down and sweeping his arm toward the ground by way of cordially escorting her and Bee into the living room to join him and Karl for a tour of his prized possessions and a lengthy chat.

Although some German-Americans acquiesced to being watched or questioned because they understood the necessity for cautious scrutiny, it was unbearable for an elderly gentleman like

Herman Behr, Sr., who was dearly and emotionally attached to his family's place of origin and whose uncle had fought valiantly for the Union Army in the Civil War, to suffer the indignity of unfounded suspicion. And it was terrible to stand by while his beloved culture was debased. Names of things of German origin, in which Herman had taken great pride, and which had all been well assimilated into American culture, were roundly disparaged and replaced: Hamburger became a liberty sandwich; sauerkraut, liberty cabbage; frankfurters, hot dogs. Cincinnati removed pretzels from free lunch counters. More importantly, churches, bakeries, and German newspapers were placed under strict watch. Some were banned outright. In many locations the performing of German music and the teaching of German was prohibited.

With each new transgression, Karl's father grew more indignant. But Karl could only respond that, although infuriating, these restrictions paled in comparison to the atrocities that had continued to build upon the horrific occurrences in Belgium that Karl could never stop thinking about:

From the 19th to the 24th of August, 1914, after crossing a bridge, using human shields, German soldiers had raped and murdered hundreds of civilians in Louvain. Afterward, they set fire to the church of St. Pierre and to the university library, obliterating its priceless rare book collection.

Every day the challenge for Karl to find a way to satisfy his craving to fight their fierce intimidation had grown even more urgent than it was the day before until he was consumed by his need to justify *something*—thus to erase remnants of shame, some vein of inadequacy. Most of all he was desperate to make good on the conviction he was speaking about so often—that he must follow his conscience—and put his life on the line against the murderous aggressors in Europe.

Karl sympathized with his father's disdain for prejudice toward German-Americans especially in regard to their unfair treatment, but when the two men met again—this time by chance at a corner market—Karl preempted Herman from continuing to expound on these miseries by saying, "Father, I have come to understand that when a person is caught in the hapless trap of guilt by association, or is subjected to spurious aspersions cast upon him, the only recourse he has is to stand tall and try to take action to exonerate himself."

Helen Newsom in 1913.

Karl Behr in 1914.

Newspaper article clippings from Karl's scrapbook.

BEHR-NEWSOM ENGAGEMENT.

Both Young People Were Passengers on the Titanic.

Two passengers on the Titanic, who were rescued in the same lifeboat when the big liner went down are soon to be married. Although they were not engaged at the time of the Titanic disaster, the pair had known each other for several years and had been very good friends. They are Miss Helen M. Newsom, daughter of Mrs. R. L. Beckwith of the Wendolyn, Riverside Drive, and 100th street, and Karl H. Behr, the tennis player.

Mr. Behr and Miss Newsom were passengers on the Titanic with Mr. and Mrs. Beckwith. Mr. Behr had joined the party at Cherbourg after they had been on a six months' trip abroad. It had previously been arranged that he was to meet the others and they decided to come back on the Titanic.

It was made known that the approaching wedding is not the outcome of a romance at sea, although Mr. Behr and Miss Newsom both were taken off the Titanic in the same lifeboat. It also was the boat the launching of which was directed by J. Bruce Ismay, the managing director of the line. The two have known each other since Miss Newsom was a student at Briarcliff, where she was intimate with a sister of Mr. Behr.

Miss Newsom's father was Logan C. Newsom, a banker in Columbus, Ohio. The announcement of the wedding was made in Columbus by Miss Newsom's grandmother. Mr. Behr is a graduate of Yale and for several years has figured in big tennis matches. He is a lawyer at 40 Wall street and lives with his parents at 777 Madison avenue.

An interesting engagement just announced is that of Miss Helen Newsom, the daughter of Mrs. Richard L. Beckwith, to Mr. Karl Behr, an attorney and graduate of Yale university and the law school of Columbia. Miss Newsom and Mr. Behr are survivors of the Titanic, both being rescued in the same lifeboat. The romance, which will have such a happy ending, had its beginning in the great tragedy of the sea.

Miss Newsom is the granddaughter of Mrs. William Monypeny, sr., of the Lincoln hotel, and is a niece of Mr. Ferin B. Monypeny of Governor Harmon's staff, and of Mr. William Monypeny, jr.

Mr. Behr is a well-known tennis player and held the Yale championship for a time.

The Beckwiths spend each winter in their apartment in New York. With Miss Newsom, they travel extensively.

The wedding of Miss Helen Newsom, daughter of Mrs. Richard Leonard Beckwith, to Karl Howard Behr of this city, will take place on March 1 in the Church of the Transfiguration. Both Miss Newsom and Mr. Behr were passengers on the ill-fated Titanic last April. The wedding will be small, owing to mourning, and there is to be no reception. Miss Gertrude Behr, a sister of the bridegroom, and Miss Beatrice Cook, are to be the bridesmaids. Douglas Gibbon will serve as best man.

Albert [illegible]

The Times — Feb. 23. 1913.

The marriage of Miss Helen Newsom, daughter of Mrs. Richard Leonard Beckwith, to Karl Howard Behr of this city, will take place next Saturday at the Church of the Transfiguration.

[illegible] ... Miss Gertrude Behr, a sister of the bridegroom, will be maid of honor ... will be bridesmaid. Douglas Gibbon will be the best man.

Both Miss Newsom and Mr. Behr were passengers on the Titanic.

The World. Feb. 23.

MANY inquisitive residents of Morristown were at the Church of the Transfiguration on Saturday for the wedding of Karl Howard Behr and Miss Helen Newsom, eager to see if the bride was pretty and of the sort to have social success. A champion tennis player always has much feminine admiration, so perhaps there was some envy when the bride appeared, for she is a young woman of very great beauty and she wore the most regal wedding veil of duchesse lace that I have seen in many years. One of the most interesting of the guests to me was Mrs. Max Behr, who had the famous butterfly wedding some seven years ago. She looked very attractive as she went up the aisle with her two little daughters walking in front of her, each holding tightly a little bouquet of flowers. Mrs. Behr's children are of a far more delicate type than those of her cousin, Mrs. W. G. Loew. Mrs. Karl is lucky in such a desirable catch and the fact that they are both survivors of the Titanic is less suggestive of romance to those who know than that they first met because she was a friend of Gertrude Behr when at school at Briarcliff. She is a daughter by a former marriage of Mrs. Richard Leonard Beckwith.

[...]E OF THE TITANIC LEADS
[...]ARRIAGE OF MR. KARL BEHR

MRS. KARL H. BEHR

Tennis Player Meets Miss Newsom [...]
Her and Her Mother and [...]
His Bride.

From a meeting on board the ill-fated Titanic in April of last year came the marriage yesterday of Miss Helen Monypenny Newsom to Mr. Karl Howell Behr, lawyer and tennis player. They were made acquainted at sea, and when the Titanic struck the iceberg Mr. Behr warned Miss Newsom, her stepfather and her mother, Mr. and Mrs. Richard Leonard Beckwith, of their danger.

... seeing an almost empty lifeboat ... by the deck, Mrs. Beckwith obtained ... mission from an officer to have Mr. Beckwith and Mr. Behr enter the lifeboat, and both men worked with the crew until the Carpathia picked them up. After their arrival in New York Mr. Behr called frequently at the home of Mr. and Mrs. Beckwith at No. 276 Riverside Drive, and after a few months' courtship his engagement with Miss Newsom was announced.

The marriage ceremony yesterday was performed in the Church of the Transfiguration, the Rev. Dr. George C. Houghton officiating. There was a recital of organ music before and during the service. The bride, who was given away by her stepfather, wore a gown of white chiffon and a robe of lace. Her veil was of old lace, and she carried a bouquet of lilies of the valley. She was attended by Miss Gertrude Behr, sister of the bridegroom.

TITANIC HERO TO W[...]

nnis Player — *Girl [...]e Rescu[...]*

MISS HELEN M. NEWSOM.

Plans are being made to-day for the culmination of a romance of the Titanic on March 1, when Karl H. Behr, the tennis player, and Miss Helen M. Newsom, of No. 276 Riverside Drive, will be married.

Miss Newsom, with her mother and stepfather, Mrs. and Mr. R. L. Beckwith, were all passing, too, on the Titanic. On the Titanic, too, was the tennis player. When the Titanic hit the iceberg Behr ran to the staterooms of the Beckwiths and Miss Newsom. He met the girl in the passageway, and advised her to arouse her parents.

She did so, and all went on deck. Mrs. Beckwith went to one of the lifeboats on the upper deck and found it almost empty. She asked if her husband and Behr could go with her to the boat. As they seemed to be the last on that deck, an officer in charge of the loading at [...] said that the men could go in to [...].

During the seven hours that the [...] floated after the sinking of the [...] until she was picked up by the [...] pathia, Behr was frequently at the [...]. When he was not rowing he and [...] girl sat together.

After the girl had thanked him for what she had done for her family she spoke of his rowing and feared that he was in danger, as he was wet and the night was cold.

At her mention of rowing he asked if he might not row through life with her.

"I'd go through all eternity with you," she said.

And so they are to be married.

New York Press. Feb. 21. 1913.

Another wedding of interest which has more than the usual element of romance to it to take place on March 1 when Miss Helen Newsom, daughter of Mrs. Richard Leonard Beckwith, will be married to Karl Howard Behr. Both Mr. Behr and his bride-to-be were of the steamship Titanic. It was [...] and they were among the few who were rescued ... sorrowing the wedding ... and take place in the Church of the Transfiguration, Twenty-ninth street near Fifth avenue. Mr. [...] have the bridegroom's [...] Gertrude Behr, and Miss Beatrice Cook for her attendants, and Doug[las] Gibbon will be the best man.

Left to right, Maurice E. McLoughlin, Richard N. Williams,
Karl H. Behr, and Thomas C. Bundy at Longwood, Boston,
July 24, 1914.

Karl Behr and the same group in Bundy's Cadillac.

The Preparedness Parade, New York City, May 13, 1916.

"The greatest civilian marching demonstration
in the history of the world" (*The New York Times*).

Helen, above, and with her dogs.

39

Writing On the Wall

$\mathcal{H}$ELEN CONSIDERS WAITING A CRUEL PLACE, although she is grateful to be carried along in its wake. Keeping her vigil by Karl's bed in the city to insure that he is comfortable, she watches him sleeping, remembering the times she has been in limbo before:

For more than three years after the sinking of the *Titanic*, Karl had often returned to their apartment tired from having studied British Mercantile law at the Library. By following the case histories of previous tragedies at sea, he had learned that an almost ironclad barrier was established against a ship owner's liability. Nonetheless, he continually researched ways to circumvent the Harper Act, which asserted that once a ship left port and was out at sea, insurmountable variables of natural danger and distance precluded its parent company from extending influence over the safety of passengers—thereby leaving the company little to no jurisdiction over the consequence of the ship's journey.

In spite of this intractable Act, during the first years that followed the *Titanic* disaster, claimants had compiled petition after petition against the ship's parent company. By April, 1914, therefore, the White Star Line's parent, the Oceanic Steam Navigation Company, had brought suit (Federal Case number A55–279) against the government of the United States to insure that its liabilities would remain limited. At the time, claims relative to loss of life had climbed toward six million dollars and were continuing to rise. Judge Julius M. Mayer presided over this trial, which took place at the United States District Court in New York City in June of 1915.

Recognizing a chance to help the survivors he had known on the *Carpathia*, Karl hoped to demonstrate a possible chink in the armor of the mercantile law's edict that there could be no control by a parent company over the safety of passengers once a ship was out of port.

Helen attended the courtroom proceedings on the day Karl took the stand. She listened, averting her eyes—aware of the humility Karl had brought upon himself to speak publicly about entering their lifeboat. Previously he had coveted a low profile, keeping himself removed from reporters as far as his survival from the *Titanic* had been concerned. Helen hoped (against every illusory aspect of the word) that by providing substantiation for Judge Mayer to rule in favor of the passengers against the claimant, her husband's testimony might, in some manner, be cathartic as a source of atonement for him.

On the stand, Karl positioned himself at the front of his chair with his back straight, his chin down, his hands and feet motionless, his eyes riveted on solemnity. The intensity of his concentration was nearly palpable. Disallowing any reason to doubt his testimony, he adhered to a simple and forthright effort to communicate "nothing but the truth."

"Bruce Ismay appeared to take action in the capacity of Managing Director of the White Star Line," Karl said. "Although far afield from the ship's place of origin, he was clearly recognized as having authority by the officers and passengers of the *Titanic*." Karl recounted his own recollection of Ismay's dictates on the starboard Boat Deck of the *Titanic*. "During the time the lifeboats were loaded, the crew willingly obeyed his orders to put in his specifically designated passengers and crew," Karl said. When asked to do so, as a follow up, Karl corroborated the spelling and pronunciation of the names of each officer and passenger in question. Finally, Karl ended his testimony by reiterating Ismay's order to launch the lifeboat, repeating Ismay's command to "Lower away."

On the morning of Saturday, June 26th, Helen was first to notice the *New York Times* headline: "SAYS ISMAY RULED IN TITANIC'S BOATS—Managing Director Had Charge of Their Launching, Testifies Karl H. Behr." The article stated that Karl's testimony had been perceived as having provided a substantive contribution toward Judge Mayer's ruling.

At the trial's conclusion on June 30th, 1916, the remuneration payment required of the Oceanic Steam Navigation Company was a mere $655,000 out of the total claim for loss of life, which by then had reached well above six million. Compared to what he had anticipated might be nothing at all, Karl thought this payment a considerable sum, based upon the outcomes of former similar suits. The mercantile liability law remained intractable, but Karl's testimony had garnered some benefit—even if only by way of providing a small resource to afford bread and wine at the tables of the steerage passengers he had wanted so much to help.

After the trial, as Helen watched two-year-old Sonny chase a tennis ball in the kitchen during breakfast, she commented on his agility. Karl peered over the top of the newspaper and the rim of his glasses to smile at his son and at her, but quickly returned to the paragraph he was reading. He decided not to mention it to Helen. *What,* he thought, *would be the point of bringing up all of this again?* But Karl was shocked to learn (if indeed the paragraph was true) about the extremity to which social mores and prejudice could be carried:

Although *Titanic* passenger, Mr. Masafumi Hosono, was reportedly rescued from a piece of floating wood by Fifth Officer Harold Lowe, he ended up facing a lifetime of ostracism and disgrace after he returned to Japan, merely because he survived.

40

Williwaw

$\mathcal{R}$OOSEVELT HAD WARNED that although Karl had been promised a commission in the Cavalry of Colonel Roosevelt's Volunteer Division, President Wilson's pacifist policy would not likely permit this fully recruited division to come into active service. But a letter, then a cable, arrived from Colonel Raynal Bolling in France, indicating his desire for Karl to come overseas to help with a difficult organizing job. Consequently, along with a group of twelve prominent businessmen, Karl traveled to Washington to be commissioned. A plan was announced that he was to become a Major.

When Helen learned that Karl was leaving for Washington to receive a commission and be sent to France, or so he hoped, she guarded her conviction to stay strong, telling herself that it would be best not to utter a statement she knew would only haunt him while he was away. But she was desperate to beg him not to go. The words in her throat struggled to escape as though locked in prison: *Hasn't your work on committees been effective enough? Your exuberant speeches? Will you have to take a gun in hand to perpetuate the fallacy that killing is the only means for change; for revenge that begets more revenge?* Helen felt that there was no glory in war, only consequence white-washed by pride. But instead of bursting out, her argument recoiled. She knew there could be little delineation between necessity and craving, no alternative to violence when fear is the bedfellow of peace.

Near the door, Karl was bent over his suitcase and valise, fiddling with strings to tie on an identification tag. He seemed nervous, fidgety. He stooped to clean the tips of his shoes with his palms; then he walked back into the bedroom for something he'd forgotten.

Helen looked through the apartment window at a tree she was figuratively clinging on to. She thought of reminding Karl about her grandfather's letter, which she had shown him once, years before. Instead, she listened to the grandfather clock tick, relying on its strident assurance of time's passing to steady and distract her. She swallowed hard, breathed consciously. Stared at the floor. Looked at the tree again. Listened to the clock again. She blinked. Karl walked toward her. She tried to memorize him—his smell, his incredible grin, his belief that he was doing the right thing. He kissed her gently; not too long, not so that tears would come. He said, "I love you," but his words drifted across the room. He said, "I'll call you," but the promise didn't resonate. He hugged her, but she knew he was already elsewhere.

He walked out into the foyer, then came back for the key he had left behind on the hall table. Without looking at Helen again he walked away. She heard the click-thump-click of his shoes and suitcase on the floor as he waited for the elevator. When he was past her ability to have reached him, she felt all the reasons that he need-ed to leave encircle her and she was guided by desire to stay calm. She walked to her chair by the window, attempting to take in the view beyond herself; her silence was wrapped in a voice of silk.

With everything seeming positive in Washington, Karl went eagerly to take his physical exam there, considering himself in top shape. But according to the authorities his tests indicated otherwise. His heart rate was forty-eight beats per minute and his blood pressure was too low. He was declared unfit. He could barely contain his shock and bitter disappointment.

The next day he went to be retested. There had been no mistake. He failed again.

Karl was told, nonetheless, that he would likely be called for special duty in spite of not having passed the physical, so he was filled with hope. Once all the paperwork was complete—uniforms and equipment procured—he returned to New York to await further word from Washington. Although none arrived, the strength of his intent and eagerness to be assigned to active duty was intensifying.

Biding time, Karl chaired his decennial Yale Reunion Committee in New Haven and led a class camp-out at the corner of Hillhouse Avenue and Grove Street to impress the idea of "service to country" on anyone who happened along. In uniform and carrying rifles, he and his classmates marched to the chapel where he addressed President Hadley and the Trustees, calling on Yale to breed a "sense of duty and patriotism." Across the country, students and faculty at other universities were performing similar rallies and practice exercises—even at Princeton where Wilson had once presided.

Soon afterward, Karl banded together with many of his classmates and two friends, Guy Emerson and Thomas C. Desmond, forming the Roosevelt Non-partisan League to inspire further enthusiasm for Theodore Roosevelt to gain the Republican nomination instead of Charles Evans Hughes. Obtaining use of a vacant store on Vanderbilt Avenue for headquarters, the League gathered over one hundred thousand signatures on Roosevelt's behalf.

At the request of Emerson and Desmond to stir up publicity, Karl masterminded the idea of staging a massive Saturday pilgrimage of men from around New York to go to Sagamore Hill. He predicted that trains packed with enthusiasts parading out to Roosevelt's house in Oyster Bay would rock the Sunday newspapers and spark evidence of fervor for Roosevelt. Postcards were mailed to thousands of selected Preparedness Parade groups, inviting men to board the special trains at the Long Island Depot. Complimentary passage was secured so that no tickets needed to be purchased, but everyone was urged to arrive early. Three trains of a dozen cars each were filled with men crammed into the seats and aisles. Hundreds of late-comers had to be left behind on the platforms.

More than three thousand men marched up to Sagamore Hill in columns of four with the Seventh Regiment Band as their escort. Colonel Roosevelt, elated to see so many of them, invited as many as possible up onto the porch where he made a rousing speech, which was suddenly interrupted by a great commotion coming from the edge of the crowd. Part of the porch had rumbled and collapsed; a few men jumped safely to the ground. Fortunately there were no injuries. Joviality returned. Jokes brewed about the power of the *weighted* word. Roosevelt then asked everyone to form a line single file and come inside where he positioned himself to greet each man individually. Karl rested on the sofa behind Roosevelt, his arms intermittently crossed with contentment or sprawled casually across the sofa back as, once again, he marveled at his mentor's ability to recognize innumerable men.

Press coverage of the event was commensurate with the grandeur of the scheme, but Hughes was nominated.

Inspired by Roosevelt's zeal, and after convincing Robert Bacon to join him, Karl traveled to Chicago on October 13th, 1916, where he spoke (after Mr. Bacon) at a luncheon attended by fifty prominent men. Within three minutes, fifty-five thousand dollars was raised. Consequently, with an additional forty-five thousand raised in New York, establishment of the Universal Military Training League became official.

Although already involved in a frenzy of activity, Karl also accepted Bacon's request for help in his run for the statewide Republican nomination for the U.S. Senate during the fall election of 1916. "To continue our preparedness battles together," Bacon had pleaded. "Job Hedges is in charge of the State campaign and Harry Goddard the Metropolitan. I need you to think up something original," he stressed.

Karl concocted a return postcard campaign to endorse Bacon in spite of the fact that the nomination had already been pledged to William M. Calder in the primaries. He had cards embossed and printed with golden eagles on the corner. New committees were formed through his friends who had participated on the Parade Executive Committee. Once returned, the postcards covered two long directors' tables with tall, leaning towers of response.

Despite the fact that the first edition of the morning papers reported a win for Bacon, late tabulations from Calder's home territory tipped the result to Calder by a few thousand votes.

Hostilities in Europe escalated to the devastating slaughter at Verdun—upwards of seven hundred thousand French and German soldiers perished.

Suspicion and paranoia toward German-Americans escalated across America.

A list of suppressed German affiliations was compiled.

German books were burned in Lima, Ohio.

In St. Louis, streets with German nomenclature were renamed.

Karl Muck no longer conducted the Boston Symphony and Frederick Stock was dismissed from conducting the Chicago Symphony.

In 1917, The Espionage Act forbade any action that hindered the war effort. Workers who refused to buy war bonds suffered harsh retributions.

On the 16th of January, 1917, Wilson's intelligence personnel intercepted a telegram from German Foreign Secretary Arthur Zimmermann, inviting Mexico to ally with Germany—offering Texas, Arizona, and New Mexico as a reward, along with an alliance with Japan.

President Wilson outlined his case for declaring war, in a speech delivered on April 2nd to both houses of Congress, saying that a state of war already existed. On April 6th, 1917, war against Germany was formally declared after a vote in the Senate and the House.

Three hundred of the most suspicious German-Americans were rounded up and held at Ellis Island. The restrictions continued to gain momentum, leading to passage of the Sedition Act on May 16th, 1918, which prohibited any disloyal speech about the government, the flag, the Constitution, or the armed forces. Freedom of speech was denied at home, even as Americans fought and died for it overseas.

In October of 1917, when the sky rippled like the underbelly of a whale and nothing about an assignment in Europe had arrived, Karl hurriedly left his apartment and raced downtown to meet Mr. William Hamlin Childs and Mayor John Purroy Mitchel for lunch. Over soup, they asked Karl for ideas to help create exuberance around Mitchel's lagging mayoral reelection campaign.

"In spite of some nagging health issues, I am expecting to go to France—any minute, in fact," Karl said.

William Childs was both a generous financial supporter of the Universal Military Training League, and shared its directorship with Karl. He cajoled, "If you are strong enough to go to France, then you should be able to stand the strain of organizing some kind of demonstration! I can assure you of all the necessary funds you may require, and the Mayor is prepared to render you assistance. Don't decide now. Think this matter over tonight."

Karl garnered Helen's ready vote of confidence and called Childs the next day saying, "By getting Roosevelt to speak, we should be able to jam Madison Square Garden, but this may not be enough to wake up New York. How about an old fashioned torchlight parade with all arms convening at Madison Square on the night of a mass meeting?"

"Great idea! I like it! We'll get you all the funding you need," Childs responded. "Set this for the night of November 1st—Thursday before the election."

"I'll staff the parades and the Garden meeting in case I'm called overseas," Karl said, suddenly realizing November 1st was only three weeks away.

Karl drafted an invitation from Mayor Mitchel to three hundred men representing various trades and professions, asking them to lunch with him at the Banker's Club. He also requested that the representatives meet with him at the Yale Club in two days, following the meeting with Mitchel. With time enough for only two meetings of the executive committee prior to the Mayor's luncheon, Karl obtained the second floor of the Club's recently abandoned building on the corner of John Street and Broadway. Friends rallied to install furniture, typewriters, telephones, and to hire stenographers. The office was ready for business the day after the luncheon.

Colonel Roosevelt agreed to speak at Madison Square Garden and also to review the different torchlight columns of the parade before commencement of the march. Among the devotees who interrupted their business activities to help with this effort were: W. Ward Smith, Captain Alfred Wendt, Abram J. L. Wakeman, Edwin Vogel, Philip Stillman, and C.H. Woodward.

Karl staffed the Garden meeting, led the recruiting effort, and organized the five torchlight parade columns with an aggregate number of approximately thirty thousand men. This time he agreed to serve as Grand Marshal.

The procession was solemn, spectacular, prodigious as a freight train moving through resplendent torchlight reminiscent of the fervor of an ancient ceremony. It brought to mind for Karl the Indians' procession across the cliffs of Mexico and the bonfire in Brooklyn before the Micks' attack.

Three columns of the parade convened from the north. Two from the south. Mayor Mitchel rolled down 8th Avenue in a motor car. Karl and Roosevelt rode together in a touring car down 2nd Avenue with two policemen standing on each running board.

Karl was not surprised when Roosevelt leaned away from him to eye one of the men whom he immediately proceeded to slap on the back, declaring, "Sergeant Levy! Why don't you speak to me? Didn't I make you a Sergeant?"

Sergeant Levy's face lit up as he answered, "Colonel Roosevelt, Sir, I never thought you would remember me!"

After a daring rescue at a tenement fire several years prior, Roosevelt had promptly rewarded Levy with a promotion to sergeant and had never forgotten his face or his name.

Once again, Karl felt grand by association. By the time Roosevelt appeared from the blizzard of fire, Madison Square Garden was bursting with an impassioned audience.

During Roosevelt's speech a heckler interrupted, yelling, "Why aren't *you* at the battlefront in France?"

With great commotion, police officers lunged to remove the man, but Roosevelt quickly requested he be allowed to stay, then answered him: "I wanted to be, but a committee in Washington blackballed me," he replied. "It's a very exclusive war," he added. "But I will tell you, my four sons are there."

After a concert at the Brooklyn Academy of Music, James Gerard, former U.S. Ambassador to Germany, spoke to three thousand people assembled. Karl's father was among them.

Early the following morning, Herman called Karl to mention the gist of Gerard's speech. His voice was low to apostrophize and impress. "It sent shivers down my spine," he said.

"What did?" Karl asked.

"Gerard's threat. He said that 'Any German-Americans who step out of line will be found hanging from lampposts.' "

Karl could not respond to his father in any way that would appease him. Injustices, perpetrated in response to perceived threats from German-Americans even for picayune offenses, were ubiquitous and worsening. A man by the name of Walter Mathey, who attended an antiwar conference and donated 25 cents, was consequently arrested and jailed. In Collinsville, Illinois, a German-born man named Robert Prager, accused of "disloyal utterances," was lynched. Karl knew that the sooner the Kaiser's aggressions were thwarted, the faster the misery both abroad and at home would end.

He had yet to receive an assignment in Europe.

At the end of Thursday, November 8th, 1917, one week after the Mitchel Parade, Karl stood at the bottom of the staircase leading to the second-floor New York apartment that he and Helen had recently rented. Looking up, he began to tremble from head to foot. Although he attempted to climb, he was too overcome with utter exhaustion to raise himself even a single step. The walls wavered. *They're caving in,* he thought.

Helen heard him call her. She was standing at the top of the stairs when she saw him collapse.

Rescue workers arrived. Karl was urged to go to the hospital, but he convinced the men to carry him upstairs and assist him into bed.

Helen summoned Dr. John Storer, who confirmed a dangerous weakness in Karl's heart, prescribing extensive bed rest—possibly for months. As he saw it, Karl's ebullience for defense, his clamorous activities and when Karl explained: "Everything has come to naught because I've not been called to serve." Years of unrelenting effort had depleted him. His breakdown was irreversible. "Until such a time as he can accept the impasse, assimilate the weakness, and gradually regain strength," Dr. Storer said firmly.

Unable to defeat the angst that drew him into malaise, Karl could no longer god what he could no longer hope for: To rise above exhaustion and the thwarted chance to prove his integrity by serving his country. Helplessness overwhelmed him.

Dr. Storer sent Karl to the "American Nauheim"—Glen Springs Sanatorium, in Watkins Glen, New York—a grand building in a park-like setting with idyllic views of Seneca Lake and distant surrounding hills. Access to the serene panorama was afforded by an arcade that wrapped around the exterior, where patients could stroll or be guided to take in the fresh air.

Nothing about the place, however, helped Karl to feel better. Although he tried to relax, walk, and write love poems to Helen, the majority of his time was spent devouring news clippings that his father and brothers relayed to him in their efforts to convince him he was better off not going to Europe:

Eugene Debs, an esteemed orator, American socialist, and union organizer, convicted of violating the Espionage Act by intending to obstruct recruiting, was sentenced to ten years in prison for his outspoken opposition to the war.

Elderly women were jailed in Iowa for speaking German over the telephone, after Governor William Harding had declared that only English was allowed to be spoken in public places, which included across the wires.

Police arrested citizens who had not been naturalized and were considered enemy aliens. Twenty-five thousand homes were placed under scrutiny within the barred zones of Manhattan and the Bronx.

The more Karl learned about heroism in Europe—of the legendary dogfights to score the greatest number of downed German planes, and of the mayhem described when airmen plummeted in flames, even the sickening wounds honorably borne—the more desperate he felt to be there by their side and he tried to explain this to Helen:

My darling girl,

Leaving you to live without me is difficult enough, but to be thwarted from doing what calls me, what my head and heart say needs to be done, is indescribably difficult. I know what it means to be a victim of someone else's overbearing will, and to see suffering occur for no reason other than irrational hatred or desire for superiority. I shiver with empathy for those in the circumstance of war.

I am sitting by a fire in the residence lodge. The flames sound like a river rushing over leaves and rocks. It is putting the man across from me to sleep in his wheelchair. As much as I wish it would do the same for me, the inferno draws my thoughts to Europe, to the flames that burn in the midst of the devastation. I want to jump out of my skin to be there. But of course I don't need to keep telling you that. I'm sure you must be sick and tired of hearing me complain about not being called. But if I couldn't confide in you, my dear, I would fall even farther back. Would I not?

Inside the fire that blazes in front of me there is a scene resembling a crèche—a nook tucked under beams—where I imagine your dark eyes pooled, and somewhere your love for me. How clearly I believe I would be letting you down if I were unwilling to sacrifice myself for your safety, my darling. I know you wish this war would fade away, as we all do, but it won't. Not on its own. Not without help. Today I saw pictures of a mutilated woman in Belgium. You might have seen this too? It isn't necessary to be in her presence to feel horror. It crawls up my skin. I can hear her screams— like the night we try to forget.

One day, I swear, I will save someone from such a fate. The fire is dying down and the man in the wheelchair is about to fall. I'd best go prop him up. I miss you more than I can say, and wish I could tell you that I am better since coming here. But night noises echo through the corridor and I'm reluctant to make new friendships, so I spend the majority of my time wondering how this happened to me, to us, and when it will all be over.

With endless love for you my darling—forgive me.

KARL

The following evening, Karl was resting in bed on his side with his head in the crook of his arm. He could not fathom the wretchedness of what he had just learned and he imagined his father's reaction. Fifteen hundred German-Americans had been interned at Fort

MacPherson in Hot Springs, North Carolina. Prison barracks in Georgia, were filled with thousands more.

In a letter that was lying next to Karl, Emily explained that Charlie had been identified as having funded pamphlets condoning refusal of the Draft, and that this was seen as a violation. Along with other "aliens," Charlie had been sent to the internment camp at Fort Oglethorpe, outside of Atlanta.

Emily said that Charlie was arrested by the Department of Justice before being transferred to the War Department to be transferred to confinement under twelve sentry towers "lurid with vultures," as he described the guards. He was being forced to work on highway maintenance. He said he didn't know how he could cope with the injustice of the internment, let alone combat his claustrophobia.

Far from growing stronger physically, Karl fell into deeper despair. Knowing he could not make a trip to Georgia, he was trapped and worst of all—useless. The only way he could settle his nerves and his torment was by rationalizing that nothing could get worse for Charlie now. At least, his friend was safe.

Months had passed at the sanatorium when Karl was summoned to the telephone. Emily's voice at the other end sounded deep and whispery—as controlled as she could keep it. But she wasn't able to hide the effort this was taking. Suddenly Karl sensed runaway horses ahead of what she was reigning in, but had not guessed that she was in shock. Her breathing, then her voice broke into spasms and sobs as she finally said, "Oh, Karl, there might have been something I could have done to prevent this."

Karl did not anticipate the worst, until Emily spoke the words: "Charlie was killed trying to escape from the prison barracks. I…I've been told he cut through the concertina wire—three layers. They said he ran. The guard claimed he was just trying to stop him—but the shot was fatal." She paused for a long while. "Oh, Karl, I know he would have wanted me to say something to clarify this, to honor you, somehow, but no words come to me. You were a loyal friend. You know how much he…"

"Emily, please. You have to realize something for me," Karl said, holding back his own pain in order to speak for them both, "You have to believe that there was nothing you could have done to prevent this. It was not your fault."

"But I never went to Georgia. A visit from me might have helped him settle…find the patience he needed."

"You couldn't."

"There might have been a way. I just kept thinking they would release him any day. He did *nothing* wrong. Everyone knew that. Everyone said so, but…"

"Emily, you have to promise me you won't blame yourself. Promise me!"

"I promise," Emily said, finally.

But Karl knew from the fragility in her voice, which tapered from sobs to a will-o'-the-wisp, that she would never be able to keep that promise.

Not long afterward, stilled with grief and the continuing need for rest, Karl learned that the writing on the wall and the trail of truth he'd suspected had become manifest. Although Roosevelt attempted to help Karl obtain a commission to enter the Aviation Service, and despite initial assurances that his poor health report would be bypassed, Karl believed that a commission for him would *never* come. Karl became privy to the reason why, and he wrote it in a letter to Roosevelt:

Karl H. Behr
61 Broadway
New York

December 29th, 1917

Colonel Theodore Roosevelt
The Metropolitan Magazine
432 Fourth Ave., New York

My dear Colonel Roosevelt,

...I have heard definitely with regard to the reasons for my not obtaining my commission. It seems that they have a rule in the Aviation Service that anyone (as I understand it) with a German parent could not be taken into the service, no matter what his reputation. I am told that General Squier and others in the Department had a number of meetings covering my case, as they were reported to have been anxious to have me. Their decision, however, was that they should not make an exception in my case owing to my being well known and the difficulties they would get into with regard to German-American candidates with political backing...

I am leaving for a three months enforced rest cure in the South, having overdone in work, some of which of course had to do with the war. Upon my return I shall enter some war service, exactly what I cannot tell, as I am a little in the air as to where I should be welcome. If you should learn of anything that I can put my hand to, to push the cause along, I shall be very glad to learn of it.

With very kind personal regards, believe me,

Sincerely yours,

Karl H. Behr

41

Cadenza

SEPTEMBER HAS GIVEN WAY to October, 1949. Twilight is cast at the apartment window. Helen and Karl delve into their usual evening banter after supper in their bedroom at 215 East 72nd Street. Helen mentions that she is content to be back near the grocer; how comforting it is to have her dear friends Bee Cook, Charlotte, and Karl's sisters Gertie and Margaret, within a few blocks. From his propped-up position in bed, Karl bemoans the loss of time during his breakdown.

"But if you hadn't been forced to rest, Karl, I might already be missing you," Helen counters, carrying her book to sit by the window.

"Some hero I was to you then!" Karl says, tugging shakily at the sheet. "Doc Storer sent me a million miles away where I couldn't even imagine you'd appear around a corner. When he ordered me to bed rest, I never believed it would last almost a year. Can you think of anything more challenging than doing nothing for that long?" Karl sinks. He is gaunt.

"Not for you!" Helen smiles. She walks back to him, sits on the edge of his bed, kisses his forehead, jostles and fluffs the pillow beside his head.

"I missed you desperately. I wrote you verses, remember?" Karl's angst resurges.

"You missed being sent to France even more."

"Was I impetuous, irrational, or just delusional?"

"Patriotic, dear, which is all those things; or none of them, depending on one's perspective."

Karl remembers Lloyd Taylor as he considers Helen's comment. "You have a point. I needed to prove to Father, to Roosevelt, to Fritz, to my colleagues—to Charlie—that I was as good as my word. Professing a goal pales in comparison to achieving it," Karl says—thinking at the same time—*there were times when I believed it was possible for me to be effective.* Then he recants: "You know how my brothers always managed to make mincemeat out of me!"

"They were kidding."

"And I was too dumb to recognize it?"

"You were down on yourself sometimes."

"I never thought Fritz was kidding. It was often on my mind— how he must have rued having a weakling for a brother!"

Helen looks into her lap, thinking about Fritz—how she had always liked him; how wonderful it was when he and Karl had become real friends. Under her watchful eye, the rekindled relationship with Fritz had been achieved, not because of Karl's triumphs, but more through his failures and the dissolution of false pride.

She rests gently next to Karl, knowing that time is getting short for him; he hasn't left the bedroom in four weeks. She wishes he wouldn't have to suffer, but his "good" days have grown sparse— like slivers of joy parceled out. There doesn't seem to be a clear or imperative thing for her to be doing so she tries to read, but merely stares at the page while Karl closes his eyes to rest. Although she is in suspension, waiting has now become a privilege. Helen remembers the time during the Great War when Karl was eager to leave for France—her thoughts drift back to the question she had asked him then:

"Darling, if you have to kill Germans, what will that do to you? How will it make you feel?"

"I don't know," Karl had answered.

"Like Hell," she said.

"Yes, I guess—like Hell, in a way, but..."

"My grandfather could have told you what that was like," Helen said.

"I know," Karl said.

"Then?"

"This is different."

"Yes. But is it?"

"The Germans could come here. They will come here and hurt you, our children, if they are not stopped. They are the aggressors!"

"That's what my grandfather thought, too."

"He was right to preempt disaster."

"But he never recovered from the massacre he executed in order to avoid one."

Outside, Helen sees spectral rays of light cast from a streetlamp. She stares at the tinctures of pink amethyst and flecks of gold that point from the center. Beneath illuminated branches people pause; water glimmers; mist is in the air. Everything circles. How could war ever end, she wonders. Only if everyone, at once, declared its demise? If every child born was never to cast the first stone? Nor the second! She sighs, intuiting that nothing—written or spoken, no decibel of sound, speech, cryptic or strident song, private or collective thought—could prevail to prevent cruelty born of desperation. She had honored and hated Karl's willingness to sacrifice himself, but she had willed his confidence into existence because it was what she had wanted for him. The city-river hums as she contemplates:

After more than eight months of enforced rest—twice at Watkins Glen and once during a sojourn in Florida—Karl recovered from his collapse well enough to have his previous physical examination failure waived. Helen suspected that a word from Roosevelt might have tipped the scale when Karl was commissioned Captain in the Army.

On September 3rd, 1918, she had returned to her apartment from a luncheon with Gertie, to discover that Karl was in their bedroom, frantically packing. She stood in the doorway, knowing what this meant—that he had finally received some kind of assignment.

"You've never made such a huge decision without talking to me first, Karl," she said.

"I was going to," he answered, scurrying from bureau to suitcase and back. He was curt, sheepish. "It's just that I wanted to get the packing done and out of the way before I did. I knew you'd support me. You always do, my darling. Besides, this isn't a choice; it's an obligation."

"Mmm," Helen nodded. She knew Karl's leaving was inevitable. She went to the kitchen to boil water for tea and to keep herself, again, from speaking her mind.

Karl reported to Headquarters of the Motor Transport Corps at Camp Holabird, near Baltimore, where he was given responsibility for production and delivery of supplies to Europe. Appointed Executive Officer of District D, which was comprised of seventeen states, he assumed that the position would stand him in good stead for transfer to Europe. Soon after arriving, however, his superior officer was relocated and Karl was left with sole authority over twenty-five thousand men. What occurred in the aftermath of the officer's departure was as unpredictable and inscrutable as war itself. Officers all around Karl were struck down one after another with the Spanish influenza. One quarter of them fell ill. Hundreds died—some within only two days of having contracted the disease. Once there were no more available ambulances, bodies were carried out in trucks. Soon there were no more trucks and only a few men left to drive.

Although the end of the Great War was declared at eleven o'clock on 11/11, 1918, willingness, sometimes even eagerness to die as a hero continued. Hobey Baker, Karl's younger paragon of athleticism, was killed in December when he crashed a SPAD on an airfield in France. Although he was scheduled to leave, he decided to test one of the planes that had just had its carburetor repaired.

Discharged from service in five months, Karl returned home on January 11th, 1919.

Gazing at Karl in the bed nearby, Helen leapfrogs back through time again—to a night after Karl had been home from Baltimore for a few recalcitrant days—when, in a single moment, she had come to know him, almost for the first time:

They were sitting alone, lingering at the dinner table. Candlelight glowed on Karl's face as he recounted the cataclysmic scope of the flu epidemic—the misery, the smells, the ambulances, trucks departing with men he could do nothing to save. In the crooked light, he turned his face in profile and said, as if it was just a meaningless passing thought, "I took my mask off and paraded through the sick barracks in a desperate attempt to cheer the doctors and the men."

Helen heard Karl's words as if they were sentinels to his deepest reach cutting through the night. Desire for self-sacrifice ruled him; she realized that his happiness had never rested in her keeping, alone.

Another week passes in the city. Helen looks up from her book. The sight of her grandson Peter's small face peeking around the door cheers her. "Hey there Pete," she says. "Is it time for a story?"

Peter springs onto his grandfather's bed, saying nothing. He waits for the magic to happen because he knows it will. Karl opens his eyes and begins—as he has every night of Peter's visit—the folktale he once learned in Mexico. His voice is antique; his recounting is slow and magisterial, draped with inflection:

"Once upon a time, a thousand years ago, way, way down in Mexico, there was a man whose name, Tezcatlipoca, meant fiery mirror. He was known as the Jupiter of the Nahua, and he carried a shield, which was like a looking glass because it reflected the destiny of his entire country and the people that he loved. He was brave. But most amazing of all was his ability to see the deeds of mankind in the shield and to warn against evil ones, sometimes by speaking through the songs of birds.

"Tezcatlipoca helped his people overcome all threats. He led them to the Land of Promise where there was great abundance. Maize was plentiful. Calabashes thick as elephant ankles. Gold, silver, and precious stones spilled over cliffs like waterfalls. Cotton bloomed in clouds of every conceivable color. A rainbow of birds— never seen before, with iridescent feathers and tails as long as a year—swathed the forests in music.

"Suddenly, after years of happiness, on one single day, in one single moment, old Tezcatlipoca was swept up into the air and he stayed away forever. But because he had given his shield to his grandson, and had taught him how to see the fire blazing inside it, Tezcatlipoca was elevated from a spirit of the wind to a supreme deity of the sky—source of breath and life and storm.

"He watched the world from above, and from time to time appeared in the mirror to help his grandson decide what needed to be done.

"And from that day on, whenever his grandson heard a bird singing, it was really Tezcatlipoca speaking to him in different languages:

"The mourning dove cooed: 'Oh, let's go, go, go! Oh, let's go, go, *go!*'

"Sometimes, on windy days in March, red-winged blackbirds scolded him for forgetfulness: *'Vous oubliez! Vous oubliez!'*

"On any given Sunday, sweet sparrows twittered *'Xingfu'* to wish Tezcatlipoca's grandson great happiness.

"And whenever the moon glowed in the night sky, he could hear the wise owls chant: *'You too!...You too!'* "

"I want to grow up to be just like you, Pappie!" Peter says, rising to his knees.

"Oh, you'll outshine me, my boy. Take heart! But remember; you can only do your best in one place at one time, no more than that. So you'll have to make difficult choices."

There is a glint in Peter's eye. "Can you give me the shield, now?" he asks.

"Soon; but now, have I ever told you my story about Bronco Bill?"

"That's enough for tonight," Helen says, beckoning her grandson to come with her.

Peter slides off the bed. Helen squeezes Karl's hand before she leaves him—listening to the distant approach of a train.

As the sound grows louder, Karl is transported to the first time when, as a boy, he was standing at a station platform with his mother, waiting to see a freight train, holding himself back from the track as she had said he should. He remembers the blur—Goliath streaking—how the train rocked the earth under his feet and sent him flying backward with his hands pressed over his ears. How everything and everyone in its wake seemed to be as stunned as he was by the prodigious force.

Something sounds as if it is ticking inside the wall. Karl hears breathing...*must be the sea, but it is not the sea.*

Behind his eyelids there is a swath of magenta; then turquoise, coiling and swirling, becomes a luminous blue lake where a moon-white speck spins upward from the water—it is a ball that rises as it blooms into a white rose lodging in the curve of a heart that turns inside out and folds into the form of a red-streaked iceberg being lifted in the palm of a long-fingered hand.

One-by-one, a thousand faces surround a man who stands amidst a blizzard of hats tossed to a lavender sky.

The hats fall and slide over shiny blades of grass, coming to rest at the base of two black shoes.

Everything that was once linear becomes circular; then immediately the reverse.

A melody is rising—middle C, E, then up to A.
A seagull screams.
A violin's bow is drawn back.
High D shimmers the frequency of spring green.

The sea pulses like polished memory.

Karl hears water become air at a vast horizon…
He envisions a voice of crystal, declaring the end at the brink of quivering light…

In time, he thinks…*I divine love.*

Addendum

In 1920, Karl was recruited to be Governor of Alaska. He received a phone call indicating that he had been appointed as such. After two days, however, President Warren Harding discovered that a position was lacking for Scott Bowen, his publicity manager, so the Governorship was assigned to Bowen instead.

In 1925, Karl joined Dillon Read & Co. where he worked as Vice President until his death.

Karl died on October 15th, 1949. He is buried at Evergreen Cemetery in Morristown, New Jersey.

In 1969 he was inducted into the Tennis Hall of Fame in Newport, RI.

After Karl's death, Helen Newsom Behr married Dean Mathey, Karl's friend and tennis partner whose former wife was deceased. Helen lived at Pretty Brook Farm in Princeton, New Jersey, until she died and was buried there in the late summer of 1965.

Epilogue

After Sunday lunch at Helen's house, when I was thirteen, kneeling on the floor in front of her, I asked her what it had been like on the night that she and "Pappy" escaped from the *Titanic*.

I waited for her answer for such a long time...it seemed that I might sink into the rug. The antique clock's tick resounded on the mantel. I imagined climbing through the window, out past the giant white columns, over the bluestone terrace, the expansive lawn, the "ha-ha" fence—past sheep to the willow-draped pond where we swam the horses on hot summer days.

When I pulled myself back into the room, I wondered why my grandmother was still unresponsive, until I came to conclude that I should not have asked the question, since a faraway stare had taken hold in her eyes.

Finally, she said, "I can't talk about that, dear. It was too terrible. But the worst part was on the rescue ship, waiting and watching everyone's misery."

The nineteen-fifties passed by on the farm—the milkman clanged his glass bottles at the kitchen door. From time to time, I searched for clues about my grandparents' experience on the *Titanic*. Then one winter evening, alone at home in the mid 1970s, I discovered the scrapbooks.

Some years later, I went to the National Archives to look for claims that might have been filed by my grandparents for their losses from the *Titanic*. I was informed that someone would come to assist me. I waited at a table in the room where so many before me had come in search of clues of their ancestry. A young man approached, pulling a dolly stacked high, long and wide with archive boxes.

"Good luck finding what you want," he said with a pained expression. "There's no order to these claims."

I took one box, placed it on the table in front of me and began fingering through bits and pieces of paper, finding nothing. I replaced the lid; put the box back; lifted the next one and continued the search. After looking through five or more boxes, I thought: *I've wasted the day. It's a needle in a haystack; a needle that may not even exist.* But I kept on, and in the very next box was a small note with the details of Karl Behr's First Class passenger claim:

3 suits

1 top coat

17 shirts

12 handkerchiefs

1 watch and chain

3 pins

1 trunk

1 silver pencil and knife

1 diamond ring

...I imagine him as he might have appeared, standing next to me—hat in hand; dressed in a vest, tweed pants (a bit worn at the knees), starched collar, tie and tie-clip tight, ever-so-slightly-polished shoes. Although not quite six feet, his carriage makes him seem tall and easy, as though there was nothing out of balance with the whole. His shoulders are broad, his bearing graceful. After removing his hat, he smooths his hair, runs the hat brim through his fingertips and hands it to me. His hands are fine, broad, careful, sure; the skin smooth; rivers of veins visible. I touch the soft stiffness of the hat—rolling it, taking notice of the fact that the rim was higher in front than in back.

∽

At the Varick Street archives again, some years later, this time searching for testimonies in the *Titanic* trial, I was given access to eighteen archive boxes. Inside each were claims but no testimonies. I was told that no one had been able to find details of the trial proceedings, and I too, had no luck. Therefore, what happened was a stunning surprise when, days later, at the Princeton Public Library, I was reading the *New York Times* microfiche to research Karl's tennis career. I had arbitrarily chosen to study the last weeks of June, 1915, a full three years after the *Titanic* tragedy.

While scrutinizing hours of the spinning blur of film to catch the sports section or other points of interest, a headline caught my attention. I backed up the reel and read it again:

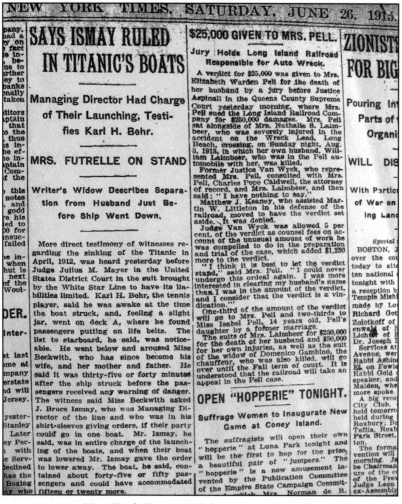

New York Times Article—June 26, 1915.

Along with everyone who watched, live, on September 11, 2001, as the Twin Towers burned with smoke hooking skyward, I thought the towers might—*it actually seemed likely*—continue to stand.

The clock on my kitchen wall hung mute. Moments of unknowing spawned Eternity. There had been no presage, no script, or sound-bite by way of explanation—nothing to make sense of a pending demise.

Suddenly, irrevocably, inexplicably—hope collapsed to dust, just as it did on the night when Helen and Karl watched their *Titanic* slide away.

Titanic and *Carpathia* Facts:

Amazingly, according to Lee Meredith's *Facts About TITANIC*, of the 35 "unaccompanied" First Class male passengers who survived the sinking of RMS *Titanic*, 28 (including Karl) were put into lifeboats on the starboard side where (in the beginning) men were urged to enter if there were no more women standing by, whereas only 2 First Class male "unaccompanied" passengers departed from the port side of the ship where orders were to load "women and children only" with some crew to row.

At the end of the blockbuster movie, *Titanic* (1997), the narrator says that survivors in the lifeboats waited and waited for absolution that would never come because they did not save anyone, but a study of the lists of survivors reveals that some were saved without an exact accounting as to how.

The man who offered Karl the use of his gun in lifeboat No. 5 was a fellow Lawrentian by the name of Norman Campbell Chambers, class of '01. In his memoir, Karl refers to Norman as an "elderly gentleman" whom he later saw on the *Carpathia*. It is conceivable that Karl might have remained unaware of their close connection.

The *Carpathia* was torpedoed by a German submarine on July 17th, 1918. The ship sank 170 miles from Bishop's Rock at the eastern end of the north Atlantic shipping route.

Research and Commentary

Starboard At Midnight is adapted from the unpublished, privately circulated, personal memoir written by Karl H. Behr. Details surrounding Karl's associations at boarding schools in Europe, at the Lawrenceville School, Yale University, the Brewster law firm, Herman Behr & Company, Squadron A, and with Theodore Roosevelt, Captain Arthur Rostron, members of the Survivor's Committee, Justice Oliver Wendell Holmes, Jr., Mayor Mitchel, Karl's tennis colleagues, the Preparedness effort, and all dignitaries including those affiliated with the National Security League, were extracted directly from his personal writings.

Charlie Engle was not in Karl's memoir. Charlie is a composite friend of this author's imagination—a mentor, a foil, and a German-American—based upon the true story of a prisoner at the internment camp at Fort Oglethorpe who was shot and killed while attempting to escape. The details of this escapee may be found on popular Internet search tools using the search parameters: "German-Americans," "World War I," and "Fort Oglethorpe," or the website:

http://net.lib.byu.edu/~rdh7/wwi/comment/yockel.htm

Henry Simmons, Jack Farnel, Sarah, Frank Purcell, Marley Ellis, Charlotte Engle, Emily, and Claude the office boy are also intuited characters.

The *New York Times* microfilm was an invaluable resource, as well as the Internet. Among the many books, movies, tapes, exhibits, and other materials, *The* Titanic *Disaster Hearings: the Official Transcripts of the 1912 Senate Investigation*, edited by Tom Kuntz, provided first-hand information.

Although Karl did not write about Oscar Raynor in his memoir, I learned about Oscar's tragic death, and of Karl's written pledge in his honor, from issues of the *Lawrence Ledger* at the Lawrenceville School archives, which were kindly made available to me. May the Raynor family accept my extended condolences.

Finally, I offer a blanket apology to any of Karl's relatives, associates of Herman Behr & Company, or other, for any inaccuracy that may have resulted from my conveyance of character in the narrative.